LIVING
TO BEAT
HELL!

Also by Joseph T. McGloin, S.J.
That's the Old Spirit!
Love and Live! (series)
Call Me Joe!
What To Do Till the Psychiatrist Comes!
Smile at Your Own Risk!
I'll Die Laughing!
(the above books illustrated by Don Baumgart)

Through Him, With Him and In Him (series)
Backstage Missionary: Father Dan Lord, S.J.
Friends, Romans, Protestants
Happy Holiday! (by Thaddeus O'Finn, pseudonym)

LIVING
TO BEAT

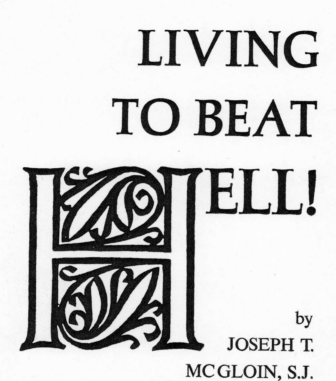

HELL!

by
JOSEPH T.
MCGLOIN, S.J.
ILLUSTRATED BY DON BAUMGART

PRENTICE-HALL, INC.
Englewood Cliffs, N.J.

To
Iñigo de Loyola—

Soldier

CONTENTS

INTRODUCTION

Living to
beat hell!

I've no really serious gripes about morticians; after all, like everyone else, they have to make a buck doing their thing. On occasion though, I've wished that a given mortician would refrain from asking with evident pride in a job well done, "Doesn't he look fine?" No matter how fine he might look, he's suffering from one serious drawback at this stage—he's dead. And dress him up as you will, he's going to stay that way.

Unfortunately, the same thing holds true for the written word—pretty it up as an author will, it's still dead. Any expression it seems to wear has to come largely from the imagination of the beholder, whose reaction can vary from the optimist's "He winked at me" to the realist's "Yep, he looks dead all right." Take the title of this book for instance. Some over-pious souls will undoubtedly look on it as uncouth, just as some self-styled clerical rebel will probably only grumble "Hell is passé—how dead can you get?" The trouble with these types is that both tend to be somewhat literal-minded and neither one is what you'd call a bundle of laughs, occupied as they usually are, respectively, in the grim business of deploring the twentieth century or agonizing reappraising. But those are their little hangups, and I can only hope here that the average reader will see in the title what the author intends—that life is a good show, a hell of a good show if that expresses it better.

Some years back I did a book called *I'll Die Laughing!* which had to do with the recipe for turning out finished Jesuits. This title was meant to imply that the author had so enjoyed his Jesuit life up to that point that he felt that when the time came, he would darn well exit as he had entered, laughing. Today whenever I meet some fellow Jesuit for the first time, I'm almost sure his first question is going to be, "Have you died laughing yet?" Since I have in my possession a clipping telling about some character who really did die laughing, I'm not so sure the question isn't loaded—especially since the unfortunate guy in the news story died laughing at one of his own jokes. I also have on hand a clipping about some poor character, one of that elite number "most wanted" by the police, who shot it out from behind a church organ and lost. When his body was removed, they found he had left only a paper bag with some lunch and "a copy of a book called *I'll Die Laughing!*"

In an introduction (which, call it what you will, is still a sales-pitch) the sequel writer is probably always tempted to point out the far-reaching success of the previous book, and, indeed, from a publisher's peculiar viewpoint that particular previous book of mine could be termed a success. The reader should also be warned however, at the very outset of this present book, that old *I'll Die Laughing!* was banned in a Jesuit house or two (undoubtedly by some unsmiling officials who might or might not die laughing to know that they thereby gave the book a fine boost) and had the further good luck to be denied a visa into one entire country. The author feels that he could glory far more in this latter distinction if it were not necessary to add that the official banner of the book had not, until then at least, read a word of it.

That book had to do with the formation of a Jesuit, and hopefully, it reflected the author's esteem of that process and his love of the trainer, the Society of Jesus. At that time it took fifteen years to mold the ordinary piece of clay—or clod as some might prefer to term it—which was all the Society had to work with in those primitive days before the evolutionary process really blasted off. And so, since that first fifteen years has been reported on, it seems fitting now to say something about the next fifteen-year stretch. It is, after all, one thing for the youthfully enthusiastic trainee to gush on about his training and morale and such; the picture could conceivably vary somewhat when described by the grizzled combat veteran who has, perhaps, acquired a less inhibited arsenal of words to work with.

There have, too, been many changes—allegedly even radical, essential changes—since the publication of *I'll Die Laughing!* These changes, too, might well have altered the picture.

The more ancient, creaking reader will recall that at that time a number of exreligious had already performed the invaluable service of explaining to the world why they were ex. The book, *I Leap Over the Wall* got a warm public welcome even though its very title—and this before the day of nuns who flew on TV as well— conjured up a somewhat ridiculous picture of a pole-vaulting nun of umpteen years, and even though the author later expressed the wish that she had not leaped over that wall at all. In this sense, of course, times have not changed in the slightest. Many publishers, in their dedicated zeal for the public good, would still much sooner offer books by those personable authors who gave up on something rather than take a chance on the more prosaic accounts of those colorless dolts who stuck with it. Too, the reading public would still sooner read about what is wrong than about what is right, about the vociferous breakers rather than the quiet keepers of promises. The divorce of famous people invariably gets a much bigger press than their marriage did—unless, of course, both divorce and marriage (not necessarily in that order) are involved, in which case a veritable journalistic jackpot has been hit.

2

The religious life has always had a few well-publicized pole-vaulters.

In our own day we have stuck manfully to our sacred tradition of showing, at least in print, far more interest in that gay, gallant corps of adventurers which leaves the priesthood or religious life (always in pursuit of still loftier means and goals) than in those lusterless louts who clearly have had neither the intelligence nor the initiative to dare such a move. We've all read often by this time about Sister Semper Fidelis whose training as a religious qualified her for a position of some prominence in her order, but who then handed down the *ex-cathedra* pronouncement that no nun could handle such a job hence she was rinsing the starch out of the old wimple and hanging up the habit, low-heeled shoes and all. Naturally, this bit of earth-shaking information was delivered at a press conference.

But there's a new wrinkle today—the priest, for example, who apparently still wants to dress like one (however a priest dresses today) or at least to be known as one, while still bitterly condemning everything which has made him a priest and the very way of life of a priest. We hear, too, from religious who seem to wish to remain such—according, that is, to their own definitions—demanding that their order adapt to their whims and theories with never an inch of vice versa. All of which is very much like saying, "Of course I'll love you; here are my conditions."

This is not to say that there is nothing to criticize in the human workings of the Church or religious orders. Far from it. There has been, is, and always will be plenty of opportunity for the dedicated critic to ply his hobby. To take but one example: I've been getting some women mad at me for years by telling them I thought religious women should look like religious *women* rather than like cupcakes or laundry bags or penguins—all of which, of course, have a certain unique attractiveness of their own, but not particularly religious or even feminine attractiveness. It has always seemed to me that the Lord has come up with a fairly good product here, one that shouldn't be ruined by poor packaging, especially on the part of those who profess to admire the other glories of God's creation. Obviously, I'm not stumping for nuns who look like either Twiggys or Sister Racquel Welches—although, on second thought, one or two of the latter in the community might cause Father to put a little more zing into the old retreat conferences.

But honest criticism and destruction are not supposed to be synonymous. We shouldn't ordinarily hang a child right away for stealing a penny, but we ought to try to correct him first and only then if he persists in his evil-doing, execute him. Too, we have to be willing to excuse in infants and very young children the tendency to blame others for their discomforts and other troubles. As children grow older, however, we get more and more uneasy if they still tend to shift all guilt to someone else. And when we encounter grown men and women who blame, never themselves, but their Church or their order for their own hangups, we are clearly dealing with the king- or queen-sized immature. After all, even a child as young as twenty or thirty ought to be able to remove the safety pin sticking into him from his own diaper.

It should surprise no one that a priest or nun might have a problem or two, maybe even very great problems. Indeed, it should, in general, be a source of some astonishment to discover anyone apparently entirely immune from problems. I suppose it shouldn't even surprise us when an occasional person who aspires to as lofty a position as a mediator between God and men can't even look up to God when he should, but can only weep with self-pity at his problems and cry to the world, "Look how I suffer." He even seeks solutions in material where the solution can, of course, never be found, as he should know. But while this latter phenomenon may not surprise us, it can sadden us when even one such man denies in practice what he professes in theory—or once professed, at least, until it was his own turn to suffer.

I am, in short, not surprised at a priest's having problems. But I deeply resent this volunteer spiritual leader's immature weeping about his problems in public. In a similar way it would have made me very uncomfortable, back in the days of World War II, had General Eisenhower burst into tears when it rained on D-Day.

Above all, I get angry when I run into good people who have become confused by the publicly paraded grumbling of priests and religious, to the extent that they now tend to be suspicious of the priest or religious who is not just happy but even enthusiastic about his work and his vocation. This is such an embarrassing attitude to the discontented that all he can seem to do about it is theorize that the externally peaceful, happy person with no time to wallow in public self-pity is just not with it, but can only be unseeing, unfeeling, and stupid. It's passé to be happy, as passé as suffering instead of yielding. Constant agonizing reappraisals

"Happiness is agonizing self-appraisal."

are the major spiritual exercise of the day—an activity combining the strenuous work and inelegance of spiritual scab-picking.

This situation may be particularly irritating and frustrating to a writer, since his tendency is to want to answer the critics word for word, sentence for sentence. But of course he can't, for many reasons. For one thing, it takes infinitely longer to answer an accusation than to make it. It takes some instant expert but an instant to say, "Mercy nuns are unmerciful and Sisters of Charity are uncharitable and Jesuits are not all like Jesus," but it would take a short lifetime to disprove these generalizations.

But there's another, still more frustrating reason one can't adequately answer the public wailer and critic. Many publishers are simply not interested in answers but only in what they think will sell. (You can, of course, hardly blame a publisher for this attitude. It might, however, be more honest for him to acknowledge this than to make his bundle under the aegis of public-spiritedness and objectivity.) For example, one of our most popular magazines, now but a memory, used to print some very heady stuff indeed in its avowed "Vox Populi" section. One soon discovered, however, that the "populi" was only a carefully selected segment of the real *populi* since this magazine for years replied to would-be answerers of its column: "We are sorry for returning the enclosed material *unread* . . . we are no longer able to consider *unsolicited* ideas and manuscripts. . . ." (The italics are mine. The words are a direct quotation.) In other words, only the writer of this magazine's choice could shoot off his mouth to millions of people, and any answer (usually none, or from someone so far at another extreme that he only substantiated the original case) would also be the magazine's choice. The "Letters to the Editor" seemed, at least to me, similarly managed—or else those who disagreed never wrote. I wrote, but was never printed. But all this, of course, appeared under the pious standard of objectivity and of a public, representative forum from editors who would have been the first to scream in horror at what they called news management.

No wonder people are confused, when the compounding of confusion and the public parading of one's pouting pays so well. It was this same magazine which first featured "a priest who wanted to marry," but one looked in vain for his identity. He signed this article with a pseudonym because he did not want to "expose his relatives to controversy or himself to ecclesiastical retaliation." Later he came out with a best seller under his own name, obviously no longer quite so fearful of these specters when the price improved. One searched, similarly in vain, for any answers in ensuing issues of the magazine. Now, the priest who wants to marry and writes about it is, of course, news; but the priest who wants to marry (as is only normal) while still continuing to put his natural desire aside for something he considers greater and often because of a promise he considers even more solemnly binding than the marriage promise—he's *not* news.

But this whole bit about celibacy and the vow of chastity is only by way of an example at this point. It is, moreover, matter for another part of this book, an important part I think. It's probably a good thing, in fact, that we are witnessing a few clerical tantrums today, since this offers some occasion for trying to clarify the problem and for airing some of the reasons for a vow of chastity and a life of celibacy (which are not, admittedly, of the *essence* of the priesthood). It is, however, also far too important and perhaps too complex a matter to package neatly in an introduction. So pant away. This matter will be treated in one of the lurid chapters which follow.

Here I'm only trying to explain why I'm writing *this* particular book. It comes to this: that amid the strident, publicized voices of discontent with the Church today, I want the world to know that there is one voice of love—stammering and inept though it seem—which I feel speaks for innummerable others who are even more silent than I. Love doesn't generally shout aloud so much as it only quietly loves. My purpose is to remind you that there is such love (not by *telling* you this, but by narrating some of its experiences), even though you seldom hear it shouting. Certainly all of us have encountered the loudmouth who makes himself seem the majority by the very volume of his unceasing propagandizing—which is really an attempted self-defense. Not too long ago the National Aeronautics and Space Administration found out that one can become a leader even if he doesn't know what he's talking about, provided he only talks *enough*. They found that students who monopolized conversations and still were always wrong were picked as discussion-club leaders more often than the quieter, and more often correct, students. This bit of information cost NASA close to seven thousand dollars, but most of us could have told them this for free.

I would like in this book to reaffirm, after these fifteen years, the original connotation of the title *I'll Die Laughing!* I still feel that unless caught completely unawares I'll be laughing like hell, at least inwardly, as I exit this life, because it *has* been great and because I feel it has given me the chance to laugh *at* hell.

Admittedly, there have been times when the laughter had to be postponed or was all inside, times indeed when laughter became doubly important because anything else would have implied a lack of faith. There have, unfortunately, also been times when the faith was foolishly neglected in self-centeredness or self-pity, and so laughter seemed impossible. But these times have been *my* fault, not my Church's or my Society's.

Somehow I've always known—although I haven't always put the knowledge into practice—that suffering and joy are not incompatible. I think I knew when I promised perpetual poverty, chastity, and obedience to Our Lord as a Jesuit that there would come days when I would seem to be torn in two in the effort to keep that promise. I had no illusion then that any vow was an immunization—from human love, for example—and so I'm sure I knew that a vow implied some future suffering if it was to be observed and not reneged upon. I think I suspected even then in my very callow youth that there might some day come someone whom I could love above anyone else on earth, someone with whom I would want to share my life. I knew that no vow could possibly preclude such a desire any more than a marriage vow could automatically immunize a person from the charms of anyone but his partner. But I also knew that whether such a situation ever came to pass or not, my promise had it covered. I knew too, of course, that should such love present itself, it would take both grace and guts (largely the former) to refrain from rationalizing away that promise.

This is why I'm a happy man—because I know that suffering, even the rending suffering that can come with love, is a part of happiness and not its contradiction. And this is why I write this book—as a happy man, a priest, and a Jesuit—not without human gripes, but not out to destroy what I love because of what seems to me some human defects. I owe all I have to God, with His Church and the Society of Jesus as His primary agents.

The play, *The Man of La Mancha*, is something rare in the theater world, a musical with a plot. It is the old story of Don Quixote put to music and marvelously and artistically transformed although it remains substantially the story of a man foolish enough to be an idealist in practice. The entire theme of this stirring play, "To dream the impossible dream," well expresses this author's ambitioned philosophy of life.

Take the air of stoicism from this play, baptize it, and you have the thought of one Iñigo de Loyola, better known these days as St. Ignatius, founder of the Society of Jesus, who once wrote:

> Dearest Lord, teach me to be generous, teach
> me to serve you as you deserve—to give and not
> to count the cost, to fight and not to heed the

wounds, to toil and not seek for rest, to labor
and ask for no reward, except that of knowing
that I am doing your holy will.

One of the great frustrations of many writers is the feeling
of inadequacy in the face of one's most intimate thoughts. The
foregoing gives some hint of the explanation as to why I write at
all; in particular, why I write *this* book.

But if the purpose of the introduction of a book (like the
introduction of a person for that matter) is to sell it, still another
purpose is to keep critics from chopping up the author for not
writing something he had no intention of writing.

Some readers of *I'll Die Laughing!* (which was fact) insisted
that one item or another therein must have been fiction. Similarly,
parts of my detective mystery *Happy Holiday!* (which was fiction;
I even used a pseudonym, Thaddeus O'Finn) were taken for fact.
An occasional reader even imagined that he recognized one or other
of the characters, particularly some of the victims, from real life.

This author can't win; readers will invariably see fact in his
fables and fiction in his fact. So the only thing to do here seems
to be to throw the whole responsibility on the reader. Where
opinions are expressed in this book, they will be fact—the fact
being that these are my opinions, right or wrong, and not
necessarily anyone else's.

As said earlier, *I.D.L.!* was written very shortly after I had
tumbled off the Jesuit assembly line. This book, *Living To Beat
Hell!* takes up more or less where that one left off. It deals with
the work of one Jesuit and is basically factual. It deals with "the
apostolate"; that is, with the apostolate of one Jesuit. It is sometimes critical since I see much to criticize even in the critics. I feel
that a little well-placed criticism can do a lot of good. Just as
one purpose of the earlier book was to dispel the old idea of the
Jesuit as some sort of murky, lurking political intriguer even from
his earliest training, so a by-product of this present book should
be to further ridicule that same old fairy-tale image in action.

God's grace works with human nature, but it doesn't change
that nature essentially in itself or in its clumsy operations. This
is a great mystery—how something as inept as human nature can,
with God's grace, act with such magnificent gracefulness. Not
even the greatest saints have been turned into angels, but have
remained quite human—sometimes, let's face it, less than charm-
ingly so. (One sometimes wonders, for instance, about those old
saints, some of them still not scratched from the approved membership list. They were considered virtuous because among other less

9

sensational reasons, they allegedly never bathed, thus providing strong evidence, if any were needed, that they had not yet become angels.) No one should be particularly surprised to find smallness next to greatness in a person, pettiness along with great zeal, and selfishness side by side with great love.

It has probably always been true that most zealous persons—perhaps because of that very zeal and its natural impatience—have tended to regard their own bailiwick as the only important area on earth (much as some gag maps show the relatively microscopic state of say Massachusetts covering most of the United States). One of my truly saintly Jesuit friends, Father Charlie (Dismas) Clark whom many knew as "The Hoodlum Priest," used to gripe—before he realized his detractors weren't really worth this form of stooping—that some of the blinding lights of the academic world seemed to think that only their own apostolate was really an apostolate at all, while his work was more in the nature of a second-rate hobby. And yet, even the saintly Father Charlie was not above retaliating in kind on occasion, somewhat more expertly since he had acquired a certain impressive eloquence from his good thieves.

I've heard some of our more soft-spoken Jesuits expressing concern on occasion at a fellow Jesuit's somewhat earthy language; I've heard these more earthy types knocking around (usually more interestingly and amusingly) the milk-toast manners of their detractors. But the truth is that the softer-spoken apostle is going to touch people unreachable by the more uninhibited one, while the saltier character is going to get at souls who can be attracted only by salt. The marvelous providence of God comes up with apostles for every type of person, and it is something less than reasonable to criticize another for his lack of one's own unique talents and personality. It may well be that one of the most horrible horrors of hell is the awful sameness of its inhabitants.

But reasonable or not, the tendency to consider one's apostolate the *only* apostolate persists, so that today one is either working in "the inner city" or he isn't really working. Why, the question goes, are you wasting time on people who obviously have so much already while others are in such great need? But just as working with only the well-heeled *can* mask a certain love of comfort and security, so this seemingly very pious question can show a unique materialistic outlook and a lack of faith. Material things *are* important, but not so important that their absence provides the only guide to the apostolic arena and their presence an indication of "No spiritual help needed." Anyone but the totally inexperienced apostle will know that the materially comfortable and the affluent have as great need of some sort of mediator with God as have the destitute. In fact, one obscure worker in both inner and outer cities said that it was harder for some of the well-heeled to get to God than for a camel to squeeze through the eye of a needle, a trick which would seem to call for some assistance.

And, of course, one could say the same thing about the exclusive apostle of the rich, the irremovable pastor of Our Lady of Mink parish. *His* is not the only place apostles are needed either. Not even the apostle's apostolicity is immune to pride. An "apostle" can be darned proud of himself whether he works with rich or poor, looking down his apostolic nose at those who work elsewhere unless, of course, he is really an apostle without any quotation marks.

I have always felt that I was trying, at least, to live and work in the only real inner city there is—the inner city of humanity and grace. To me the inner city is not a limited geographical area at all, but the universe, and it is God who assigns us to our section of it. We could easily mistake our own little ghetto of pride for an inner city were we to do all the choosing ourselves according to our likes and not necessarily with regard to our talents and to God's fairly clear, even when difficult, providence.

In my own imagination somewhere there is an inner city where I belong and where I can most generously serve God, but its nature is known to God and me alone. But this is *my* idea, and maybe it will never be God's. Whether it is His idea or not, it would be a mistake to spend my time daydreaming about it, because there's an inner city to work in right now, the inner city of *His* choice where He has placed me now. This inner city may, in fact, be tougher and demand more generosity than the inner city I imagine, because the latter is solely my choice and has nothing to do, as far as I can see, with my limited talents or God's unknown will for me.

In what we like to call the practical order my inner city so far has been wherever someone thought he *needed* me. At times it has been a cocktail party where someone who had thought priests spiritually allergic to booze are surprised, shocked, and delighted (in that order) to see one apparently enjoying a drink. It has on occasion been a cold, filthy attic where the old and poor and helpless were "cared for" by those paid by the county for their carefully portioned and profitable charity. Sometimes it has been a theater lobby where the discussion of a play concealed the discussion of infinitely more important things. It has been a shack where the only furniture was a hammock swinging low over a dirt floor, or a " study hall" in a warehouse where malaria-bearing mosquitoes were so ill-informed as to spare not even the prefect. Sometimes it has been a handball court where an opponent and I sprawled completely exhausted after a couple of hours of hand-to-hand combat. At times it has been the top floor of an athletic club where a relaxed acquaintance wanted to talk or a harassed waitress found a smile most welcome.

Sometimes my inner city has been the home of a friend who had invited another friend or several. And it made no difference at all whether this home was magnificent or shabby; it was still in the inner city. Sometimes my city has been a television studio where a staff member wanted to talk or someone, seeing the show, would call in and ask if he could drop over. Sometimes it has been my own room next to the phone, when someone had found the word "Jesuit" in the phone book and often enough in near despair had called up to talk to "a Jesuit," and had had to be satisfied with this one.

My inner city has been a bus depot in Amarillo, Texas, at 2 A.M. or a railroad station in Omaha or Topeka, Kansas, or an airport in New York. It has been a crowded street in New Orleans, or next to a stalled car perched on the shoulder of a freeway, or the streets of Laredo, the restaurants of Mexico City, a home in Cuernavaca. It has been a hotel or a cab or Central Park or a stadium or a bus or train or plane or the shore of a lake. Often enough, it has been the lecture platform with an audience of thousands or only a handful: adults or kids or mixtures of whole families of several generations. It was once a restaurant in a bus depot where I was alone with a "bird-bath martini," and the hostess and a wonderful little old man joined me because they wanted to talk—something they wouldn't even have thought of had there been no bird-bath in evidence.

In a way, my inner city has been wherever my typewriter has been. I have, hopefully, written to many more of its citizens than I could otherwise have reached. I have answered countless letters from strangers and non-strangers who had nowhere else to turn and who, often enough, could not work up the courage to express their problems to anyone face to face.

My inner city has been any place I've lived—when a fellow Jesuit wanted to talk, or more often the janitor or a lay faculty member, or when the police suddenly loomed at my shoulder asking where an employee might be. Oh yes, my inner city has also been the police station and the jail, the psycho ward and the emergency section of the hospital.

Just as my inner city has known no geographical limits, its citizens have not been of any certain class either. My inner city has included boiler experts and ditch diggers, truck drivers and Ph.D.s, members of the AA, AAA, and AMA. Most often perhaps, the citizens of my inner city have been teen-agers and frequently their parents. There have been entertainers and artists with their seemingly unique problems and their sometimes unique approaches to them. There have been executives and flunkies, saints and sinners (not that this is any clear-cut distinction—a saint is still nothing but a sinner who keeps trying). And always they've embarrassed me with the light of their greatness probing uncompromisingly into the shadows where I thought I had successfully hidden my own short-comings.

The citizens of my inner city have been of all colors, of all degrees of faith from the maximum down to very close to zero. They have been the balanced (whatever *that* is) and the slightly or not so slightly unbalanced. My citizen has been the man from whom I asked directions on a street, the salesgirl with whom I was friendly because we both understood that I was her servant rather than she mine, the drunk on the viaduct in Kansas City who spoke to me because my strange collar told him that he might find kindness in me.

There have, of course, been many citizens of my inner city with whom I've failed utterly, those whom I knew God would have to get at some other way. There was the young girl who came to talk to me privately in the course of a retreat. She politely thanked me for my help when she left the room, and to my dis-claimer, "I didn't do anything to help," answered immediately "You sure didn't." There have been those I have found it hard to understand, which is too bad, and certainly those who have been unable to understand me, which doesn't matter in the least.

I've loved them all, these citizens of my inner city; sometimes, indeed, too much or at least too humanly. On second thought though, there's nothing which prevents God's using even excessive love for his own all-important purposes.

This is then, to me, the real inner city, the universe; and these are its citizens, anyone. It extends everywhere, and it includes everyone, without limit. The rest of this book tells what some of it has been like to date. My constant prayer has been that I don't louse up God's grace or get in its way because He can do a terrific job if our ineptness doesn't hinder His work of grace.

PART ONE

CHAPTER
ONE

*Monday comes
but once a week—
thank God!*

O n some indeterminable day in the future the world's only surviving man, stumbling through an atomic wasteland, ◈ ◈ will chance on a sunken vault containing a time capsule. And if any cog in his mental machinery is operable at all, he'll leave the thing right where it is—for many reasons, but mostly because if he digs it up, he's almost sure to be talked to death. Ours is *the* age of talking—discussion or dialogue—none of which is to be confused with communication. Instead of getting down to work immediately on most projects, we first—and unfortunately often last—throw them around from one convention to another. Then we assign task forces, which used to be known as committees and which accomplish just as much, sometimes even managing to come up with some excellent formulae and language whose meanings can be explored at future conventions.

Many of the happy expressions of our age have been conceived in a test tube, and yet some of us regard them with almost parental pride. There is, for example, hardly a dedicated conventioneer today whose eyes don't brim with tears at the word "charism," since by it he acknowledges that no less a personage than the Holy Spirit has knitted his bag—and maybe even that of the whole convention.

That must have been a dramatic moment indeed when the delegates at a Jesuit conference, enlightened by this very charism, tagged themselves and their religious brethren as "hyphenated persons" rather than ordinary mortals of only one syllable.

Now when word of this filtered down out of the noosphere to those of us in the barysphere, we were, initially at least, a bit shook—which is an ever present hazard at our level. The term seemed to carry a hint of schizophrenia, and one is always a bit sensitive these days about his mental health anyhow, since he feels he can't possibly be normal if those he reads about are. On closer examination, however, we were relieved to discover that "hyphenated," like so many other charism-created expressions, didn't really mean so much at all, at least nothing really new. It only indicated that there were Jesuit priests and brothers and scholastics, Jesuit pastors and teachers and missionaries and poets, and even some blessed with a double hyphen, like Jesuit-bird-watchers. (One of the very formulators of this expression, or at least a vigorous applauder at its formulation, later added still another hyphen to his already considerable collection by attempting marriage. It can be a heady thing, this multiplication of hyphens.)

Whether you call him hyphenated or only dedicated, however, a Jesuit ordinarily does do something within this profession of his, maybe many different things. Missionaries have been mathematicians, and teachers have been artists and even writers, and pastors have been inventors or more often, as they'll tell you themselves, janitors. Father Charlie Clark (or Dismas as he called himself) specialized in turning all thieves into good thieves, Father Gerald Kelly in moral theology, Fathers John and Bill Markoe in the Negro apostolate, Brother John Renk in butterflies, and Father Dan Lord in everything. The Society of Jesus was founded as a free-lance order with the emphasis on missions. From her very early days she also became very involved in teaching. But her members have never adhered doggedly and exclusively to any one task. The Society was founded as a mobile force, ready to move where needed at the Holy Father's wish, prepared to fill vacuums or even "to fight the unbeatable foe" on occasion. And the only real shame that can come to a Jesuit is getting taken by that very beatable foe which is himself.

In that primitive, less selective day when this author slipped unnoticed into the Society of Jesus, one's ambition was to be a Jesuit, with little or no explicit thought of any particular hyphenation. Today there seems a greater awareness of one's career within his vocation, and so there is a greater advertance to the Jesuit-scientist or the Jesuit-artist or Jesuit-teacher or Jesuit-so-and-so. On the other hand, we were not completely unaware of the hyphen in the background either, since we knew that either God was already aware of our peculiar talents (and some of them were indeed peculiar) or else we would soon submit a complete list to Him.

The first hyphen we acquired made us into Jesuit-religious, closely followed by that of Jesuit-students. One bit of knowledge that helped uniquely towards my own perseverence was the realization that the student bit, at least in its formal aspect, was to be temporary, even though a rather long temporary. Similarly, one bit of ignorance which uniquely helped towards the same end was my lack of foresight on how long a teacher or writer has to study, privately and informally at least, if he's to avoid being shallow. Informally we were, in fact, permanently hyphenated as students, since it would be ridiculous to imagine anyone's posing as a professional who had ceased to be a student of that profession, as ridiculous—and dangerous—as an illiterate M.D.

Quite soon in my own Jesuit course hyphen began to follow hyphen: teacher, missionary, youth worker, and even a semi-hyphen vaguely expressed as "writer." (The writer's charism was never vigorous enough to create a more glamorous term.) At the same time, it became quite obvious that a lot of avocations were simply not my own thing, although other Jesuits were able to handle them with the greatest eagerness and efficiency. Such, for example, were the formal student bit and parish work which were seemingly just not for me. These are, of course, only two examples from an embarrassingly long list.

In God's Providence (which finds some weird caulking with which to plug up holes) "writer" has, I guess, become pretty much my hyphen, although the reader should know that I was once introduced as "an expert in teenology," whatever that is. And since writing, at present at least, seems to be my thing and since I did work a long time with teens and write for them and about them, one may well wonder why this book begins with a chapter on teaching instead of on one of these two apostolates. The truth is, though, that no matter what other work he does, the Jesuit *is* a teacher—whether he teaches formally or informally, orally or in writing, or only the toughest way there is, by example. Working with teens *is* a form of teaching—except perhaps for professed teenologists who are usually far too busy collating their surveys. So is writing. The book which teaches nothing (and doesn't even have a regard for interesting reading) *is* a nothing, a total failure.

Although this chapter has something to do with teaching, it's certainly not going to be a teachers' manual. If it were, it would have to be committed by someone else far more experienced, infinitely more wise, and exactly 100 percent more convinced of the worth of teachers' manuals. My own teaching experience is only a noontime shadow next to the experience of countless others, as I taught full time for only thirteen years and part time for another eight or so. And yet if I can produce here only one usable idea or puncture only one phony balloon for only one reader, it will be more than worth the presumption and the effort. And if that idea turns out to be interesting as well as usable, then my cup damned well runneth over.

My attempts at teaching took place in three distinct eras and locales: regency, that three-year period between a Jesuit's philosophical and theological studies when he is pulled unceremoniously and abruptly down to earth as he tries to teach considerably more than he has learned; ten years of teaching as a priest in a Jesuit high school for boys; and a few years of part-time teaching in a girls' academy. Regency itself, even under ordinary circumstances, throws one abruptly into a very real, practical world, and so it

19

should normally be a great step towards maturity. My own regency was a somewhat exceptional one for those days since I was sent to Belize, British Honduras, to teach in St. John's College.

Getting to British Honduras was something of an experience. When a young man who has been in somewhat of a hothouse for seven years, rapt in the rare atmosphere of philosophical learning and academic degree work (and who has never even bought a train ticket for himself) is suddenly told to go to British Honduras, it is comparable to being told: "Take Colonel X's place in Apollo XX."[1] By the end of the trip (which was in the company of several embarrassingly uninterested cows on a cattleboat) an insatiable love for travel the hard way had me hooked forevermore.

Regency is, however, more than an experience. It's also an unbelievable maturer; and combining foreign missions with regency, I feel, further accelerates this maturing process. And so it's my conviction that if we Jesuits take seriously proposals to do away with regency, we're out of our collective mind. However, if the voice of abstract theory does prevail and regency is scratched,

Like St. Paul's apostolate, mine sometimes called for a luxury ocean voyage.

a couple of years in the Peace Corps or in a "peace corps" of our own devising would, I feel, be an acceptable substitute for acquainting our men with the real problems of our world. Many returning members of the Peace Corps will tell you that when they come home, they can't help feeling they're returning to a relatively trivial life. After handling great responsibilities abroad, they seem to be expected to act like infants once more. I recall that on my return from Belize I was met by two good friends whose first words were, "Let's go have a milk shake."

After theological studies and tertianship (another couple of Jesuit customs whose days may be numbered) that ever-dwindling number of Jesuits who are going to teach get at the job. It was my own good fortune after a seven-month stretch of pastoral purgatory to teach for ten years at Regis High in Denver, another place and set of experiences I couldn't forget even if I wanted to.

At Regis I tried to teach some English, a bit of journalism (unfortunately, mostly to those who wanted—or more honestly needed—the credit and to a few dilettante types who felt the literary world couldn't possibly wait for them much longer), a lot of religion, a marriage course, and what was laughingly referred to as Latin.

At the beginning of what turned out to be my final year of teaching at Regis the principal was embarrassed to stumble onto a senior Latin class whose existence he hadn't suspected and which he certainly didn't know what to do with. Ordinarily, seniors who were still taking Latin were at least fairly good students since Latin used to be part of the more difficult course. But this gallant band of seventeen young men, no doubt sensing the challenge, had decided (back at that moment of truth when they had had to make up their minds about their future studies by way of electives) that they would just as soon continue to take Latin. There they were—probably through some secretarial error—still reveling in all the thrills of the Latin classics, undaunted by any concern that they still had a lot of back work to do in English.

In many subjects, the Jesuit high schools of the United States make use of a common syllabus which prescribes certain material to be covered. The powers-that-be, moreover, knowing the sneaky creative bent of their fellow Jesuits, leave little to chance; and so they also prescribe "province exams" covering this material, ostensibly to compare inter-school achievement but in reality to see if the material has been covered.

The Latin syllabus listed sections of Virgil's *Aeneid* for the artistic and literary enjoyment of seniors. But neither Virgil when he created his very lovely poetry, nor our prefect of education when he dreamed up his equally lovely—in its way—syllabus, ever envisioned this particular Latin class. They couldn't even spell Virgil's name twice in a row, nor did they, logically enough, see why they should have to. As for poetry, they not only couldn't spot it in Virgil but poetry was for finks anyhow. Moreover, the syllabus called for what was for them an impossible coverage of material, perhaps twenty or thirty lines a day. These Latin scholars might have been capable of one or two lines on a good day in midweek when all conditions were ideal for concentration and they had no other interests at the moment.

Since the syllabus did, however, lay down this quota of lines, we gave it the old college try, with predictable results. Luckily, somehow the Jesuit minds behind the syllabus had left a mini-loophole and provided no test on the stuff at the end of the *second* semester. And so while I felt some faint obligation to continue to expose this collection of scholars to *some* Virgil during this second semester, I didn't feel that I had to turn them loose on it every day. So we improvised a program of Virgil on Mondays and Wednesdays (Monday was neither their best day nor mine anyhow) and selections from the Latin Old Testament on Tuesdays and Thursdays. As always I gave a test on Friday.

This system sounded great to them largely because they knew they could easily lay their hands on the English Old Testament, and because some of the stories were bound to be more interesting than those included in the Virgil syllabus. They were a bit shook, however, to find that the biblical references were not marked on their mimeographed selections from the Old Testament, and so they had to read gobs of The Book looking for the right passage. Probably in fact some of them spent much more time trying to find the passage in English than they would have used up translating it themselves—although this is by no means certain, of course. The pleasant by-product of this project was that they did read a lot of the Old Testament and enjoyed it—although I'm sure a scholar of the Scriptures would be horrified to hear that any such subterfuge is ever necessary to get anyone to read the Book. But then he probably would have been horrified at my scholars anyhow. Nonetheless, we had some fun, and my students learned—a little.

Their quarterly exam consisted of individual Latin sentences (paragraphs were always a bit too much for them) to be translated from Virgil and from the Old Testament. Unbeknown to them I slipped in one sentence from *Winnie Ille Pu*, but it didn't bother them in the least or even slow them up. The sentence was *De apibus semper est dubitandum* ("One is never sure about bees"), and they attacked its translation with their usual confidence. Of course, not being familiar with *Winnie,* their translations were less than perfect. They did, however, show the Old Testament influence—such as one translation "David slew Goliath."

We had a unique situation at Regis in those years, and as far as I'm concerned, it ought to remain unique—unless that is, it can be rendered non-existent. I doubt if any high-school teacher or administrator is ever completely happy when both a college and the high school are under a common roof and a common thumb as they were then at Regis. I felt, as some others certainly did also, that the high school usually finished a poor second in the arrangement. I was once informed, for example, that a letter to the high-school alumni was "subversive of the college" and that the high-school alumni dinners I had initiated were frowned on "because some of the high-school alumni were kidding some of the college alumni and giving them inferiority complexes." So I began with sharp and unusual insight to suspect a certain anti-high school and pro-college bias.

In general, however, the rivalry between a high school and college on the same campus was not unhealthy—at least when it existed horizontally rather than vertically. There was, for instance, the day at about 11 A.M. when a new jet plane on a test flight flew too low and broke about seventy-five windows in the building which housed the high school, some college offices, and most of the Jesuits. That noon at lunch when I asked Father Frank Bakewell if he had heard it, he said that he had, adding that he also "heard that it woke up two of the college faculty."

The truth is though that the faculty, religious and lay, college or high school, with which I was privileged to serve or associate with during those ten years at Regis are remembered both as professional associates and as friends. Naturally, however, one can't list them all.

I can't, however, omit mention of the principal of Regis High in those years, since I feel that he, Father Jim Eatough, was not just one of the best principals in the business but also one of the finest teachers. In fact, the latter undoubtedly helped to make him the former. He inspired all of us, too, by always teaching some new course or other himself to keep his hand in and to better understand his teachers.

There was another outstanding man connected with my teaching days in Denver: Dr. F. Alan Murphy, then psychologist for the Denver public schools. He introduced me to the values of his profession, overcoming my initial skepticism with his great professional know-how and patience. In my work at that time and also in my dealings with people ever since, I have found the things Dr. Murphy taught me to be of infinite value, and I'll always be grateful to him for the realistic, practical training he gave me in his field. I only wish I could have done as much for him in *my* way. Above all perhaps, he taught me not to play God with the minds of my fellow human beings or with my supposed knowledge of those minds. At the same time he showed me how to recognize those who did need some special help and how to obtain that help for them. His tutelage gave one valuable insights into other people—and even on rare occasions into oneself.

In 1954 the Missouri Province had been split into two provinces, with the division becoming official the following year. Although Denver remained part of the Missouri Province, I belonged to the newly formed Wisconsin Province. Like several other Wisconsin Province men, I kept hiding out at Regis. But then sometime during my tenth year in Denver I was found out, and the two provincials began to fight over me. The argument came down in essence to "You take him," and was promptly answered by, "No we've had him. You take him."

And so at the end of that year I was picked up on waivers, rather than traded, to Minneapolis in the Wisconsin Province, where I was to spend more time on writing and less on teaching. I considered it a stroke of luck at this time to fall into a part-time job teaching a course on sex and marriage, which I had already taught for ten years. There was only one negligible difference this time: I was to be teaching girls instead of boys.

Jesuits run boys' high schools and they sponsor, if no longer run, colleges which are usually co-ed. Since all my teaching had been on the high-school level, I had never had the pleasure of teaching young ladies, or even girls, formally. But I had dealt with the species in huge numbers in the youth groups of Denver, and so I knew something of their *modus operandi.* But to know something of one category of female types is by no means to know all; and to know these kids on the open range or even in a retreat is not the same as encountering them herded into a classroom. The man who claims to know much about women has to be either telling the truth or not. If he's telling the truth, he's not just a genius but one such as the world has never hitherto known. If he's not telling the truth, he's either just a liar or too stupid to realize how wrong he is. It's amazing, I might add, how many books and articles are written about women by men who are neither geniuses or liars. It is, in fact, something of a rarity to find even a woman who really knows other women.

One does, however, occasionally get little glimpses into the shadowy and mysteriously fragrant world of the female personality, perhaps uniquely so in a girls' academy. The first thing the male type notices in such a school is the somewhat strange attitude

No man is an island—except maybe the poor guy stranded in a girls' school.

of the workmen in the building and about the grounds. You get the feeling they're about to throw their arms around you, an attitude you mistake at first for Minneapolis friendliness until you realize it's really the overwhelming joy of a man who has long been stranded among women.

Come to think of it, there was one other occasion when I encountered such a phenomenon. A man knocked on our door and greeted me with the initially startling remark, "Father, I live with nine women." I'm sure I treated this with the good psychologist's "Well now, there's nothing abnormal about that; happens all the time." But I was relieved, nevertheless, to learn that he had eight daughters. There were, I swear, tears in his eyes as we talked, tears of joy at being able to converse with someone other than women for a change—although I'm not sure women really converse so much as only wait, more or less patiently, for you to finish what you have to say.

As you dodge, whistling gently to yourself, through the halls of a girl's school between classes, you wonder if these are really the creatures boys can get so absorbed in that they tend to forget all else. Their hair is sometimes a mess and often enough their dress is at least careless. They wear either too much makeup or not enough. They push and shove and giggle, and you wonder how far away from womanhood they really are. Probably only about as far as the nearest mirror.

I should hasten to add that the regulations in a Jesuit school usually keep the boys looking as close to human as boys get. But even so, at proms and such, you find it hard to recognize in the sleek, sharply dressed teen-aged boy the same casual kid who slept in your class just that morning.

Occasionally as I taught, I would see the younger girls exercising on the lawn, which was a still greater disillusionment to the sheltered male who had imagined that women are issued in only one delightful standard form. But the defenses are down during exercise period, and so is the camouflage. And so one marvels at what technology can do.

But these are surface musings. It's in the psychological area that a teacher had darned well better realize how vast is the boy-girl difference. Indeed, it would profit any husband or wife, prospective or actual, to realize the same fact.

From a time which must have been fairly close to birth I had always known that there is an enormous psychological difference between boys and girls. But I doubt if I had ever known before this teaching experience how wide the gap really is. I never realized for example, how terribly important it could be to a teen-aged girl that she wear either a white or blue-black hair ribbon. Nor did I realize that this ribbon is not just a supplementary, superficial bit of decoration, but infinitely more. Not one girl in this school would have dreamed of wearing a hair ribbon of any other color. And why? Because no *other* girl would ever wear any other color. Simple. They wouldn't wear the *same* dress as others socially, but they wouldn't be caught dead in a very different *length* of dress from the others.

As in the boys' schools I had taught in, here too I was something of a counselor. Now a boy will meet his counselor in the hall and simply make an appointment to see him, or else even go to the counselor's office unannounced. But the girls didn't do things this way. Occasionally on my desk I'd find a scented little note which chatted casually for a sentence or two and then offhandedly—as if it didn't matter in the least—ask for an appointment. It makes no difference to me of course, what method is employed so long as I can be helpful to the students.

In a counseling situation boys will often tell you about their dog for about an hour before getting down to the real point of the conference. Girls do the same thing, but the difference seems to be that instead of talking about their dog they often tend to talk about their girl friends and the latest gossip. Boys and men certainly gossip plenty. But I doubt if even the man working on his degree in womanology will ever be able to match the dread indirect effectiveness of the tiniest female. They're born experts, and they improve from then on.

I found the young female sense of humor, too, quite different from that of a boy. Boys love irony when it's properly handled and not unfairly or crudely used against them. But girls seem slower to accept this—maybe because of that eternal feminine striving for "equality" which only produces an inferiority complex in those who are already, in so many of their own ways, superior.

One day the gals had hauled an enormous stuffed wolf into the classroom and set up the monster in the back of the room on a sort of counter running around the back windows. Undoubtedly they were interested in the teacher's reaction to this caper. Being a guy who has known a lot of wolves personally, I didn't react at all. As far as they could tell, I didn't even notice the wolf until they had forgotten all about him. Halfway through the class period I pretended to see him for the first time and then quietly told one of the girls in front, "Tell that new girl in the back that if she's going to stay in class, she's going to have to wear a uniform like the rest of you." Then I went calmly on with the lesson. Maybe a few did titter. But the majority didn't seem to see anything funny at first, and finally when they did, acted as though I had insulted them. And what a way out idea *that* is.

While spring days and class rings and dreams of proms cause an air of some absentmindedness in boys' schools, the depth of the male coma ordinarily isn't even close to the female variety. Girls become absolute zombies at this time, off in another world, and there is little one can do to bring them back to reality, or what is currently passing for it.

Now these aren't just generalizations, and whimsical at that, but they're relative trifles as well. There was, however, one difference between boys and girls which seemed more serious to me. When I walked into the classroom at this school for the first time, I walked in with all the confidence of a veteran teacher handling a subject he had worked at for years—a course in sex and marriage—one, moreover, he liked to teach. The results of this course were always obvious and gratifying. The knowledge the boys gained seemed to produce a wholesome matter-of-fact attitude towards the whole beautiful subject.

But there were differences right from the start. For one thing, in all the years I'd taught this course to young men, I'd never encountered the slightest hint of disrespect for the subject, but rather an honest awe of it and the sincere desire to learn about it in an objective, professional manner. With the girls in general there was this same respect, but it wasn't so completely universal as with boys. The venom with which some girls can curse their lot as women, the near-hatred a very sensitive or depressed girl can manifest for the very fact that she exists because of a parental sexual act and her consequent disdain for sex itself—these bits of bitterness have, as far as my admittedly small experience has taught me, no general parallel among normal men.

In teaching a sex-marriage course to boys for ten years I have encountered appalling ignorance of the subject, despite, of course, the quite understandable pretense of knowing it all. I'd be suprised if more than one in fifty boys had gotten any adequate sex information at home. I felt certain, though, in launching out on the same course with girls that their knowledge would be better than that of the boys.

It turned out, though, that where the boys' ignorance of the subject had been appalling, that of the girls was utterly incredible. In a basic test on anatomy and such the class average for juniors and seniors was right up around 8 percent.

But ignorance is one thing, and complacency in that ignorance, or even the determination to preserve it, is quite another.

And here I ran into another surprise, a thing I'd never encountered in a single boy—the occasional girl who was not only ignorant of the whole subject but was directly opposed to learning anything about it. As one actually told me, in writing of course, "Leave us, please, with our romantic illusions." From what I was able to learn in this case, it seems that mother was almost certainly responsible for this attitude in her daughter, and the tragedy is that by this time this ignorant young lady has probably done some poor unsuspecting guy the favor of making his life sheer hell.

I don't mean to pummel the girls or to set myself up as a woman hater; if challenged, I could dig out a few testimonials to the contrary. I dearly loved teaching those kids, and the vast majority of them reacted beautifully, in accord with their beautiful nature. It was a great thrill, for example, to see them drop the pose of sophistication society seems to demand of the teen-aged girl, and to act like the kids they still in part were. It was delightful to see a girl stumbling over her own feet and then laughing about it instead of feeling she had publicly humiliated herself. It was awesome too to realize that you were teaching a woman one moment and a little girl the next. All too soon the girl would be gone, and it was exciting to know that you were helping the woman who would take her place. And so because I so admire the picture of what a girl or woman should be and usually is, I deplore the exceptions all the more.

Teaching is a thrilling business, if I can judge by my own experience. It's a great joy to see a young mind *seeing* a truth—and not just remembering or guessing at an answer—for the first time. It's a thrill to see a mind progress, even though such a sight is of its very nature only possible either very rarely or over a long, long haul. It was a joy to see boys and girls alike growing—mentally and spiritually, as well as physically. Maybe that's why I preferred high-school teaching over the higher educational department and why I consider it so vastly important. But then I'm sure the dedicated college teacher has reasons for *his* preference too, and reasons I'd respect.

CHAPTER
TWO

Down the up staircase

Clearly, my teaching experience is not as long as some others in the profession. But because I did teach for some ❖❖❖❖ time and saw some of its results and because I still feel I'm something of a teacher, even though the audience is much more remote, there are some educational phenomena today it's hard to keep completely quiet about. Being a kindly, gentle man, it's very much against my nature to do any griping; and yet I feel it's time *someone* did, so I just elected myself. And since this chapter *is* largely griping, I'd suggest that the reader who doesn't enjoy other people's gripes simply skip it and go directly to Chapter III which is less argumentative and, I hope, more pleasant.

The things I have to gripe about are germs. Unchecked, they could very well corrupt the whole educational field, since they've already damaged a good section of that field. It's my belief that the most serious disease in the field today is a growing permissiveness, further fed by what I call discussionism and dilettantism. Actually, these afflictions strike all types of education, public and private. Yet there are those, even those within the fold itself, who seem to think, or at least to say, that only Catholic education suffers from any defects at all. And so I'd like to include a kindly word or two here for the latter type of dedicated critic.

When one stands back for an objective look at education today, he sees some pretty frightening pictures flashing before his eyes. It's true that deep within the educational field some very thrilling things are indeed taking place, especially perhaps in the training of the very young. Unfortunately, there are also some pretty weird practices at work too. And hopefully, what I have to say here might prod some of the hitherto silent into getting on their hind legs and howling a bit about these atrocities.

For my first gripe let me introduce the subject of *permissiveness.* This is a little gimmick originally created perhaps by the league of grandparents, those lovable people who are so adept at spoiling their children's children, and by those educational theorists who have always managed to avoid practical experience. Unfortunately until they learn better, brand new teachers and parents do like to believe that the annoying (and apparently depopularizing) responsibility of discipline is passé and that permissiveness should characterize education—which is much like telling some gullible salmon that he ought to float downstream since it's so much easier than battling his way up.

Few if any disciplines are entirely successful in bridging the gap between theory and practice. In the educational field there's simply no substitute for facing the reluctant student every Monday morning after each weekend lost in correcting homework.

If one were looking for the most efficient means of destroying an entire civilization, he wouldn't have to look beyond permissiveness. Much, although by no means all, the chaos we see on some college campuses today is, in fact, due to permissiveness— from the time a theorist-trained mother indulgently wiped Junior's oatmeal off her face instead of stuffing it down his little throat, up to the time a college official smiled indulgently and handed over his job to the supposed learners in his "care." One hears too of experimental colleges with no curriculum, no schedule, no anything except the study of what one wishes and the neglect of what one decides to neglect. One such experimental college announced a few years ago that "the only requirement is the study of Urdu," which is to provide a window into non-Western culture and "to utilize an Urdu-speaking faculty member from Pakistan"— certainly a mature reason from mature educators for making only Urdu compulsory and keeping all else voluntary. But if some college campuses are beginning to resemble an uninterrupted Fort Lauderdale or even Fort Apache, we can expect still more startling things in the near future. One reads about experimental elementary schools where the kids pack their own weapons, where the curriculum offers a choice of arithmetic, mixed nude swimming, sewing, golf, knitting or casting small idols, or fooling around, and where any sort of guidance by adults is considered interference, and so taboo.

This gives a picture about as cheering as the *Lord of the Flies,* and it probably fails to alarm us because we know it's—still at least— an exception. And yet it *should* alarm us, because it's permissiveness brought to its logical conclusion which comes to barbarity— sometimes certainly the barbarity John Courtney Murray described as camouflaged in a Brooks Brothers suit, but nevertheless barbarity.

If we look into the learning process, we discover that even the very mature don't always learn best in studying only those items of their choice. Often enough, one learns through being exposed— even reluctantly or accidentally—to things he never dreamed existed and by forcing oneself or (horrible thought that it is) even being forced into listening to something in which he had no initial interest. The best one can hope to achieve from a studious avoidance of those things he doesn't want to hear is a bag of assorted information. He could well be forming only a psychopathically prejudiced personality as he clutches his little bag.

It has probably always been the case that the permissive administrator or teacher will do his thing by occasionally chopping down his fellow administrators or teachers. This, of course, is calculated to get him a rating of neat or cool from the student he coddles as he builds up this image of his own creation. I read recently of the dean of a woman's college who said that her girls would "play dead" in front of a certain teacher, because as this dedicated apostle of charity and solidarity put it, "They know it's a waste of time to argue with a fool."

Now either the teacher in question really was a fool or he wasn't. If he wasn't, then this clever administrative analysis should be vulnerable to the same libel laws as any similar statement—on campus or off. The fact is that some students (and administrators too, it seems) are quite likely to mistake plodding, unsensational and non-iconoclastic teaching as foolish. If the teacher really was a fool, then the first thing to be realized is that if one can't learn anything from even a fool, he's pretty much of a fool himself. More importantly in case the epithet really did fit, the proper thing to do would seem to be to get the poor fool, who somehow got this far in teaching, something more in keeping with his peculiar talents. In this particular college he might well have been made a dean, for example. Who knows—he might have a hidden talent for pointing out to the students the fools on the faculty?

The second gripe I'll air here is a first cousin of permissiveness, and it's known among psychologists as the discussion syndrome. This phenomenon is the *exaggeration* of a very good tool of good teachers—discussion, like booze, is neither good nor bad in itself, but indifferent. A moderate use of both for some good reason may be not only helpful but fun. Overuse them or exaggerate their importance though, and all you've got, respectively, is a silly drunk or an immature teacher, or maybe both at once. Taking booze on an empty stomach, disastrous as it can be, isn't even comparable to discussion originating in an empty head. As one of my teen-aged friends described the latter, it's nothing more than "confirmation in error."

The trouble is that the person afflicted with the discussion syndrome carries this mentality into all his fields of endeavor. Father Elvis, for example, tries to direct a retreat and finds himself at the center of the same sort of riot he inspires in the classroom. So he gives up, holding discussions and songfests and maybe a kite-fly instead of directing a real retreat while still calling it a retreat. And suddenly Father Elvis is neat and keen and cool and all like that—as esteemed, in fact, as those teachers who can always be talked out of assigning homework.

The discussion mentality spreads to unbelievable lengths and

Reading even pious truths aloud doesn't always grab the young.

undreamed-of conclusions. If discussion is the educator, who needs teachers? And if one can learn the will of God through discussion, who needs the Church or religious guides or the priesthood? Through discussion college students can learn to run a college much better than administrators, so who needs *them?* And discussing religious hardly need superiors.

Truth is "there," says the discussionist, and all you need do to experience it is open your mouth. Far and away the most boring teacher this author ever encountered used to maintain, his prose throbbing with the same high degree of emotion which character- ized his teaching, that it was impossible for a teacher to be dull if he was presenting the truth. To him, you served up the truth much the same way as hamburger or pizza, and the student, drooling in anticipation, couldn't help but gulp it down.

This is usually and quite understandably the mistake of the new teacher. He figures he's offering the kids a batch of manna and they can't help but like it, but he soon discovers that they'd still prefer some of the old leeks, onions and garlic.

But, while this is the normal and pardonable mistake of a new teacher, it's amazing how many apparent veterans seem to think that all one must do is expose the kid to the Scriptures, for example, and let him discuss them; and mental and perhaps even spiritual ecstasy simply must follow.

Since the dedicated discussionist is bound sooner or later, to find a good deal of time on his hands, he may well decide one day that the only valid kind of teaching is by example. And so he reconvinces himself that he's really teaching when not teaching. Or he can, in another symptomatic rash, echo the words of a no doubt great educator: "They can learn more on the picket line than in class." In a sense, of course, they can. They can also learn more on the battlefield. But in class, especially if they should be lucky enough to have a teacher present, they should be able to learn why there are picket lines or battlefields in the first place. And then they might just be able to do a better job on both fronts or maybe even help to avoid both, and some day perhaps picket lines and battlefields will become unnecessary because men will have learned.

Discussion, like most other things, is a perfectly good gimmick as long as it's skillfully used and in the right proportions. It's probable, in fact, that an under-use of discussion is just as bad as its overuse. Heresy is truth gone wild, and an enlarged heart is just too much of a good thing. So is too much discussion. So are two heads on one set of shoulders.

There may be some nice flowery words which could describe my third gripe, but I don't seem able to think of them at the moment. Sorry about that, but it seems to me that one great cause of many weaknesses in the educational field today (and especially in that field of minor-league theology called religion) is what can most accurately be called *dilettantism.*

It seems an inborn instinct of human nature to become so impressed with one's own thing and one's own opinions that one fails to notice, or at least to value, anyone else's. The reasonable maturing human being, willing to learn and able to progress, will sooner or later get over this. The superficial dilettante, however, will continue to see only the world of his own creation, regarding all else, when noticed at all, as satellites so far out as to be vague and unimportant. He's a dabbler and often a pedant in disguise. In his own eyes, of course, he's more an unrecognized expert.

Maybe one of the most obvious characteristics of the dilettante is what might be called The Year-One Complex. His world has just begun, and whatever may have preceded his public life and messianic mission was just a block of rock in the evolutionary process. Even in a field where one encounters tremendous generosity, self-sacrifice, and frequent heroism—on the missions—one will sometimes hear a newly arrived missionary ask, "Why has nothing ever been done here?" If he's a real missionary and not just there out of some mistaken search for glamor, he'll soon realize that if nothing had been done, he wouldn't have even the poor living quarters he has.

Year-One teachers are constantly coming up with new discoveries, astounding things no one seems to have thought of before. In our day, for example, legions of teachers have discovered that discussion or dialog is a fine pedagogical weapon—and we can expect new insights like this almost every day.

A dilettante is an *aficionado*, or fan, who lacks the skill or thoroughness of the real participant. And yet he pretends to be the master, drawing universal truths from his very limited information or experience, often guided largely by his emotions. He's the specialist of the half-truth, the discoverer of the long overused cliché. Some dilettantes today are able to quote many a lovely expression from their favorite, half-understood authors. The dilettante as teacher is undaunted by the restricting limits of his knowledge, managing to stretch it far enough under a confident cover of clichés and a liberal use of the discussion method.

But if I'm griped at the permissive and the discussionist and the dilettante in education, I'm far more frequently thrilled by the great teachers I've seen in action and sometimes been privileged to work with. And maybe in retrospect I can see some of the qualities of those teachers much more clearly than when next to them.

38

While the superficial teacher's qualities begin outside on the surface, those of the good, sometimes great teacher begin within; and so he knows the value of study and contemplation before he ever opens his mouth. He's not a talk now and it may make sense later type. When he does talk, he will already have thought it out rather than only groping for it in speech; and so he has something to say, something beneath the words and even the clichés.

He really does become involved instead of just talking about it; and he becomes involved, not with some vague remote object of pity, but with those nearest to him, his students. He doesn't *use* his students so much as letting them use him. He serves them. He sees in them, moreover, not some bubbling blob of humanity, but individuals, each with a unique personality, unique reactions, unique wants and yearnings—but with a common destiny. In a family, father and mother are either going to realize that their children are individuals, or they're going to fail as parents. They just can't expect John to be as clean and sweet as Jane, and they can't, usually at least, expect Jane to kick a football as far or be as fascinated by frogs as John is. In any classroom there is a comparable situation, and the real teacher will knock himself out to know *each* student, to know, for example, when to push and when to pull both class and individual. Push a kid at the wrong time, when you should be either pulling or leaving him alone, and you've lost him—maybe forever.

As a human being himself the teacher respects and appreciates the human beings before him. Moreover, he loves them—not with the gushy sentimentality of a flower child, but with genuine esteem for them despite their faults, and not because he sentimentally closes his eyes to such faults. He loves them as children of God, no matter how they may appeal or not appeal to him personally. And so loving them, he's concerned as a teacher with seeking their good unselfishly.

Certainly, one of the most basic requisites for a teacher has to be unselfishness, from the unselfish giving of his time all the way to his refusal to seek himself in his students or even their success. Many of the faculty gripes about poor students come not so much from a genuine concern for the student as from the frustration of the teacher and his inner feeling of failure. And if there is one thing the teen-aged psychologist (and they all are) can spot quickly, in a teacher or parent, it's selfishness.

Until the teacher learns that visible results are not what count (after he's done his best), he's not really a teacher—because he's not unselfish enough yet.

There's a certain mystery about the effectiveness of teaching, just as there is to that indefinable term "leadership." You'll find a brilliant man who simply can't communicate and a hard-working teacher of medium talent who can teach up a storm. Occasionally you'll see high-schoolers making life utterly miserable for a muscle-bound, heavy-bearded teacher or prefect, while a small, soft-spoken one can hold them by his or her very presence.

One answer to these seeming contradictions has to lie in the degree of alertness and interest of the teacher. Young people seem to know at once when a teacher's mind isn't entirely on them, and so they tend to go elsewhere also. The good teacher or prefect gives the impression that he has no interest whatsoever except this job of the moment, and he never gives the impression that he'd sooner be somewhere—maybe anywhere—else.

Now clearly no one could sustain such an impression without, usually at least, really liking what he's doing. This is, I believe, the difference between the great teacher and the merely good one; the former genuinely enjoys teaching, and he loves and enjoys his students. Naturally there will always be times, like most Mondays,

It's hard to explain exactly a disciplinarian's success or failure.

when even the best teacher will walk into a classroom with something less than peak enthusiasm.

Another thing the genuine teacher will make sure of is that it's he who walks into that classroom and not some phony personality he's assumed. He has to be himself—which doesn't mean complacency in one's own drawbacks, but working with what one has rather than pretending to have the qualities, good or bad, of others.

One of the greatest retreat masters in the business, Father Dan Campbell, S.J., used to give the senior retreat at Regis High in Denver each year. I had heard Father Dan one of those years just prior to going out to direct a retreat myself; and so instead of being Father Joe McGloin, I did imitations of a poor man's Father Dan Campbell. The kids spotted this, of course, long before I did but I finally spotted it too. And so that was the last time I tried to be anyone else but mediocre little old me.

Given then, the prepared, alert, interested, sincere teacher, the means he uses are going to differ with his own personality and that of his students. Some means, however, seem very nearly essential to any teaching process: questioning, oral and written testing, repeating (always in different ways), relating one bit of knowledge to another and both bits to all knowledge, related reading and reporting, genuine, active discussion, and writing. None of these gimmicks works by itself, but all require careful preparation and a teacher who can awaken interest and maybe even inspire a bit of his own enthusiasm. And all of them are helps to making knowledge one's own and not just a memory lesson.

Certainly it must be obvious to anyone that the requisites for a good teacher are very much like the requisites for a good parent. And so is the final characteristic I would name, that dirty old word "discipline." The fact is that the full-time parent and the full-time teacher alike won't have the problem with discipline the part-time absentminded excuse for either one will have. How inconsistent our society can be when it demands discipline in the business and professional world and allows it to be eliminated in education and home training—even in marriage for that matter.

The trouble is—more so today perhaps than ever before—it's the relatively few dilettantes who make the headlines rather than the many, many good teachers.

Some time ago a teaching nun commented—in a magazine, of course, and in a neat reversal of that selfless outlook supposed to be essential to the good teacher *and* the religious—that *she* could do as well teaching in a public school. She went on in a burst of flawless logic to say with no apparent doubt or hesitation that the "Catholic schools are on the way out." Only in the fine print could one discover the incidental fact, "Of course, I'm only in my second year of teaching." And this was September!

There undoubtedly *is* a financial problem connected with Catholic education, just as there is with any private education. On the other hand, it isn't just private schools which feel the financial squeeze—there have been instances of public schools being closed because they lacked funds—although the double tax burden is doubly hard on Catholic parents.

PART TWO

CHAPTER
THREE

Wall-to-wall
teen-agers

Walter Mitty and I were soul brothers long before I ever made his acquaintance. Years ago when I contemplated my ◇◇◇◇ future, I quite easily saw myself as a tennis pro, an eminent doctor, a diplomat, a cop. All of these accomplishments were incidental, however, to the conviction that I was certain to be worshipped as the adored head of a household of fifteen kids, their incredible mother, and fifteen Great Danes, one for each child. At one point, in fact, I even had a dreamer much like myself talked into all but fourteen of the Great Danes.

Not even in my wildest dreams of those Mittyish days, though, did I ever see myself as a Jesuit. And even when that impossible dream became reality, it never occurred to me that as a Jesuit I would ever have any more to do with youth than trying to hold a

I had, of course, often visualized the success of my future vocation.

gang of them at bay in a classroom. Teaching, I felt, was darn well going to be it, and come 3 P.M.—especially on Friday—*that* apostolate was going to flake off, even as my devoted students would reluctantly trudge off for home.

Now I suppose every would-be teacher envisions his future students as Pavlov's dogs in more or less human form, drooling for knowledge at the first bell and sprinting for home at the last. And of course, every non-teacher knows perfectly well that a teacher has only a six-hour day. At least some of the pastors who asked for our help on weekends seemed to wonder what we could possibly have done otherwise with all that free time. It takes exactly one day of teaching to burst this pretty balloon. In the first place, they *don't* all streak out at the final bell. There are always a few characters who perversely prefer to stick around for awhile. There are also some who would clearly prefer not to stick around any longer, but who do so anyhow—in some cases because a teacher, having failed to touch their hearts that day with love, is now going to see if maybe a little fear won't turn the trick.

Then too, so many school activities seem to begin when the school day ends that you wonder why you bother with the regular curriculum at all. There are annual publications and school newspapers, drama and glee clubs, athletic and debate teams, organizations of the next set of protests, and all those other activities billed as "extra-curriculars"—even when, as sometimes seems the case, they would probably fit into the class day much more logically than some of the other stuff presently indulged in for academic credit.

Quite often a number of the inmates will stick around after the bell just to talk—about their studies, maybe, or at least about their lives. And the teacher who really is a teacher will soon discover that he may well be living up to his name more thoroughly and literally after the dismissal bell than he managed to do before it. Certainly it's here too that much of the real rapport between teacher and student is created or perhaps strengthened, and where a school's morale, if it's to have any, is born. The teacher is, in fact, a full-timer; the classroom, contrary to those *a priori* convictions of the neophyte or the non-teacher, is the arena for only the minimal part of his vocation.

When I was sent to Regis High in Denver in the autumn of 1951, my assignments were quite simple: teach English Literature and Religion, serve as moderator for the student magazine, and do some counseling. To a guy who had wrestled with the Jesuit course of study and was somehow still alive it seemed like a relaxed, healthy setup. Then one day the principal, Fr. Jim Eatough, met me in the hallway and blew the whole peaceful bit, as he casually

mentioned, "I'd like you to see what you can do with that sodality."
At the time I thought in passing that someone in a somewhat
earlier day might just as casually have suggested to a man named
Socrates, "How about a nice, cool glass of hemlock?"

In theory and in its simplest description—too simple—the
sodality is a way of life within one's state of life. It outlines certain
principles by which the laity could live more perfect lives. And
so, centuries before the retroactive prophets of our age of discovery broke the story of lay perfectibility to a startled but happy
world, the Jesuits who dreamed up the sodality were aware of the
possibilities.

It would be beyond the scope of this book to attempt any
thorough description of the sodality in action. But one of the
greatest working sodalities I have ever seen is not called a sodality
at all, but is known as the M.F.C., or *Movimiento Familiar Cristiano*
of Mexico. The last time I had any close contact with this group,
there were over twenty thousand couples involved in its workings
in Mexico City alone. You would find a daily schedule for the
family posted in the home: Mass, meditation, and so on. Profes-
sionals in this group give their time and talents to helping those
who need them most, with architects teaching the poor how to
build houses, seamstresses teaching them to sew, doctors instructing
in health and medicine, and so on. One close friend of mine has
formed a group which finances the complete education of many
children. This group managed, in fact, by very hard work and a lot
of holy chiseling, to con people who needed it less out of half a
million pesos one year and a million the next for people who needed it more—which is a lot of money anywhere (a peso was eight cents).
Maybe one can best sum up the spirit of M.F.C. in a short prayer
they sometimes use: *Señor, dales pan a los que tienen hambre, y
hambre de Ti a los que tenemos pan.* (Lord, give bread to those who
are hungry, and to those of us who have bread, a hunger for You.)

In other words, this Mexican organization displays all the
essential elements of a good working sodality—the attempt to
perfect oneself and others, a goal which includes apostolic work as
one of its means. The trouble was that the sodalities we had experienced in our own youth had been nothing like that. They
were pure blah. And so I felt that the organization was a predes-
tined loser and that I was being saddled with a distasteful job that
traditionally had to be done, one that less recent members of the
faculty than I had shrewdly refused to have anything to do with.

And so in my ignorance the work with sodalities began with
an attitude you might correctly call somewhat short of enthusiastic. This attitude wasn't improved any by the discovery that

when I drew the short straw on the sodality directors' raffle, there were all of sixteen sodalists (out of 350 boys) in the entire school. And of course, all I knew about the sodality then was that you herded the kids together for meetings; I had no idea what they were supposed to do once the gates were locked.

But there were at least two things I hadn't forseen while priding myself on my blind obedience in humbly shouldering this distasteful burden. First of all, I had no idea then how well a real sodality could satisfy that great hunger of the young for a challenge. And second, when I first encountered those sixteen sodalists, I couldn't possibly have imagined what sixteen boys were capable of. In retrospect I've often realized that there must have been many a jolly green giant around the time of Christ too, who had wondered what those twelve slobs could possibly be capable of.

Very quickly those sixteen began to teach me—not directly about the sodality, but rather that it was worth finding out about. It began to occur to me that this sodality thing could be worthwhile and that starting almost from scratch might not be such a tragedy either.

The first big break seemed to come almost by accident—the suggestion that each of the sixteen bring a friend to the next meeting. One young guy alone (now Father Bob Sullivan, S.J.) brought fifteen friends to that next meeting, and by the end of that school year we had about two hundred sodalists, good ones. By the end of the year too, we were beginning to find out what a sodality was all about.

Even our school sodalities soon got too big—luckily as it turned out—for the available faculty manpower. So we divided the crowd into small groups of around fifteen, directed at their weekly meetings by a senior and a junior who had already prepared the meeting in conference with one of the faculty moderators. Any teacher knows that he learns an unforeseen amount from his students, not just in preparing his class material but when he tries to put it across to a class. And so the boys in charge here turned into some pretty terrific, knowledgeable leaders, as they realized you can't hand something on unless you have it first yourself. They also, as a by-product, began sometimes to appreciate *their* teachers more. As time went on, some very good literature was showing up on what the sodality was supposed to be and how meetings should be conducted. *The Queen's Work* in St. Louis, under Father Dan Lord, S.J., had always given great help to those who wanted it. Now some of the theologians at St. Mary's, Kansas— men who had previously in their own regency days been saddled with sodality work—put out a set of booklets that fit our unique school situation. Like myself these men had come to see the sodality's potentialities, instead of only spending their time griping about not being assigned to some job which was clearly more apostolic—like handing out sweat socks for the athletic department.

Since many of the other schools in the city had sodalities and we had much to learn from them, we were soon getting the city's moderators and sodalists together for meetings and for days of recollection and discussion. It's funny how some chance remark can clue you in on whole attitudes and psychologies. One such remark from those days still stands out in my mind: "I didn't know there were that many good kids around." From then on this was the idea beneath just about every meeting and convention we held—to make sure the kids knew they had all kinds of company in their ideals and principles, and that the loud-mouths were then, as always, a minority.

Just as we had once divided our own school's sodalists into smaller groups, so now we began to divide the city's sodalists into neighborhood groups. We called them "cells" until a parent—a Mr. Maple or Cedar or some such name, I believe—objected that cell was a commie word. So we traded the word cells for units until, of course, the communists, no doubt hearing of us, also substituted units for cells and so we had to switch back. These groups, units or cells, met once a week all over the city, and they were the forerunners of a youth organization.

After the cells or units had been operating for awhile, some of the young people suggested that we set up a city council, made up of representatives from each school, to meet periodically and then communicate what they had learned to their respective schools. This was a tremendous step forward and it would be impossible to forget the three young people who were its prime movers: Jeannie Cattermole (now Mrs. Robert Brun), Barry Dawson, and John Castellano—all now raising a few sodalists of their own. As time went on there were to be many like these three, too numerous to mention. But one remembers pioneers.

Soon we had two councils of about seventy-five members each in operation: a senior and junior group, to insure continuity and an executive board to plan meetings and so on. Naturally, the rules for membership in these groups were stricter than those for the ordinary sodalist—something the young people had no trouble understanding, although a few of their adult leaders, especially some with a status symbol mentality, would occasionally miss the whole point.

Our executive board used to meet every couple of weeks on Sunday mornings. After Mass at Regis we'd head for the nearby Ernie's Supper Club, which at that time had a back room we could use for breakfast and our meeting. At one of these breakfasts we had some hotcakes, and I later griped to my good friend Ernie Capillupo about the white syrup he then served instead of maple syrup. Ernie didn't say much about this—at least not much for him, which meant only a few hundred words. But the next time we met he greeted me cheerily and called out, "Here's your bottle, Father," as he reached under the bar and pulled out a bottle which turned out to be maple syrup but which looked—especially considering its storage place—exactly like bourbon. To the startled customers in the room at that hour Ernie explained happily if inadequately, "Always uses the stuff on his pancakes."

After another of our meetings I emerged from the back room with a few bills in my hand to pay Ernie, whose cash register was at the corner of the bar. Also at the corner of the bar this particular morning was a customer who obviously had propped himself up there for awhile and who, on seeing the priest and the bills, demanded, "Hey, what kinda game's goin' on back there?"

Out of Ernie's back room, too, and from that particular group of kids came a whole series of articles about a mythical character named Father Robin (since he was depicted as something of a hood, robbing the rich to help the poor) and about four of the kids he worked with. Ernie was surprised and delighted with the series, only noting on seeing the opening article, "Hey, you make my joint sound like a dump." A few minutes later I heard a friend, or most probably a relative of Ernie's, say, "Hey, Ernie, he makes your dump sound like a joint."

Our purposes in getting all the kids together and organized were many: communication, encouragement, a sharing of ideals and principles, joy in good company. And yet, our purpose was single too: to get as many young people as possible to help instead of hurting each other, to give them a sense of solidarity in the things they knew were important and right. And we used every means we could find to further that purpose.

One great help was the result, once more, of a casual suggestion at one of their get-togethers—to have their own magazine. Some of the kids began the *By-Line,* as they called it, as a little leaflet sort of thing run off on the Good Shepherd Convent's mimeograph and then on an offset machine. Finally, it became an eighty-page printed magazine, its cover in full color, going to some four thousand subscribers around the country and even outside it. Andy Martelon and his brothers, just then beginning their AM Printing business, made the publication possible in those years; but since they also were just beginning, we were able to help them in some small way too.

We also did a TV show from time to time. There's really nothing comparable with doing TV shows with the young, because some of them are invariably so frightened (and still more scared to show it) beforehand that they come pretty close to getting sick, but then once it starts, they're usually charming and relaxed and honest and open and all the rest, usually having a ball in fact. So does the whole studio staff.

In thumbing through the final issue of the *By-Line,* I came across a paragraph, almost at random, which will tell better than I can what the kids thought of and expected from this organization. I remember the boy who wrote this—no mystic, but just an ordinary, good guy.

> This history [a foregoing sketch of the history of the sodality] should give us an idea of what the sodality is meant to be in the light of its past history—a means of genuine, solid sanctity and apostolicity. It is *not* a club, not an unrealistic antidote to juvenile delinquency that would cure all juvenile ills by social or blind, unmotivated do-good activity; nor, on the other hand, is it an ivory-tower type of spirituality. No, it is a genuine, all-pervading *way of life,* touching on every aspect and moment of life— a way to sanctity, personal and apostolic. Moreover, it is manly and womanly—a challenge to any teen-age American with two virtues: life and courage. Only the dead and spineless *need not apply.*

I'd say that gives a pretty good idea of what it was all about.

All this time our get-togethers were growing both in frequency and the numbers of persons attending. Soon city-wide became state-wide, then district-wide, and finally and for some years, at least on occasion, nationwide.

We Americans have to be the most profuse discussers in history, and so quite naturally we are great convention people. There are, however, conventions and conventions. Some are invaluable, while others remind you more of a pack of middle-aged boys and/or girls who have suddenly found themselves away from home and mother for awhile. But no matter what their nature or effectiveness, all conventions have at least one thing in common: they cost money. Conventioning is big business. As a matter of fact some conventions as such are simply not worth the time or effort or expense involved. And while there are undoubtedly many more useless adult conventions than those for teens (for one reason because there are more adult conventions of any type), still one tends to look on a youth convention *a priori* as fun and games and a little mild mayhem.

Our conventions, or "youth congresses," were not, however, begun as only fun things; nor did they operate as such. True, they were *fun,* hopefully in about the same proportions as life itself is fun. Getting a youth convention organized is work, so much work that only an utter idiot would attempt it without overwhelmingly good reason. Now it was perfectly clear to me that here, particularly in the members of the two councils, we had young people who had more to offer their contemporaries than any number of sermons or sets of instructions. We figured that no young people could come in contact with our central group without profiting from the mere contact. The youngsters at the heart of these conventions were the same ones who were giving their Saturdays to the poor and orphans, who knew that this life demanded character and who lived accordingly, and who were deserting childish and selfish immaturity gracefully and courageously.

At the time of the conventions I had a lot of hazy ideas about why we held them—even as in the middle of all of them I swore never to get involved in another one because I was going to enter the Trappist order at the conclusion of this one. But even years later I was still discovering more reasons why the Lord had pushed us into them—whenever I'd meet any of the kids who had been there, for instance. A short time ago I ran into a priest who had brought some of his students to one of the early conventions from somewhere in Texas. They had arrived late, when in fact, Bishop Bernard Sullivan, S.J., was already celebrating an afternoon Mass for the group which was jammed into the hall. This was back in the dark age when, as we're now told, it was clear that no one could possibly be participating in the Mass because everyone was so silent. And yet, this priest still remembers how impressed he and the kids with him had been when they had come into that hall, jammed with wild teen-agers, hushed and thoughtful—not, clearly, with the hush of boredom (since they don't hush, for long at least, with boredom), but with reverence and understanding and communion with God and with each other in God. (I hasten to note that I'm not knocking our newly found external participation in the Mass, nor the vernacular. But it is at least possible that in concentrating so zealously on this external participation we may, up to now at least, have lost sight of a certain inner and deeper appreciation and participation. It will be nice when we get both.) Had this single effect been the sole result of that entire conventions, all our work would have been justified.

The convention "just grew," so that we were involved in them almost before we realized it. There had been local single days of recollection and discussion, then local double days, then non-local gatherings and finally nationwide three-day conventions, or congresses. The first conventions, or Rocky Mountain Youth Congresses, were centered at some of the schools in Denver. This soon became an impractical setup, however, so we had to look elsewhere. Fortunately, we didn't have to look far, since the Denver Elks generously offered us the use of their hall. We had only one convention at this hall, but it was a beauty, with some seventeen hundred young people in attendance from many parts of the United States. Strangely perhaps, out of all those delegates, I particularly remember two black girls from a southern state, fresh from their contact with their then governor's historical and "disinterested" attempt to keep *his* schools lilly-white. I found these two sitting on the steps of the Elks Club at about 7 A.M., having come in by bus. One of my boys immediately took them to the Shirley-Savoy where Ike Walton, the manager, welcomed them as he did all our kids with the most tremendous courtesy. If our hospitality fell short of that of their home state, they didn't say so.

We were able to stay at the Denver Elks for only one convention, because we outgrew it even before getting there. And yet, crowded as we were, in retrospect this seems to me our greatest convention in many ways; at least it was the most fun. Maybe it was because the conventions were new and fresh and not yet *too* big, so that there could be a livelier, less impersonal atmosphere, and a looser discipline perhaps, that the larger crowds were going to demand. Whatever the reason, it was great.

But if we're going to talk about the evolution of these conventions, we're going to have to discuss a dirty subject: money. The best convention program in this world isn't worth a hoot if very few can afford it. Our potential delegates were a pretty good cross section of America. While some of them wouldn't have blinked at a fairly healthy tab for a three-day youth convention, most of them (and their moderators, too, incidentally) couldn't have afforded too much. And so for every conceivable and inconceivable reason, we had to beg and scrape and fight to keep the costs down. It soon became clear that the costs of a large convention can't be kept down without the presence of someone who is a bit shameless about getting the job done. And that's my sole excuse for becoming what my friend Will Jurgens termed a clerical chiseler.

Delegates to our conventions paid twelve dollars for the whole bundle: lodging, transportation around town, four main meals; everything, in fact, except minor meals and snacks (I hasten to point out that a teen-ager's snacks are never really minor), souvenirs and such. Several parents, in fact, wrote to ask if I would hold on to their kids a bit longer, since it cost more than that to feed them at home.

Since the Denver Elks hadn't charged us for the use of their building, we had to look for something larger at about that same reasonable price. Up to now, we had met with nothing but kindness and cooperation—from the Elks, hotel men, restaurant operators, musicians. But now as we approached an auditorium and arena world, it was like walking into a cold, cold climate after enjoying a nice warm room. To put the matter as briefly as possible, the arena or auditorium would have cost us about five thousand dollars for our convention. It would be necessary, of course, to pay a full crew of stage hands full days' wages because one of them would have had the harrowing and exhausting responsibility of turning the lights on in the morning and off at night. There had to be a complete crew of janitors too, and an auditorium full of paid ushers—even when we could easily have handled these jobs ourselves.

The final chapter in this incredible tale of horror concerned the meals. We would have to serve some ten thousand meals, and this would call for another complete crew to put up and take down tables, plus of course the costs per meal. Happily, I have forgotten what this latter figure was. I tried to duck that cost anyhow by proposing that my friend Ed Rogers at the Denver Drumstick serve the meals in paper boxes as he had done so beautifully at the Elks. They were ready for this one too; that would cost me twenty-five cents for each meal served, plus of course whatever I would pay Ed. So naturally, at the mention of this latest $2,500, I had a few questions, like who got this little stipend and for what? I don't recall that there were any really precise answers, but my impression was that the recipient of the money was some sort of official village caterer who would "pick up the boxes" at this ridiculously low salary.

By this time, it was clear, of course, that we had long ago left the practical order, so I had two speculative questions: First, what were those janitors—already into us for some five hundred dollars—doing while the boxes were being picked up by someone else for this

54

laughingly nominal fee? And second, were there any openings on this job? If I could pick up boxes at the rate of twenty-five cents per box, I figured I could make at least $150 an hour, and that beat the clerical chiseling bit. Now certainly I'm not knocking Denver's late-fifties convention facilities any more than I'd knock anyone else trying to make an honest buck. The city has lots of conventions, so there must have been some point here I missed. All I'm saying is that clearly *we* couldn't afford it, and to be honest, nobody concerned took any steps to *help* us afford it.

Only about seventy miles south of Denver is a lovely town, Colorado Springs. I had spent a year there, but I was not well acquainted, since that year had been spent in a hospital bed staring at Pikes Peak, a view that impressed me for only the first few minutes. But Colorado Springs is a convention town and a good one, and it was reachable from Denver, so I took a look. Not knowing anybody of influence in the Springs, I followed a hunch and tracked down the editor of the *Colorado Springs Free Press*, Ed Byrne, catching up with him one day in the bar at the El Paso Club. To my surprise and delight Mr. Byrne not only liked the idea of our convention's coming to the Springs, but he promised to help sponsor it— with all the publicity he could give it and "buying the kids their first meal." It sounded too good to be true, but true it was.

One step led to another. The Colorado Springs auditorium, it turned out, would just hold our group of between two and three thousand. There was a fifty-dollar fee for it, but the Chamber of Commerce would take care of that. The meals would be served, and reasonably, by the Antlers and Alamo hotels with no charge for picking up the boxes. Our final meal—a chuck-wagon dinner following a field Mass in the Garden of the Gods on Sunday—would be handled by Joe Reich one year and Mike Edwards the next, professionally and reasonably. Despite the fact that many of the motel and hotel rooms in the Springs go at around sixteen dollars, the hotel men there, as in Denver previously, agreed to $2.50 per night per person. The fact that it was November and that I could send them two to four hundred head each at this price alleviated the pain somewhat. Actually they were glad to help, and many of them even threw in some transportation and rescue work and such as the convention progressed.

Transportation was a major item. Getting the kids to the city wasn't any great problem since we had great cooperation, particularly from Floyd Roberts of the Continental Trailways and Dwayne Fleer of the Burlington. But the hotels and motels were a long haul from the convention center, and our final day's activities would be at the Garden of the Gods, twelve miles from the auditorium—a good brisk walk. The first bus company I checked with came up with a four-thousand-dollar figure for the three days—not a bad figure either, but one I could only admire because I just didn't have it. By the time we left this office, we were down to sixteen hundred dollars and I caught Will Jurgens watching me a bit more carefully after that time. Unfortunately, this bus company mogul later had second thoughts and decided he couldn't do it for sixteen hundred dollars after all, so we had to look elsewhere.

Will and I went to Continental Trailways to see Floyd Roberts, who simply nodded and agreed to everything. Floyd was undoubtedly horrified later on, realizing what he had agreed to; but he did it, probably with a bit of manipulating to make things come out nice and even. Floyd gave us eight huge buses to and from Denver, and we were to use them for all three days. The big snag was going to be on Sunday when eight buses just couldn't do it, since on that day we would have to bring all the kids to the Garden of the Gods at the same time. While we were getting pretty good at filling buses, two thousand just wouldn't go into eight. I'm probably not at liberty to say how the problem was solved the first year, but I don't think it will hurt anything in this day of ecumenism (retroactive I hope), to mention how Floyd took care of it the second year.

On the final day of our convention that year, while the kids were eating their way through the chuck-wagon dinner, wagon and all, Floyd pointed up the hill. "Look at all those buses, Father," he said proudly, "twenty-three of them."

"All I see," I told him, "are eight." But there *were* twenty-three of them. "How did you do it?" I whispered.

"Well," Floyd answered, "I'll tell you. Each Sunday the Council of Churches hires fifteen buses to bring the Air Academy cadets to the Protestant churches in town. The buses weren't doing a damned thing for a few hours, so . . . ." Floyd smiled with satisfaction. At this late date I still smile in appreciation for this generous, if unvolunteered, ecumenical gesture by the Council of Churches.

These were our major financial hangups, but there were others too, of course, and so many people allowed themselves to be chiseled that it would be impossible even to list them. One year the Pepsi Company supplied all the Pepsi the kids could drink (which isn't really much, only about enough to float an ark), plus paying for the dinner boxes, plus later putting a Pepsi machine in my office in which I kept the beer until, after a year or so, some vice-president decided the machine wasn't paying off. Other companies did similarly nice things for us. I seem to recall a lot of free candy and pop that one of my adult helpers, Officer Joe Hale of the Denver Police

Department, inadvertently sold on the train between Denver and Colorado Springs. Dale Seiders at the Antlers cut his meal prices down so far that no one but a clerical chiseler would have the guts to try to get them still lower. Karl Pehlman did a twenty-minute 16 mm sound documentary of the Congress which I still have—at about one percent of the going rate.

There were many memorable moments before, during, and after these conventions, but one that particularly stands out in my mind for its unique sort of poetic justice concerns the motels. Once things got rolling and after my own initial meetings with them, it was Will Jurgens who contacted the motel and hotel owners, gathering all the information on how many delegates they could take and so on. One day I was in Will's office when a certain motel owner called. The conversation, I believe, went something like this:

MOTEL OWNER:

How come that priest is boycotting us Catholic motel owners?

WILL JURGENS:

He's not boycotting anybody. We can use your motel. Father's paying two dollars and fifty cents a night per person. How many kids can you take?

MOTEL OWNER:

The lowest I can go is seven dollars and fifty cents.

WILL JURGENS:

(starting to burn) All the others are going at two dollars and fifty cents. Father can't pay you seven dollars and fifty cents.

I don't know exactly what followed on the other end of the line here, but what it came to was that our Catholic friend wasn't willing to come down. He seemed to figure that since he was a Catholic, I should have been paying him $7.50 a night instead of the $2.50 those non-Catholics were accepting. Will seldom gets really burned, but I could see he was now. His final sentence before hanging up couldn't possibly have been improved on: "Listen, I know this priest, and he doesn't give a damn about what you are. All he cares about's your motel rate."

But even chiseling and cutting down on costs as we did, we still couldn't have broken even without donations from "patrons," and this meant just plain begging. Our patrons included every sort of person, all of them with only one thing in common: an interest in seeing the kids get something worthwhile and memorable from this convention. In looking over the list of patrons now, I notice ads from people like the Kerdy Wrecking Company, who couldn't have expected much direct business from their ad—or maybe they could at that. I remember one luxurious home where Will Jurgens accompanied me in my search for funds, where all I heard for an hour was how much this couple was already giving to every conceivable charity and a few more. As time wore on, it became quite clear that they were single-handedly supporting at least the whole Catholic Church, not to mention the United States Government. It became equally clear that we would be lucky to get out of there with the change in our own pockets.

When we did finally emerge, tearfully and clutching a five-dollar donation, all Will Jurgens could seem to manage was, "You'll have to make more than five bucks an hour." It helped to remind myself of the infinitely poorer people than these who had come across with twenty-five or even a hundred dollars. I remember, too, a group of young guys the summer before who had emptied their pockets in my hands before entering the Jesuit seminary, and so had become "patrons" of the coming congress. It's possible, of course, that I may have suggested this give-to-us-poor bit.

When I look back on these conventions and the money involved (it must have been a thirty- or forty-thousand dollar turnover), I have the sense of its all having been a somewhat frightening dream—at least the financial part of it. I can remember having up to twenty thousand dollars in my old room at Regis, sorting it out on the floor and then bringing it to the bank in a paper bag—something which only a money-unconscious religious could possibly get by with. Sometimes I tremble at the thought. On the other hand, I sort of wish I could walk barefoot through a bit of the stuff right now. It's too bad to have to consider money first when discussing these youth gatherings, but it had to come first. No money, no convention; it was as simple as that.

Naturally, there was a lot of other planning too, much of which the young people themselves gradually took on. There were speakers to contact and potential delegates. There were, in fact, something like ten thousand letters to be sent out, programs and schedules to be drawn up, entertainers to be hired, chaperones to be conned into the job, panels to be prepared, hotel rooms to be assigned, trains and buses and planes to be met, and so on. There were memorable surprises and seeming contradictions—like the sunshine, strong enough in November to give the kids a sunburn at the Garden of the Gods' field Mass and chuck-wagon dinner, while some Californians who had never seen snow before found enough of the stuff behind the rocks to have a snowball fight in the sun. In fact, we always had good weather even though it was November. There was the year we lost our electrical power just when it was time to sum up the panel discussions for the whole group, and were lucky enough to have Father Joe Freeman, S.J., on hand to take over—a man with a built-in bullhorn.

We tried to keep the right balance of seriousness and fun at the conventions, opening and closing them with Mass. There was a get-acquainted party the first night and a dance on Saturday. There was always a talent show. There were bus tours of the magnificent scenes to be found in Colorado Springs and the vicinity, such as the Garden of the Gods, the Air Academy, the Broadmoor district, and so on. The great NORAD chorus sang for us one afternoon, and the Air Academy Choir sang at our concluding field Mass. Two of the talent shows stand out in my mind. At one of them two Pine Ridge, South Dakota, Indian boys brought down the house with their native dance. They really deserved their first prize, even though I had forgotten to appoint any judges and so had to judge the show myself. That was right after they had made me an honorary member of their tribe, something which might have led to a charge of bias had anyone known who the judges were. The other talent show I remember was one in which a little blind girl won first prize. She deserved it too. But even if she hadn't, the judges would have thought twice about giving it to anyone else, with that big seeing-eye dog staring at them meaningfully all the time she sang.

The young people themselves were, of course, the chief workers around the convention. There were, however, a number of things requiring adult help, and I was lucky enough to get two tremendous groups of people interested—one in Denver and one in Colorado Springs. Every name on that list, when I look at it now, brings back the memory of their enthusiasm, loyalty and friendship. I wish it were possible to talk about all of them. Since we were centered in Denver, it was naturally the Denver group which was most intimately concerned with the congresses. Like the teen-agers, the adults seemed to help, each in a unique way, to contribute his or her thing to a successful congress.

John Doyle deserted his regular job for the entire three days and his wife Lois stopped whatever she'd been doing, and so both always seemed to be where they were most needed. Just before the opening of one of the congresses John and I had been casing the Antlers Hotel, as was our custom, when on the fifth floor we happened upon two very tough and very seedy-looking characters

In a simple, heart-warming ceremony I was made an honorary member of the tribe.

indeed. They were in turn checking out the hotel, probably because that built-in male radar which detects the presence of girls still operates even when submerged in alcohol. John and I immediately suggested to these two citizens, in a kindly way, that they had best get into the elevator and head for the first floor and then keep right on going. We were, in fact, courteous enough to see that they did make that down elevator. There were a couple of other matters to take care of just then, so we didn't ride down with these gentlemen. A bit later when we got to the first floor, John muttered, "Oh, oh," and nodded towards the front doors, where our two guests were even now holding meaningful dialog with Mike De Francia. Now Mike is one of the nicest people I know, and he has a very high boiling point. But he is also just about as tough as he looks, and that boiling point, high as it is, sometimes gets reached all at once. Besides, they were standing in front of glass doors. So John and I joined the group and eased our friends out of the hotel and into the street. "Those two guys," John remarked, shaking his head, "will never know the favor we did them.

They'd have gone through that glass in a couple more minutes."

Another of my "specialists" was Officer Joe Hale, the Denver policeman who like all good cops was never off-duty. Joe was a safety officer in those days and he had worked a lot with kids—in fact, I know that Joe scrounged the money to get countless kids an education when they couldn't have made it otherwise. So he was not just at home at our conventions but at work. It didn't take long for the kids to find out that the nice man with the wavy gray hair had them pretty well pegged. There was the dance, for instance, in the auditorium with several thousand kids milling around. Joe suddenly came down from the top of the balcony and threw a young guy out of the place.

"How come?" I asked.

"He didn't belong," Joe said.

"How did you know?"

"He had on army shoes."

Anybody who can spot army shoes on a crowded dance floor from the top of the balcony isn't a bad guy to have on your side.

Then there was the young character who had been merrily shooting off firecrackers for some time and he had gone to dinner, only to return and find John Doyle, Kindly Old Father (me), and Officer Hale sitting quietly in his room casually holding the rest of the cherry bombs, clearly waiting too with an unasked question.

For the sake of discipline I always acted a bit over-eager on first nights to catch any little thing I could make something of an example of, for the smooth functioning of the rest of the con- vention. (Any teacher who *is* a teacher will tell you this isn't bad policy in the classroom as well.) One year a few otherwise bright young men were so stupid as to think Officer Hale would fall for something as cornball as stuffing the bed with blankets and pillows to make him think they were there. Not only that, but these young men were among my very trusted council members, so I had no choice. I can still remember those poor young fellows standing there as I called every possible form of transportation between Colorado Springs and Denver—plane, bus, train, bicycle, and dog sled—asking when the next trip was, answering "Not soon enough," and then asking John Doyle if he wouldn't drive these three home. They were, of course, on quite a spot, since their folks would know they had been sent home. I didn't send them home, but I did strip them of their council membership—which had to be done. Some- times discipline does hurt the discipliner more, but I had others to think of too.

But if Joe Hale was efficient, it was his wife Hazel whom the kids thought was the cop in the family. When we bussed one bunch of boys, the Hales with them, into their motel, it immediately became clear to Hazel that the teacher who was with them wasn't the alert sort you look for in a prefect. Her clue to this suspicion came when he got off the bus, put his suitcase down in front of it, and absently watched as the bus ran over the thing. So Hazel saw her duty and done it—lining up the boys much as any good top-sergeant would, assigning them rooms, and pushing them into same. It was a good show, and we had no trouble from that motel, although I'm not sure if their teacher got on the right bus at the end of the convention.

Unfortunately, when you mention one name you leave out innumerable others. But there seems no way out of the difficulty. Our Colorado Springs group too was great, with Will and Betty Jurgens, Wayne and Margaret Sheley (her only serious lapse being her sometime calling me Holy Joe), and Dale and Denny Seiders in the forefront. Dale at the Antlers not only helped with his hotel and catering, but he became a patron as well and also did things like putting on the hotel marquee: "Welcome George Marvin Trio" alongside of "Welcome Father McGloin." There was also Rex Morgan, then a Colonel I believe. He did a sort of *Tonight* TV show out of Denver on which I later appeared (right after Tempest Storm— which would be about as thrilling as Richard Nixon following Salome). Rex did a bang-up job on running our talent shows, and somehow managed to finagle the NORAD Chorus for our entertainment at the convention. I remember hearing him mentioning, as he tried to get this arranged by phone, that "the Secretary of State is vitally interested in this convention."

One of those years I wrote to J. Edgar Hoover asking him if he would speak to our kids. I had written him once before in my life— when I was about fifteen years old and had ambitions to be a G-Man—and this busy man had taken the time to send me a hand-written letter explaining that my name was going on file and that when I got my law degree, I should apply again. But what shook me on this occasion, over twenty years later, was the way his reply began: "It was nice hearing from you again." Incidentally (not that it matters), Mr. Hoover didn't speak at the convention.

Among the Colorado Springs group one little old man stands out in my memory just now. He never missed a meeting, applauded everything enthusiastically, (today he would undoubtedly be shouting, "Sock it to 'em"), and never volunteered to do a thing. I suppose he just liked to go to meetings and rev up the enthusiasm.

Andy Martelon printed our Congress programs. He did a beautiful printing job, but I still wonder to this day how he was able to time things so well all those years, never getting the programs

Somehow he didn't seem to show that keen alertness you look for in the good prefect.

to us one minute ahead of time, but never really late either.

A number of priests and religious were on hand too, and some of them even helped out. The teen-agers were quick to notice, as I certainly was, that every time I turned around at some of those early conventions there was a tall, smiling Franciscan quietly standing nearby like some friendly balding archangel, either ready to do whatever needed doing at the time or already starting on it. This was Father Silas Oleksinski, O.F.M., and I think at that time he had safaried in from somewhere in Texas—San Angelo or one of those remote reaches. Fr. Silas is a superb man, a great friend, and a real inspiration to the kids—without ever preaching a word to them. But then everyone I've been going on about here was not just an aide but a friend. I'm not suggesting that all was perfect; there are teens as well as adults who can be petty. But we were lucky enough to have a minimum of both and to be able to handle both efficiently, usually ahead of time. In general, we encountered only greatness.

So often in the midst of the controlled confusion of a youth congress, there were things which struck us as hilarious. I'm sure

Even an exotic priest is afraid an exotic dancer might possibly be a tough act to follow.

they weren't always that, but the situation made them seem that way—much like the urge to laugh in church at something which wouldn't even be funny anywhere else.

Teen-agers, like everyone else, have to feel that they're being trusted. On the other hand, since they *are* still teen-agers, the trust one puts in them is not quite the same as that given a full-fledged adult, "full-fledged" including that rare combination of both age *and* maturity. To look on teen-agers as completely mature and so to throw them entirely on their own, even in situations where the mature adult would have trouble escaping unscathed, is clearly ridiculous and pathetic. So is the other extreme of treating them like infants or prisoners. The only realistic attitude is the recognition that they are schizos, alternately adults and children, with no one completely able to predict which personality will come to the fore when. The children's personality, however, is most apt to take over at least sometimes when they are in a large group—just as it has been known to do in an occasional group of grown men or women, especially perhaps convention groups.

64

At any rate we had chaperones, some of whom were old hands at the job, others unsuspecting beginners. Jack and Mrs. Hill, as I'll call them, fell into the beginner's category. But Jack at least took on the job with all the confidence of a man walking into a group of rioting female prisoners, secure in the knowledge that the masculine aura of authority alone will quickly calm the storm. The couple didn't really have any great chaperoning problems. But they did discover that when two hundred girls get together, they can tend to act a bit giddy. As for the girls, they sometimes tend to forget, under such circumstances, that they're getting to be big girls. So they're not above chasing each other around hotel corridors and in and out of rooms, sometimes without bothering to don their mother-hubbards or the equivalent over their often somewhat skimpy pajamas. Jack chuckled tolerantly at this sight at first; in fact, for maybe the first ten times he told them to get out of the corridors and back into their rooms. They always politely answered, "Yes, Mr. Hill," and obeyed, only to reappear as soon as Jack had gone back to the TV set. He was, in fact, about to can the kindly tolerant stuff and blow his top when Providence stepped in—in one of its many and unlikely disguises—and took care of the situation.

At a time when the kids were having a carefree, squealing time playing tag in the hallways, a seasoned conventioneer (very well seasoned, in fact) chanced into their part of the hotel from his own sector—the Well-Diggers' Convention, I believe it was. Now to a guy who may have been boozing it up pretty steadily for a few hours with his fellow well-diggers and who is, he thinks, stumbling off to his lonely room, the vision of a whole colony of gossamer-clad dryads prancing around the corridor must come as something of a pleasant surprise, much as manna from heaven once surprised the Israelites in their desert. "Girls!" the happy conventioneer shouted gratefully, spreading his arms wide and moving in to join the festivities. He must have been sure then that it had all been a dream because that many girls couldn't possibly have disappeared that fast. But the Hills had no more prefecting problems *that* night.

There were, of course, crises to be handled from time to time. There was the girl with a heart attack and the boy with a ruptured appendix—both of which ailments turned out to have a closer relationship to the stomach and too much pizza than to the heart or appendix. There was the girl who screamed that she had seen a man at her window—certainly one of the tallest men ever to hit Colorado Springs, since his head reached the sixth floor. (Of course we did have some delegates from Texas.) Naturally, there were the usual prefecting problems one would encounter anywhere—a bit of noise and high spirits occasionally accompanied by firecrackers.

When we were first arranging living quarters for the kids, we encountered what seemed, to me at least, a contradiction. Hotel men told me that they could fit twice as many girls as boys into a hotel, largely because girls don't mind so much sleeping together but boys usually prefer not to. And yet despite this fact and the extra loot involved, veteran hotel managers said they would still prefer to take boys. Only one hotel manager that first year told me with an ingenuous grin that he would prefer to take girls. He asked for girls. Girls he got—about two hundred of them, mostly from the same school. That year at least, I checked out each hotel personally at night and then dropped in again early the next morning to see if it was still there. When I got to this particular hotel the following morning, the manager—good soul that he was, and in his first managing job of course—asked me, tears in his eyes, if I would ask the girls not to turn on all the electricity at once—radio, TV, lights, ironing equipment, hair dryers, the works—and so knock out his circuit breakers. He also wanted me to tell them to stay out of the corridors. I promised to send him a couple of well-diggers.

A couple of high-spirited conventioneers can be the chaperone's best friends.

We collected all sorts of odd bits of information like this as the conventions unfolded. One of the most important practical bits of knowledge again came as a surprise to me at first. And that was the omnipresence of sharpers. Our first year at the Elks a little girl slipped on the stairs and almost fell, only to be practically caught by a lawyer who just happened to be on hand. He informed us a short time later that he was suing us and the Elks for some exorbitant sum, total disability, shock, and so on. This guy wasn't an ambulance chaser, mind you; not even a super-charged ambulance could possibly have stayed in front of him. Fortunately, his prospective "client" refused to go along with him. But we were ready for him and his spiritual relatives the next time.

It would be impossible to include here anything approaching a complete list of the subjects handled at these Youth Congresses. Even the structure of the conventions underwent a rather thorough evolution. When we began, we did a lot of talking *at* the kids. This in turn changed to talking *with* them; discussion, if you'll pardon the overused and misused term, but discussion prompted by something positive to start with. Finally we got to where we wanted: an opening and a closing talk by an adult speaker with something to offer, with the young people themselves handling everything in between. The program for our final congress, for example, shows about thirty panels of four teen-agers each, prepared to stimulate and lead the discussions. There was an adult in each room, with instructions to say nothing unless it was absolutely necessary. It seldom was. There were only four panel subjects, and so every delegate to the convention could get to a discussion of all four subjects if he was fast enough. At the end of the day all the panel discussions were summarized and discussed further before the whole crowd. *That* was a busy day.

In skimming through the summaries of the congresses (and trying to disregard the nostalgia they bring even now), I see topics like these: The Christian Leader, Closeness to Christ, Teen-Age Example, *Living* Your Faith, Vocation, Your Faith and Your Family and Friends, Your Faith and Your Fun, Intelligent Dating, Maturity. Sometimes the subjects were so worded as to challenge the teen-agers just to answer them. We found, in fact, that this was really the most effective way of putting things and the most stimulating of discussion. The entire theme of the final congress we had was Are Teen-Agers Slave or Free? and the panel subjects merely further questions amplifying and detailing this one: Do teen-agers do what they know is right, often despite the crowd, or are they not really slaves to the crowd, meekly going along with it, right or wrong? Are teen-agers not slaves to materialism, out for pleasure at any cost, or have they really the courage to love God? Isn't some form of delinquency *natural* to teen-agers, since they are slaves to worldy patterns of right or wrong—in their conversation, fashion, recreation, entertainment, shows, reading? Don't teen-agers take their social or dating patterns from the crowd slavishly, or are they really free to follow the dating patterns they know are right psychologically, socially and morally?

As can readily be seen, if these subjects were practical, they were also goading. And the young people handled them beautifully with their usual honesty and directness. Once again, our purpose was to let them discover that vast numbers shored their own ideals and that the phony loud-mouths they sometimes met were a distinct minority. And the purpose was fulfilled, completely so.

The kids were magnificent. They were, of course, still kids and you can't expect two or three thousand youngsters to tiptoe around for three days at a convention and communicate only in sign language, or at most in controlled whispers. I found it frustrating, bordering on irritating, to return from a convention, washed out, completely emptied of energy or ambition, and to be greeted with "I hear those kids really tore things apart." Probably the most horrible thing the two or three thousand youngsters did for three days was make noise or try to stay out an hour later than was permitted. As a matter of fact, in the years I was involved in these conventions, the only time I ever heard such criticism of the kids came from those who were far too busy—presumably with the Lord's work—to be present, much less to help out. Or they looked on such conventions as something of a nuisance, since they might, for example, cause some of the kids to come a few minutes late for the Sunday afternoon football game.

It would be nice to look back on those ten years now, and seeing a still going organization, be able to say with some pride, "I had something to do with starting all that." But this, alas, is impossible, since the entire organization—city councils, city organization, *By-Line* magazine, youth congresses, the works—all went down the drain as soon as I left Denver for Minneapolis and a full-time writing assignment. To say that word of this elated me would be about like saying a man could rejoice in the death of his daughter. I accepted it as a *fait accompli.* But at least for those years we had a great thing going, and I would do it all again, even knowing its short life expectancy. This comes home to me most strongly when I run into any of those great kids, now adults, who taught and helped me so much more than I did them. To say I was, and am, proud of them doesn't even come close to expressing what I feel. But since I did work so long with so many young people,

I'd like to generalize on youth a bit at this point—especially since we've become a youth-centered country and world. I'm no teenologist, but it would, after all, take special studies in stupidity to have worked with some twenty thousand young people and still have learned nothing about them.

CHAPTER FOUR

The hope
of
the future

Unfortunately, in our day when one uses the word "youth," too often it tends to conjure up the ◇◇◇ picture of the young—screaming, looting and often shooting on campus or pushing the dean out of a window. And while that's a headline picture and so presents only the sensational, still it *is* a real picture of one group of youth—that much-publicized segment which seemingly goes to college not so much to learn (and often not even to register) as to teach the teachers or disrupt or both.

One of the saddest pictures I've seen lately was a young guy, a recent high-school dropout, on a TV interview show. This boy, who claimed to speak for all high-school students although he had met only a very few, said that what he (and he claimed, "they") wanted was a world without rules, so that he could, for example, "dance in the street" if and when he wanted. When he was asked, "But what if your dancing in the street interferes with traffic or with, say, an ambulance on an emergency run," his only answer was, "I'd discuss it with them, and maybe they'd want to dance in the street too." But the pathetic part of this whole incident was that his father, on the same show, agreed with the boy substantially, or at least said sadly that it was okay for him to think and act as he did.

Not too long ago my great friend and dog Sam F. Spade was graduated from obedience school, and I was showing her (that's right, her) off—insofar as she will agree to show off—to a friend and his teen-aged daughter who had just gotten a pup of her own. "But," the girl objected, "doesn't obedience training cut down on the dog's freedom?"

I thought about that, and it suddenly seemed quite clear to me that the obedience training, far from cutting down on ole Sam's freedom, had actually increased it. Without this training I could never let her run free—because of the danger to herself primarily, and had she been anything but the lover she is, the danger to others. And yet with this training, she can be trusted and so have far greater freedom than she could otherwise enjoy without interfering with the freedom and security of others. It's the same way with people: We gain and practice freedom through obedience and sacrifice and all the rest. And without these, what we have isn't freedom at all, but only selfishness, chaos, and danger.

Today's young people are as idealistic as ever, and that idealism can be one of the greatest sources of hope for our country. But the fact is too that youth is often sold out on its ideals by its very youth. There are destructive forces at work which are all too skilled at misdirecting these ideals, using them to destroy while flattering youth that it *is* mature, knowledgeable, and far more capable of decision and ruling than any of its elders—no matter how little "elder" they may be or how skilled and experienced.

Often enough, the *cause* some of the collegians allegedly espouse is most valid and important: the causes of civil rights and racial equality, for example. But their means of achieving a good purpose are often immature and so bound to have just an opposite effect—something we can see happening right now as minority militants demand, not equality or integration, but superiority and segregation and even a weekly paycheck for going to college at all.

The non-student and professional agitator are, in fact, experts at using youth's immaturity for their own purposes. A few years ago I heard a speech delivered by a prominent American communist to the student body of one of the largest universities in the country. This man had been banned previously, but a small group of faculty and representative students had gotten the decision reversed, convincing all concerned of the maturity of the students and their ability to distinguish truth from error for themselves. The speech was really a masterpiece, with the students booing maturely and applauding with equal maturity—exactly where the speaker had decided they *should* boo and applaud. He was willing to take all the booing they had to offer to put across the few points he wanted—especially to further convince them of their complete maturity and their ability to distinguish clearly truth from falsehood.

One can—in fact, must—believe in youth and still have no faith in the self-constituted spokesman for youth, whether that spokesman is young or only wishes he were. The glib dilettante who constantly claims to speak for youth is usually speaking only for himself. Youth, moreover, is not the whole of society but only a *part* of it, maybe not even its most important part. Youth is obviously "the hope of the future," but if we completely neglect the valuable present for that future, always living in some material future instead of making use of the present, we're living unrealistically and sometimes psychopathically. We can't neglect the future even in our

74

present, but on the other hand, we can't neglect our present either.

One of my problems is that I keep thinking the much-publicized generation gap works both ways, and so it is the responsibility of *both* young and not so young. But another problem I have is the realization that those who first coined the cliché "Never trust anyone over thirty," are now over thirty themselves, and they're finally right—I don't trust them.

But the vast majority of our young people never tie up a college president or burn a science lab, and so never make the headlines. When, in fact, one writes about youth, his journal-isitic lead should be something shocking, so his readers will know he's writing about the young. Something about rebellion or the new morality or pot always makes for a nice opening. As far as content is concerned, all the writer need do is pick a few old surveys or polls out of the files. Most teen surveys have at least one question like "Do you sometimes hate your parents?" And one can leap to universal conclusions from any answer given—such as the rebelliousness of youth, the universal failure of parents, the need for both to see a psychiatrist or if that's too expensive, to check in with some less costly counselor like the Holy Spirit.

Now strictly speaking, all that one can learn with certainty from a survey is that the people who stood still for the thing answered thus and so. One can't even be sure, in fact, that they're telling the truth. As a matter of fact, if some surveyors would only watch teen-agers at work on their surveys, they would be less likely to take them at face value. There's probably no other group in existence so fond of giving the startling answer rather than any of the anticipated responses. Where their elders are forever trying to keep from making waves, teen-agers are always eager to cause a real splash.

Now I have the greatest respect for polls and surveys when they're honestly worded—with no patsies like, "Have you stopped beating your wife?" included among the questions—efficiently presented, and then interpreted with a touch of genius. Finally surveys, like psychological tests, have to be taken in relation to all the facts one can gather about the individual involved, and not only applied blindly to the individual because this was the way some group showed up. In other words, the surveyor, like the psychological tester, has to resist the temptation to play God. As Doctor Anthony Standen noted in *Science is a Sacred Cow* (New York: Dutton and Company, 1950), the famous Kinsey survey-report should not have been called *Sexual*

Behavior in the Human Male, but rather, more accurately,
"The sexual behavior of 5,300 men who were willing to talk
about it."

Almost everything depends on which of his pet theories
the pollster or surveyor is out to prove, since one can, in fact,
"prove" just about anything through the use of some figures
and either the suppression or the interpretation of others. We
are, in fact, engulfed in a great flood of the things today—in the
Catholic Church, for example, as those who decide to disagree
with some church doctrine or other invariably take a survey
among their friends or think-alikes to back up their position.
They never seem to realize that those who consider their disagreement a lack of faith and their survey only the pathetic search
of the self-seeking for company invariably refuse to answer
it at all, even should they accidently happen to be contacted.
If one should come upon a survey favoring the abolishment
of the human male, the first thing he might suspect is that
it might well have been conducted and answered by some of
the more militant members of the women's lib movement.

Some time ago 3,500 sets of parents were asked, among
the other survey questions, how many of them made their
children wash before meals. And quite righteously, something
like 97 percent of those parents said they did, indeed,
insist that their children wash before meals. Then, however,
the surveyors asked the children of these parents the same
question, and there was a slight discrepancy, with only 17
percent of those same children saying their parents had ever
even mentioned the subject. So give or take 80 percent for
complete accuracy.

When it comes to oral surveys, there are still greater
difficulties because of the human penchant for wanting to be
part of the crowd at all costs, for not wanting to stand out at
least as so different as to seem odd. This may be especially
true of the teen-ager who, despite his quest for individuality,
is desperately careful never to be considered *out of it* or *square*
and who has to be constantly proving himself part of the crowd.
I once encountered such a survey, in which a teacher asked
a group of some seventy-five girls how many of them were
going steady. And of course, as soon as the first one said she
was (as was only to be expected of the first girl asked), almost
all of the others in that room had to echo the same boast or lose
face, all with an equal degree of truth. The girls each added,
as a matter of fact, that they went steady with some boys I
knew very well, a group I also knew contained only four steady-

76

goers at the time, none of whom went with any of the surveyed girls. All we seemed to have here was, at best, a survey in wishful thinking.

But certainly one of the most ridiculous surveys of the whole collection came some years back in an alleged survey of the teen world. Even the teen-agers thought it about the funniest thing they had ever read, with most of them never coming in contact with even one of the teens described therein as typical. Among other startling things, the surveyor said in effect: we have created the typical or composite American youth—a remarkable statement if ever there was one, since not even God came up with an atrocity which anyone could call typical. The typical or normal individual exists only theoretically, in fact, and this because you and I are left or right of that no-man's land which is normal or typical.

In a psychological test one doesn't end up with a straight-line profile—down the 50th percentile range, for example—any more than his face or bodily profile is a straight line. He, or she, will ordinarily show a jagged profile, bellying out a little here and in a little there. Psychologically, he or she will land in the 40th percentile in one category, the 60th in another and so on. Since I'm trying to be completely honest here, I'll have to admit that I did in ten years or so of psychological testing see one straight-line profile, or very nearly that. Not only that, but the straight line traveled right along zero all the way—in all categories except one where it was up near a hundred. Happily, that one category was self-confidence, so the subject, despite having absolutely nothing else, did have a maximum degree of happiness.

But, getting back to that teen survey, this is the profile, as I remember it, of one youth who won their "typical" endorsement: A sniveling boy in Podunk, a tall youngster—six feet three—who, in the last two years, has owned three cars and a motor scooter and who says he might like to help the unemployed, but he won't because he knows " they'd just want a few hundred dollars or something. . . ." Just what's typical here I'm not sure. Even a person who has never spoken to a teen-ager in his life should have trouble swallowing that one.

There were, of course, some very good, valid points in this same survey, but there were enough bloopers like this one to keep it utterly ridiculous on the whole.

But if the polls and surveys make some ridiculous claims, the headlines are even more laughable—until, of course, you

Some of the press do a convincing imitation of the Pied Piper.

suddenly realize to your horror that there are people who
still read them exclusively and even a few who believe them.
Of course, if you can get ten million Americans to believe
some political candidates, it's not surprising they still believe
headlines too.

Actually, I've reserved another setting for opening this
jar labeled "Press," so I'll leave it unopened for now. But we're
talking about youth, and if any single group ever got a lousy
press, it's the young. True to the code of printing all the news
that's fit or unfit to print and headlining the routine stuff
sensationally, many newspapers and magazines simply will
not feature anything worthwhile done by a teen-ager or a group
of them. There are, of course, exceptions to this general
principle. Now and then, as a sort of sentimental sop to the
nice little old ladies of both sexes among the subscribers, the
press dons its halo and comes up with some *Reader's Digest*
type of story about a couple of teen-agers who stopped to

change a tire for some helpless old lady—not too helpless to drive, of course. And so, periodically, in between scandals, it comes out that teen-agers are fundamentally good, nearly as good, in fact, as we were when we were teens.

But for the most part, much of the press—dedicated as it is to its thing which is selling papers and such in fulfillment of its vocation of informing and educating an ignorant public—will print, or at least feature, those items that do sell papers. And so we read mostly about the teen-ager who smokes pot and steals and rapes and destroys. But we see very little about the teen-ager who builds, who plugs away at his studies for his future good and that of others; the teen-ager who obeys, who shows real courage in conquering himself and his problems, who really bleeds with bleeding mankind, and who prefers a job which will do some good and not just make money and more money. We read plenty about the teen-aged delinquent— in fact, it's doubtful if the press misses any such at all—but we read little or nothing about the teen-ager going his quiet way of being a good, growing, maturing human being, maybe even sometimes to an almost heroic degree. He's just "not news."

During many of my ten years at Regis, 80 percent of the student body and upwards received our Lord in Holy Communion every day—and I never saw that in the paper (perhaps because, like some Catholic "experts," the press might have deplored a Catholic school's producing only good practicing Catholics). But let one of those kids break a window or push a car in the lake and *that* would make the paper readily enough.

Sure, take the surveys and polls and use them, but use them with a great number of grains of salt and with what you know and with what the teen-ager himself teaches you. Take the headlines too and use *them,* but don't forget the vast percentage of kids who never make the headlines and who are never asked to participate in a survey or poll.

So that's my gripe with polls and surveys and headlines. And having gotten that off my chest, let me get on to a somewhat revolutionary way of talking or writing about teen-agers—from experience and direct contact with them. I don't want to fall into the hole I've just dug and universalize on what a relatively few teen-agers have shown themselves to be. All I'm saying is that in looking back on those years of work with teens—work which consisted of dealing with them externally, but also in counseling and retreat work where one gets at their inners—certain of their characteristics stand out in my

Pushing a car into a lake is always good for a headline.

mind. I feel too that these characteristics were always there, sometimes visibly active, at other times only potential, waiting to be summoned up by the right incantations.

One other thing I would say by way of preface: The characteristics outlined here are, admittedly, *youthful* characteristics, so much so that when we see the young without them, we suspect that something's wrong. But they're characteristics too which can remain with a person as long as he makes the effort to keep them. And in this sense, one can remain young as long as he tries to. So it comes to this: These are characteristics of youth, yes, but as long as you have them, you too are young; and when you've lost them, you're no longer young but wound out. Maybe this has some relation to a phenomenon we've all seen—the young person of eighty and the old person of eighteen. I don't buy that old bromide about being as young as you feel, because a sick young guy can feel desperately old and an old drunk can feel amazingly young.

But I do think one is truly young as long as he hangs onto these characteristics of youth.

I doubt if anyone would dispute the fact that the young have a supply of energy so vast that it's just barely credible. Like the man said—if it weren't true, you couldn't believe it. They go, go, go, until they drop from exhaustion, long after an older person would have had sense enough to throw in the towel. Finally, they usually seem to reach a point of sudden collapse, only to revive later and cut loose with just as much energy as before.

It has often occurred to me that the manufacturers of breakfast cereals are making a terrible mistake by boasting of more energy and more vitamins in their cereal. After listening to countless tired mothers (who were not, of course, too tired to talk), I've come to the conclusion that more energy is just exactly what they *don't* want to serve up at breakfast. Someone could, in fact, make a mint if he'd come up with a breakfast cereal liberally sprinkled with tranquilizers—in the form of sugar, let's say. At least, he'd earn the undying gratitude of a host of harassed mothers. (There is, seemingly, no other kind of mother today.)

Going with this appalling store of energy—almost synony-mous with it, in fact, since when one is missing, so usually is the other—is an enthusiasm which has no counterpart at any other stage of human development. Where an adult, at least in age, might yell genteelly at a horse race or with less restraint at a TV set during the weekend football game, a youngster would be more likely to get out and run alongside the horse to urge him along, or to shake the TV set. The enthusiasm young people showed for those doused lights of the cultural and musical world, the Beatles, was of an essentially higher intensity than any imaginable adult enthusiasm. In fact, on many an occasion, it seemed more like hysteria.

But even if the young are double-charged with energy and enthusiasm, they still have to be plugged in or they don't even light up. A teen-ager can, in fact, be as inert as any rock or clod unless he sees what he considers some good reason for being enthusiastic and making use of his energy. In a moment here we'll talk about how one can try to plug them in, but first let's mention just one more of their seem-ingly innate characteristics.

It's hard to find the exact word for this one, but you can begin tentatively with "honesty." The suggestion that teen-agers are honest, however, brings on a variety of reactions.

Some look incredulous, others tolerant of your condition, most perhaps only stunned, as though this had never occurred to them and was never likely to. And always, but always, you'll hear from the lord of the manor whose window had once been broken by a teen-ager, or who knew someone who had had a hubcap or even a car stolen by one, and who therefore knows for a fact that teen-agers are not honest. All of which reminds me, remotely at least, of a dedicated citizen named Glockenspiel or some such, who wrote me indignantly after reading an article of mine on racial injustice that he had once seen a Negro hit a boy with a lead pipe, and therefore. . . . Which reminded me in turn, as I answered him politely and gently, that there might well have been someone named Glockenspiel or similar who way back in the forties graciously held the oven door and stepped aside politely for Mr. Cohen to enter, and therefore. . . .

Therefore nothing, as a matter of fact.

At any rate, to label teen-agers as honest is not to imply that no teen-ager is ever dishonest in the ordinary sense of that word. There *are* teen hoods—maybe not as many yet as there are adult hoods, but at least some. It's true moreover, that far below the efficiency level of the bona fide hood, there exists a teen-ager who would on occasion pick up a loose hubcap—or perhaps even one not so loose but attached to a whole car. There are teen-agers, I feel sure, who would and do cheat in exams. By and large though, challenged to honesty rather than pushed towards it without motivation, the teen-ager *is* honest, even in the literal sense.

But I don't mean the word honest only literally here. Perhaps I mean more that *insight* which is honest, and an openness and frankness accompanying this insight. It's not honest, for example, but rather completely dishonest to judge a man only by what he looks like without bothering to get at what he is inside. It's not honest to shout to the world that another race is inferior to one's own, when the sole basis for that judgment is a generalization on individual defects (real or imagined) or only on appearance. It's also a stupid blunder to lump all of remotely like appearance under one moral and social as well as physical category.

But most teen-agers are honest enough to judge a person, not by what he looks like, but by what he *is*. And this isn't only honesty; it's also intelligence. It takes a pretty studied idiot to think he can honestly judge people solely by appearance, and in fact, most of us would be in serious trouble were that to become universal procedure.

This honesty is the basic reason for the teen-ager's usually being completely color-blind—until taught otherwise, of course, by his "leaders." As the song goes from *South Pacific* (which might have had something to do with the play's being banned from some of our country's cultural preserves), "You've got to be taught. . . to hate all the people your relatives hate." Until some such adult apostle sees his tutorial duty and points his whole charism at it, the young are too honest and reasonable to buy this sort of bilge.

But there's another element involved in the honesty of the teen-ager, one complementary to this instinctive insight they have in judging people by what they are—they speak and act accordingly. There may be people who see the truth but still don't always speak and act by it—such as the allegedly non-prejudiced person who still hasn't the courage to express any disagreement with the prejudiced mob. But the teen-ager feels that truth is to be broadcast, not supressed. And once he thinks he's caught onto some fragment of truth, he does throw it around—and sometimes to the embarrassment of a few others. If you want the perfect nickname for someone, ask a teen-ager; because with his built in X ray and his penchant for outspokenness, he'll come up with something so fitting you'll wonder how you missed it yourself. Teens are, fortunately or unfortunately, capable of this not just with their contemporaries but with adults—like with teachers, for instance. Adults might, for example, find it difficult to discover or even suspect any attractiveness inside the hairy nests it sometimes inhabits today, but the teen-ager often seems able to meet this challenge too and find something the hair—and the psychological hang-ups which often fertilize it—would otherwise conceal. Teens are also capable, of course, of discovering hidden ugliness when *that's* there, whether it's camouflaged by a beard or overpowered in Aqua-Velva, Chanel No. 5, or Right Guard.

In this line, perhaps one of the most typical (if you'll pardon the word) pictures of the teen-ager I can recall was one featuring a cute little girl maybe fifteen years old, dressed as a drum majorette, and a young guy maybe twenty-five years old. This latter character was clearly a man with a mission, and he was out to impart—undoubtedly since he saw no way to impose—his certainties on a stupid world. He carried a sandwich board, with a few of the stupid inanities of the segregationist scrawled across it: SEGREGATION OUR WAY OF LIFE, THE BIBLE SAYS NEGROES ARE INFERIOR, that sort of stuff. And walking along behind him in this picture was this little majorette, calmly yet determinedly slugging him over the head with the baton. This teen-ager recognized stupidity when she saw it. She knew the truth that he apparently wasn't aware of. And so she was taking the only direct way she could think of at the moment to send him a message. Maybe this isn't a pedagogical technique which can be universally recommended. But it can be effective, on occasion at least.

Another facet of this honesty of the teen-ager might be "non-sophistication," or in its best sense, "simplicity." We've probably all encountered the youngster who has become pre-sophisticated, who has never really been allowed or allowed himself to experience the things of a child. Even in his early teens you'll find this poor guy sneering at things he should be reveling in unashamedly and honestly with a simple childlike enjoyment. Unfortunately, our world *has* made sophisticated monsters out of many of our teen-agers. Instead of having fun as kids, they sometimes get hung up on all the adult games—like sex and booze, and drugs—because these are the only kinds of fun the adult world has dangled before them from infancy. And so, sadly, there are today many youngsters waddling around in ill-fitting adult shells, waiting for time to make the adjustment—which, of course, time alone can never do. There's something terribly pathetic about a sixth-grade girl all set for the elementary-school prom, decked out in a formal and complete with orchid corsage. What can she possibly do for an encore in the next few years?

So teen-agers, then, are energetic, enthusiastic, honest. Great. But even the parents and teachers who have seen flashes of these dormant potentialities are anxious to know how they can get the kids to get going on using them occasionally. If I could answer that question for every individual teen-ager, I wouldn't be fooling around writing this book—I'd be too busy counting my money. But while no one can tell you how to get any given teen-ager pointed and moving in the right direction (any more than he could do the same for any given adult), still I think there are a few further potentialities of the teen-ager which can help in the process.

The very first thing one has to realize about a teen-ager is that he *is* and wants to be an *individual*. Now, on the surface that might not seem completely accurate, since many, if not most of them, seem often enough to be the greatest conformists in the world. Even their fads are first cousins to conformity, as one shaggy head of hair and/or beard leads to another, one mini or maxi skirt to another, one straight scraggly hairdo to another, and so on. It's all too obvious that teen-agers have to be part of some *in* crowd or

What can she do for an encore after the sixth-grade prom?

they're frightened and embarrassed—much as life today can become unbearable for the girl with naturally curly hair, although a few years ago she would have been the envy of all her fellow henlets.

This is all true, but it's true too that even as the teen-ager has to be a member of some group, he also has to be himself and not just an indistinguishable blob in that group. This is the contradiction he lives with and fosters. He has to be *in,* yet still an individual; he has to differ from others as an individual, but not to the extent of being out of it or an oddball.

The same is true in their family life. Most teen-agers love their parents and family, even though they'll probably fight them on occasion. But the strange—or not so strange—thing is that when they get to school, an unsuspected phenomenon often takes place. It's not that they don't feel free and even compelled to indulge in that great indoor sport known as griping about your square parents, but they usually reserve this criticism as their own exclusive prerogative. And so if you join in heartily, agreeing with them and adding perhaps a few original critical comments of your own, you'll often have a fight on your hands. They'll take some of the arguments they've battled against at home and use them against you.

They usually, in fact, have a sense of family solidarity, even when they make sure the family never suspects it. On the other hand, every family and every parent has to realize that their demand for individuality is very real and ever present. No young person wants to be known only as one of the Smith girls or . . . boys. He's *Joe* Smith or she's *Jane* Smith—and don't you dare forget it, at home or at school. I've known youngsters who simply quit studying because when they did well, some unsuspecting teacher came up with "Oh, another of those Smith kids, smart." I've known boys who did their darndest to be dirty and rough and argumentative because they were constantly told (and there are nearly infinite ways of telling even without words) what a nice neat older sister they had. I'm not sure what would happen were you to constantly drum into a younger sister that she had a beautiful person for an older brother.

The recognition of this quest for individuality, which is so natural to all of us, can be a real weapon. And then the trick is going to be to discover what it is that *this* individual teen-ager can do in a way somewhat unique to himself. Maybe some little guy can only haul out the garbage at home more efficiently, he thinks, than anyone else—even when, objectively, his mother knows that she could do it better herself and even save time. At school the teacher has to be on the lookout for this proof of individuality—in the unique way a student can read or reason or draw or run or dance or write on the board or clean the erasers or even just hold his breath.

Whatever it is, he has to have his thing, which is not quite the same as everyone else's. In the production of our *By-Line* magazine all the jobs were, to some degree at least, unique. There were those who could write—some who could do fiction, others editorials, others fillers, and so on. There were those who could take pictures and those who could process the film and print. Some were good at layout, some could draw or print. There were those who could distribute the magazine locally and those who could mail it nationwide, those who could sort the magazines and tie them in bundles, those who could re-tie them when they fell apart, and those who could bring them to the post office. There were those who could sweep up the room after an issue was finally in the mail, those who could file the old photos. But there was something of a thing here for all concerned. The mailer, for example, took pride in his mailing, although he might not have been able to take as much pride in his attempts at writing.

Miss this clue of individuality and you miss the teen-ager.

Going with this quality of seeking individuality while still hiding in a crowd is that characteristic of the young that I'd consider the most important of all: The characteristic whose presence assures us we're still young ourselves and whose absence warns us we're getting all wound out. Put simply, the teen-ager, deep within those inpenetrable recesses of his own mind, wants nothing to do with mediocrity. He has to be challenged—and greatly at that—or he's just going to stay inert and indifferent, probably with an all too obvious bravado which tells the world, "I don't care." This is, in fact, part and parcel of his individuality. It causes only harm to challenge the teen-ager who's capable of being a great TV technician to become a lawyer instead, when he hasn't the interest nor perhaps even the aptitude for law—even though daddy may have had. Challenge him to be a *great,* an *outstanding* TV technician though, and you get somewhere.

I'm completely convinced that this is the greatest single clue to the workings of the teen mind. Why does he do nothing at home? Why does he balk at doing his school work? Because, rightly or wrongly, he hasn't seen any challenge there and so no reason for his interest. It's up to someone to *show* him the challenge. This isn't to say, either, that we should hold out some vague, futuristic ideal to the teen-ager—maybe that too—but rather that we have to show him the challenge in a dirty room, a stack of dirty dishes, or a couple of hours of unfinished schoolwork. This is precisely where the skill of a parent or a teacher (ideally, the parent should be part-teacher) comes in, and so the parent has to recognize the challenge first himself instead of seeing only the drudgery. And this will mean getting beneath the bare action itself to the reason for doing it. It will also mean keeping a youthful outlook.

But there's no need to remain abstract; there isn't a single characteristic I've named here that I haven't seen in action in the vast, vast majority of teens with which it was my great privilege to work. From the first, they were involved in all the do-good projects youth organizations or sodalities everywhere are accustomed to push. They collected stamps for the missions, and sometimes money. They worked with the nearest orphans—taking them to football games, coaching them in their games, or sometimes even teaching them. They collected food-baskets for the poor at Christmas, usually lifting the food from their own homes and then bringing it to school for redistribution to those they felt were poorer than their parents.

Now these were all good projects, and the young people did them well. But good and well aren't enough for the teen-ager, and one didn't see here that hysterical brand of enthusiasm they're capable of when really interested and, above all, when challenged. Actually, in those early days, I didn't know just what was lacking— I'm not sure I realized that *anything* was—until one of the kids put me wise.

At one of our so-called days of recollection and discussion we managed to blend about eight hundred kids into a chapel built to hold maybe three hundred uncomfortably. Near the end of the day we held a sort of general discussion, and two items from that discussion still stand out in my mind. There was the girl who stood up and began, "I disagree with everything that's been said here today," tears in her voice. What had been said so far was, indeed, worth disagreeing with, since one boy had scathingly denounced all sodalists as phonys—to an extent, I might add, that some of the kids later suggested he might have been planted. The fact is, he wasn't. But he did unwittingly give me an idea along that line for future meetings.

This turned out to be the turning point of that meeting and, in fact, of our youth activities. "If you disagree with it," she was asked, "what do *you* suggest? What are we supposed to do if we're going to stop being the phonys he claims we are?"

In the course of the discussion that followed, there emerged the second item I remember from that meeting and the concrete clue, I'm convinced, to any effective work with teens. "Instead of just saving stamps for the missions," one girl asked innocently enough, "why don't we save a million stamps?"

88

Just as casually one day, someone might have said "Let's throw that tea in the ocean." The very word "million" was, in fact, exactly the clue we needed. Everybody, but everybody, had always saved stamps for the missions, but who had ever heard of saving a million stamps? It was a unique idea and a challenging one, where only "saving stamps" had been mostly a sort of nice blah.

They did it too—a million stamps. And that's an appalling amount of paper; if the reader should think this only a harmless or even useless little hobby—this stamp-saving—he's never been on the missions. A few of the right stamps can make all the difference between Christmas dinner and no Christmas dinner there.

It was the reaction to that "Let's save a *million* . . . " that really got us going. It was quite obvious that only something unique and big and challenging really turned on the young. The sort of thing, however good, that anyone else could do or had done was greeted with a shrug and a So what? There's a contradiction here, of course, between a teen-ager's sometime argument to his parents—Everybody else is doing it; why can't I?—and his attraction to those things no one else, to his knowledge, has attempted. But any good teen-ager has to be allowed a reasonable quota of contradictions.

Never again did we suggest to anyone how easy a project might be, but we emphasized instead how tough it could be—still possible, of course, but so tough that not everybody could do it. "We need you" was the theme, and "We need the ability that only you can bring to this project, tough as it is." And the kids bought the compliment.

These young people had always worked a bit with the city's orphans, but now they began to put their sensitive young insight and honesty to work too. They saw that while the things they had done with and for the orphans up to now were all good—entertaining them and so on—still there were other, perhaps less glamorous things which could be even more effective. And so they came up with seemingly simple things, like quietly sitting next to a little orphan type while he or she did some schoolwork. To the non-orphan that might not seem like much. But to the orphan, who's always with his own contemporaries or some prefect, to have an older person, a sort of big brother or sister, think enough of him to take the time to just stay near him—that *is* something earth-shaking.

One of my students took to this project with great enthusiasm and, I should add, managed to up his own grades during this time. Apparently he met a smart orphan, and we're not sure who was watching whom do whose homework.

Then there was the boy who always brought seventeen orphans to the football game each Sunday afternoon—in his car, with five seated in back, five standing, four seated in front and three standing, all so jammed in that they couldn't possibly have spilled out. At one of the games this young guy was constantly distracted by one of the kids who kept jumping up and yelling that he wasn't an orphan. His benefactor pushed him back into the seat each time and told him just to shut up and watch the game. At least he kept doing this until he counted heads and found he had eighteen kids instead of the seventeen he had set out with.

There was the high-school girl who helped to cure a little orphan of a speech defect—with no technical knowledge, but with a lot of love and patience and the recognition of a worthwhile challenge, and never a doubt about being able to help.

The teen-agers continued to collect Christmas food baskets for the poor too, but their instincts told them that this wasn't perfect charity either—collecting a lot of food for the poor and then letting only a relatively few of the collectors distribute it. And so they began to turn also to a project which a number of other teen-agers in the city were already doing—working directly with the poor along with the Dominican Sisters of the Sick Poor. Soon there was a large group spending their Saturdays scrubbing and painting and teaching and even cooking for the poor of the city—none of which, of course, they would do at home. Somehow or other it seemed no challenge at home, but it was here.

Two of these boys once went to help out in a home where an old couple had a rather unique phobia: They were deathly afraid that they were going to run out of oatmeal, and so they had stashed about fifteen cases of the stuff in the corner. And as these two spiritual descendants of Robin Hood told me later, "They wouldn't part with any of it, but we did manage to get away with two cases." Rob the oatmeal rich to help the oatmeal poor.

Some time after this project had started, I asked one of the boys who had helped to get it going to explain it to the city council group. He had no time to prepare, no prompting from me or anyone else, and his first sentence went almost exactly like this: "This is the greatest project we've attempted. But if you can't do it for the sake of Christ, don't even try it. . . . "
Just one of those superficial, giddy teen-agers talking to about seventy-five to a hundred of his similarly giddy contemporaries. And no one there seemed to think he had said anything extraordinary at all. Maybe he hadn't at that.

By the time we got a letter from a missionary in British Honduras, Father Robert McCormack, S.J., asking if our sodalists could send him a few books for the library, it was perfectly obvious that it would have been a mistake to approach them about only a few books. So instead, I read them the letter, changing, however, "a few books" to "a library." Soon enough, over six thousand books had been gathered together, and money collected for packing and shipping them. But then the crates were bummed off a crate maker, the Denver Trucking Company agreed to take the shipment to New Orleans, and the United Fruit Company carried them the rest of the way to British Honduras—all for free. So the money too was sent along to a happily surprised Father McCormack to buy shelving for his new library. Maybe some of the books were not the greatest, since they were for the most part United States rejects; but they were quite a beginning. Besides, it's just possible that some United States rejects are better than some United States non-rejects. At any rate, these young people, who wouldn't have been overly interested in sending "a few books" to the missions, were interested in sending a whole library.

The final characteristic of the young that I would mention here can, like all these qualities, carry its owner far off in either direction. And yet this characteristic, which comes down to the lack of any fear of consequences, is the very first requisite for perfection. It is, in fact, this quality that sometimes makes the teen-ager, naturally a good driver, also a menace because he has no idea that he might hurt anyone, himself included. This is one reason the Air Force likes young pilots, even apart from their superb reflexes.

This is, in fact, the reason those of us who are not saints are not—we fear the consequences. This is also why the young have a better crack at perfection than any other segment of society, if they'll only *use* what they have. If the goal is worthwhile, the young will take even very painful means to get it.

To me this youthful quality was most typically illustrated in the picture of a couple of teen-aged boys in East Berlin, standing on a curb, with the huge gun of a Russian tank pointed directly at them. And they were in the act of fighting that tank with the only weapons they had—a couple of rocks. This may seem foolish and foolhardy to the non-young, but not to the really young. Not to a young guy named David, for example, who got a lot of mileage out of a rock, along with his youth and faith.

So these, when I look back, are some of the great qualities I saw in the young people I was lucky enough to associate with for ten years—their energy and enthusiasm, their honesty, their craving for individuality along with their hunger for the challenge, and their disregard of consequences when a thing seemed worthwhile. It seems to me that it is the greatest duty of adults to show them what things are really worthwhile, and this—first, last, always—by example.

Something else occurs to me too, when I think of these characteristics, all of which we can keep as long as we don't let ourselves get wound out or old, and which, in turn, keep us young in the best sense of that term. Christ said that ". . . Whoever does not accept the Kingdom of God like a child will not enter into it at all." It occurs to me that maybe this is what He had in mind: if we're to have any part with Him, we can never let ourselves lose these best qualities of youth.

PART THREE

CHAPTER
FIVE

"What about that guy who's just writing?"

When natives of Hollywood notice this collar I wear, they know I'm either made up for some movie or TV role, ◇◇◇ or starting a trend in black Nehru jackets. You must, after all, expect this sort of thing from people who can seriously use an expression like " . . . the Hollywood Bowl and those other religious places."

Apparently all travelers—even some of the sober ones—like to while away the time by talking with a priest, and they almost always begin by asking, "Where's your parish, Father?" Not bad for openers—that; but the reply I have to give, "I don't have a parish," seems to bring on a variety of reactions, all of them tinged with suspicion. The pious-type questioner clamps his—or her—jaw shut in disapproval, and you can sense the shrug of the playboy type as he imagines he's stumbled across a clerical swinger. A priest, they figure, has a parish

The priest in Hollywood is often mistaken for just another bit actor.

and if he hasn't, he must have been silenced or defrocked, a rebel of some sort or maybe even a democrat.

When I try to explain that I'm a priest-writer, there's usually a nod of partial understanding, even though I often get the idea it says more "I'll humor the guy" than "I see." God knows how they'd react if I said, "I'm hyphenated."

Writing has become another of those hyphens, but it's still mainly a job, at the moment an all-absorbing job. And it's no more and no less a job than the priest-pastor or the priest-teacher or the priest-anything else. Sometimes on the darker days at least, it seems to validate Graham Greene's remark that "for a writer as much as for a priest there is no such thing as success."

Back in those dark ages when not everyone was a writer, I met the great Bob Casey who by that time had worked for countless newspapers, had been a correspondent in two major wars, had published about sixty books, and was, you might say, beginning to become fairly well-established as a writer. I was pretty well-established by that time myself, having sold a short story for five dollars and several significant articles at a less sensational price. And so, aglow with the enthusiasm of the living author in the presence of another writer, I asked Mr. Casey how he felt about his writing now and if he was still thrilled by it and by seeing himself in print.

"I ran into Marguerite Higgins on the train," he said, "and she answered your question. 'An artist,' she said, 'can sometimes get a lot of pleasure and a real break out of just painting for himself, and a pianist can sometimes enjoy playing the piano alone. But who ever heard of hitting a damned typewriter just for enjoyment?' "

Writing, in general, is a job. It's only that the writer is a little more in the public eye perhaps than some other workers. I'm often embarrassed, in fact, at some of the publicity and relative renown my job carries with it, when I think of the lack of recognition of those in my own Order who really deserve it—the missionary working under incredibly discouraging conditions, the teacher pushing himself courageously into a classroom Monday after Monday and year after year, the parish priest selflessly giving himself and his time to his people, the counselor patiently and sometimes endlessly listening. You could draw up a long, long list of unsung heroes in the Society of Jesus alone who will never make a headline, never write a book, never be introduced as a famous author, or maybe never even be introduced at all. And yet these are the really big-deal people because they do their jobs solely for the Lord with no danger of dedicating their lives to seeking human recognition. *That* takes enormous faith and just as enormous courage. If an author gets praised for a book, a teacher ought to be recognized for lighting up the ablative absolute and a pastor for helping to prevent moral, or sometimes physical, suicide.

Among the questions a writer hears—and asks himself—the most frequent one has to be Why? More often than not, the question becomes more specific: Why should a *priest* write?

I once asked one of the pro football players I played handball with why he stuck with his tough game: football, that is. Money, of course, was one element but by no means the only one, especially since the ordinary pro player doesn't draw anywhere near as much as the relatively few glamour boys of the sport do. The real motive, without which ordinary money wouldn't swing it, lies in the simple answer, "I *like* to play."

And despite the often grueling work and the frequent discouragement and the sometime loneliness, I *like* to write. That's one answer. Another reason is that a writer begins, sooner or later, to see little vacuums he hopes he can fill. He thinks he sees a need for someone to see what he has to say, or he feels compelled to challenge something which has appeared publicly—in a newspaper or a speech or in the theater perhaps.

There are, I feel, so many bloopers and absolute untruths being perpetrated in the communications field today that I must, as a priest and as a writer, take some small steps to try to counteract them. There is, for example, little relationship of headlines to news stories today and, all too often, little relationship of the news story itself to the total truth. In general, the press' handling of the whole birth-control controversy, to take but one example, has been a mockery of truth from the scare words "population *explosion*" all the way to the fantasy that Pope Paul had dreamed up the Church's doctrine all by himself. So is the survey and poll-proven myth that a majority of Catholics—and many non-Catholics, for that matter—don't back him and follow that backing in practice.

Or consider the publication offering bonuses to religious attending a meeting of their Order if they will slip the editor a report on the things they have sworn to keep secret.

Why does a priest write? A priest who can do so *has* to write— if only to give the lie, as far as the communications field will permit, to this sort of phonyness. Maybe his contribution will amount to only about the same percentage the old joke attributes to the tobacco in cigarettes, but he can at least do this much and try to do more.

But as a priest and religious, concentrating these days as I am on fiction and films and such, I'm particularly stumped when I encounter someone who wonders what on earth a priest is doing in *this* field.

It seems perfectly obvious to me that if a priest is supposed to be influencing people, then he should be trying to do so in the widest possible fields. In a classroom I could be putting an idea or two in front of maybe a hundred kids a year. In a parish I might be able to needle a similar number mostly on Sundays. But with one book I can get to thousands of people, and with one good movie or TV script I could annoy millions. Fiction, good fiction that is, would certainly have more influence than any number of my sermons—which is no comment whatsoever on the sermons of others.

These are just a few of the reasons I write, and write fiction. Once that question, *Why* do you write?, is out of the way though, another one is invariably forthcoming: How did you get started? Often enough, in fact, a writer asks himself the same question although wording it a bit differently—more like: How did I get into this mess? One begins to write, I believe, much the same way he begins his visible and vocal life on earth—unaware of what's happening, but still screaming because he has a pain some mysterious place or other. Undoubtedly everyone, writer or not, has read things which caused him to mutter, "I can do better than that." Then some take the trouble to try, and others don't. The former sometimes become writers, but the latter only join that vast throng of wishful thinkers who say, "I always wanted to be a writer," but who really mean, "I would like to have written" rather than "I am going to write."

When I search for the catalysts of my own writing, the picture becomes very nearly psychedelic. I can hear a great teacher, a superb prose writer himself, Father Louis Doyle, S.J., praising an opening sentence of my adolescent college attempts at writing. I can see a paragraph I wrote "just for fun," and I can remember a great friend and greater man, Father Bill Fitzgerald, encouraging me. Then there was that first page of print with my name on it. I can sense the thrill of having someone enjoy a thing I've written, the sense of fulfillment in having chopped and added to and polished a single paragraph until it sounded like something. But maybe these resurrected subconscious beginnings are of interest only to myself. So let's get to the nitty-gritty, although it may turn out to be a little more gritty than nitty.

I'd goofed around with writing, much as I'd doodled on occasion with music and drawing, but it never really got serious. In those few years as a Jesuit I'd written careless, spontaneous little things, even—God forgive me—some verse for our bulletin boards. During the three years of the study of philosophy I tried to put some of the earth-shaking philosophical truths I imagined

I had learned into article or pamphlet form. Looking back on those attempts now, I couldn't possibly elevate them by calling them amateurish or sophomoric or adolescent. They were simply awful, although I, of course, thought they were great. But then, they did show desire and the willingness to stick my neck out—and those are indispensable elements in this writing racket.

It was a day like every other day in Belize, British Honduras, and I was doing the night watch in our warehouse study hall. It was 8:37 P.M. when Father McCormack, then headmaster of St. John's College, walked into the room.

"Say," Father Mac said casually, "I'd like to have you put on a play in a couple of months. It's a custom."

"Fine," I told him. "What play would you like?"

"What play . . . ?" He seemed genuinely surprised. "Oh, that. I don't think we have any plays down here. At any rate," he concluded happily as he headed for the door, "I'll leave that up to you. Feel free."

I can't remember just what turkey I disinterred for that first production; but whatever it was, it taught me that it would be easier to write one's own play, knowing what actors and scenery were available. I wrote and produced about six plays in those three years in British Honduras—not because I wanted to write at first, but because I had to. And one great impression remains after these years and after the thrill of seeing so many of my attempts in print—there is *no* thrill like seeing your own play suddenly come alive before you, except maybe the thrill God might have felt at creation.

But you can't start out with play writing without coming to imagine that short story writing would be easier. For one thing, the short story writer doesn't have to worry about the limitations of his available actors and scenery; he can go hog-wild, into exotic lands impossible to crowd onto a stage and with any character imaginable.

So I wrote a short story—something about how my father had met my mother, or at least her version of it. That story brought me my first check as a writer—for five dollars—and so with this con-crete recognition I was hooked. I had now become an author and not just a writer—or so I imagined. During the years of theological study I wrote mostly articles and short stories, with the greatest encouragement coming from *Extension* magazine and its great editor at the time, Eileen O'Hayer. But the writing always stayed on the side, even when I eventually got back into the classroom. It was, in fact, an ironclad rule, purely of my own, that there would be no writing at all during the school year, because of the possibility of its interfering with the teaching and the increasing amount of youth work at the time. Fortunately, my summers were free for writing in those years. And I spent most of those summers in St. Louis at *The Queen's Work* building. Since anyone who spends the school year in cool, colorful Colorado and the summer in hot and humid St. Louis would seem to be out of his mind, I'd better explain a bit.

I had, of course, visited *The Queen's Work* before for one reason or another and had come to know Father Dan Lord. He was, in fact, an idol of mine in just about any category you could name—as a man, a religious, a friend of youth, and, perhaps above all, as a writer and director. Everyone knew Father Lord and thousands still remember him. I tried to describe him in a book called *Backstage Missionary*, but how can anyone describe a man who could do everything and almost did? Next to the vibrant Dan Lord, my book on him was a dud for two reasons: I probably idolized the subject too much, and secondly, I couldn't seem to get at all the sources I needed for a good job. This latter blank wall remains still at least a partial mystery to me.

Father Dan Lord had built the sodality in America. He had also built *T.Q.W.* with its enormous pamphlet business, the office buildings on South Grand, its magazine, everything. To say that he did this single-handed wouldn't be true and would be unfair to some wonderful men and women who helped. But he was certainly always the moving genius, and without him it most probably would never have been done. To name but one item—he could have been a millionaire from his pamphlets alone.

Among other things Father Lord was a great cultured gentleman. He was also a great entertainer and humorist. Like any good, unaffected humorist, the joke was often enough on himself. Later on when I was traveling a lot and giving talks and lectures myself, I remembered one of his stories especially—for some reason or other.

Father Dan was scheduled to speak to about five hundred librarians, mostly nuns, at I think the Thomas More Book Store in Chicago. He barely made the deadline, since his train had been late, and so when he arrived, he asked if he might visit the men's room first. There was, however, a difficulty to this, since he was cornered in a small room to one side of the main hall while the rest room was on the other side, with five hundred women in between watching in eager anticipation for the guest speaker to appear.

Dan noticed, however, that there was a row of blackboards up front, so he decided he'd just hurry along behind these to the rest room. He hadn't noticed, unfortunately, that the row of black-

Father Dan Lord may be one of the few lecturers who was applauded while entering the men's room.

boards came to a sudden stop about fifteen feet short of the rest room, and so as Dan emerged, he was greeted, his hand reaching for the rest room door, with thunderous applause. And so he bowed politely and disappeared into the wings.

By the time I started going to *The Queen's Work* regularly for the summers, Father Dan was gone. But there were others, such as Father Bakewell Morrison who became one of my closest friends. Father Bakes was a delightful genius, a genuine one and not the *ersatz* type so common today who makes sure "intellectual" is added to his ID tags. He was also as completely outspoken (and he had the lungs for it) as anyone I've ever met. He loved to start an argument and then sit back and listen to it develop. He was a short man with a barrel chest, and when he walked, he looked like one of Captain Ahab's boys on leave. Father Bakes had a heart condition, and so he didn't go many places; but when he did it was something of an education, although often embarrassing, to go along. I seem to remember a little discourse on motherhood in that booming voice of his in a hospital elevator one day, with a very pregnant lady among the passengers. We were visiting Father Gerald Kelly that day, and Bakes read the patient's chart for us—and for the rest of the world—with great emphasis and probably a few additions. He was interested in everything and he spent his last summer, in fact, studying Spanish. I thought he had also developed an interest in plants when I saw him carefully cultivating some stuff in a flower box. It turned out, however, to be a practical rather than an intellectual project: growing mint for mint juleps.

One morning Bakes didn't show up, and we found him in bed. He'd died quietly in his sleep—maybe the only quiet thing he'd ever done.

Father Fred Zimmerman was in charge of *The Queen's Work* those days and he was a most thoughtful host as well as a good friend. He was succeeded by Father Jim McQuade and Father Joe McFarland, both fine Jesuits and also good friends of mine.

Throughout the years there were two men at *T.Q.W.* who did a day's work every day, quietly and unassumingly, without fanfare and disregarding, I'm sure, a lot of headaches. Father Al Heeg was sheer genius with children, a quality helped along by a certain charming childlikeness of his own. Father Herb Walker for years carried on as editor of the magazine and did a tremendous job for its many young readers.

The lay staff of *T.Q.W.* was made up of the typical self-sacrificing sort of person who makes publication and promotional centers like *The Queen's Work* possible. Catherine Roberts, now Sister Catherine Roberts of the Cenacle Religious, was the librarian. Florence Flaherty was Father Walker's secretary and was even kind enough to do some typing for me, despite my frequent reminder of the "exorbitant salary" she got. Marian Prendergast devoted most of her life to being Father Lord's secretary and she later helped Father Charlie Clark the same way—as an unpaid volunteer— which meant a salary only slightly less than the usual *Queen's Work* salary of those days.

Father Puggie Dowling, who had so much to do with *Cana* and *Recovery Incorporated,* was there. Puggie was what he himself described as a "foodoholic," and on his frequent trips to the hospital the old charmer would soon have all the nurses talked into bringing him food buried in bouquets of flowers.

Puggie was as outspoken as Bakes Morrison and also unique. Father Charlie Clark walked into his room one hot, humid day to go to confession and found Puggie typing, stripped down to his shorts. "Just a minute, Charlie, " he said, "till I put something on." So he put on a stole.

Father Charlie Clark, or Dismas as he called himself for the sake of his hoods, was a boarder in those days too. It would be hard to imagine a more dedicated man than Charlie, The

Hoodlum Priest, as the movie called him. He loved his cons, and indeed so did we, at least those we met from time to time working in *The Queen's Work* building. There was one tall, dignified-looking executive type who ran the elevator for awhile, quite a step down no doubt for one of the best con men in the business. There was also a young guy who had been a lifer on the "habitual criminal" bit, although as I remember it, his life sentence had come on the occasion of his stealing a truck tire. He was one of the most handsome, personable young men I have ever met, and he could neither read nor write. If it hadn't been for the selflessness and persistence of a Father Clark he might never have been paroled.

Not all of Father Charlie's friends had done much of their time inside a seminary or a Jesuit's living quarters. One day a cigar-chewing gentleman visited Charlie's room and was immediately dictating things to Charlie's male secretary. "Put down a new bed. My God, Father," he went on, "ya need an easy chair and a desk. Put those down, Archie—we'll pick 'em up somewhere. . . ." It took all of Father Charlie's persuasion to convince his friend that the poor furniture in his room was really all he wanted. If I remember correctly, though, somebody delivered a barber's chair a few days later. It had probably been repossessed for installments or something.

For all his efforts to identify with his cons by acting tough, Charlie was a gentle man and in voice at least, if not always in vocabulary, soft-spoken. When he was organizing his Dismas House in St. Louis, he acquired many friends in that neighborhood, among them some Italian fruit marketers who always filled his arms with produce before he came home in the evenings. One day, he told us, he had been talking to two "boys" in the presence of "Mama," a matriarch who knew no English and who constantly rocked back and forth fingering her Rosary. Her black eyes glistened as she regarded Father Charlie and spoke rapid Italian to her boys. But what alarmed Charlie somewhat was that every now and then, loud and clear, came a phrase that sounded very much like "sunuvabeech." Naturally this made Father a bit curious and even alarmed him a bit, since she did seem to be talking about him. Finally, he asked the boys what Mama was saying, and they laughed as they told him: "Mama is a little bit afraid of having hoods coming to live in the neighborhood, but she says if you're going to live with the sons-of-bitches, it'll probably be all right." The Hoodlum Priest saw to it that he remained just Father Clark with Mama.

But a book could be done about Father Clark, just as it

could about Father Lord. I'm not sure if I've run into any bona
fide saints in my life, but if I have, Charlie Clark and Dan Lord
are among them. And if that's what saints are really like, I approve
of them.

There was a constant flow of visitors through the building,
and so you never knew who was going to turn up next. One entire
summer found us with a recognizable ethnic group: Kelly, Lynch,
Connery, McQuade, Morrison, and McGloin. Fathers Gerald Kelly,
John Lynch, and John Connery were moral theologians, the best
in the business. With this congenial group, in fact, we had planned
a mild domestic celebration for one evening; but just about that
time Father Bakes up and died—as Father Kelly put it, "most
inconsiderately," which is exactly the way Bakes would have put
it himself.

Even with the well-deserved reputation of St. Louis for heat
and humidity, *The Queen's Work* building was a great place to
write. We had the sixth floor to ourselves, safeguarded in fact
by a somewhat thought-provoking sign in the elevator: No Women
Allowed Above the Fifth Floor. A stranger might well have
wondered about those lower five floors. The chapel, rec room, and
dining room were partially air-conditioned, and I did much of my
writing (after the basic typing) on the roof. In fact, I often slept
there too when things got too hot inside.

St. Louis is, I think, an interesting and active city. To me the
Muny Opera, the outdoor theater in Forest Park, was gorgeous and
its summer shows delightful. Father John Lynch was once invited
to attend with some friends, but his hosts then decided they would
"wait until the following week, because Cole Porter's *Can-Can* is
the current show and only the dirty-minded would want to see that."
I had, of course, already seen it twice when Father Lynch happily
relayed this story to me.

These were productive summers too, and I was able to turn
out quite a number of pamphlets and articles and not a few short
stories. In the six years following Father Lord's death I did a
monthly bit for *The Queen's Work* magazine and these articles
were all done during those summers. A book entitled *Call Me Joe!*
was put together in those years, as was the aforementioned
Backstage Missionary. And I began the trilogy for teen-agers
Love and Live! here, finishing these books off later.

Something went out of the place when Bakes Morrison left
us, just as something had gone out of it—much of its heart, as a
matter of fact—when Dan Lord had left it. Bakes' departure plus
a number of smaller reasons caused me to discontinue my St. Louis

In St. Louis during the summer you sleep where you can—or try to sleep where you can't.

summers. Then too, I was moved from Denver to Minneapolis where writing conditions were still better than in St. Louis.

The Wisconsin Province of the Society had bought a house in the city of Minneapolis to make use of while they were constructing their novitiate and juniorate at nearby (about twenty-eight miles away) St. Bonifacius. It was a lovely place facing on Lake Harriet, the nicest of twenty-six lakes within the city of Minneapolis. The house was ideal for putting up those Jesuits who didn't fit anywhere else—which isn't so bad as it sounds, but only says that there are men whose work and schedule just don't fit into the regimen of a school community. There were men in the house representing the Apostleship of Prayer and some who were running the Mission Bureau. Now and then a Jesuit studying at Minnesota or another nearby university would stay with us, and occasionally someone writing a dissertation or something even more earth-shaking would spend some time there.

When it was a question of my moving, Father Leo Burns, then

Wisconsin Provincial, gave me the choice of moving to one of our high schools or to the Jesuit Residence in Minneapolis for full-time writing. Sight unseen, I chose the house in Minneapolis. To be devoted just to writing in a school would be an impossibility—for just one thing, because as soon as a teacher got sick, you would be it. Moreover, you'd want to be it. Writing is like any other discipline; you sometimes have to lock yourself up to do it.

We had nice neighbors in Minneapolis (something I've been wanting to say in print for some time), particularly Dr. Harold Buchstein and Lee Primus and their families. The single item which prompts this accolade for Dr. Buchstein is that someone had once asked him, when we first moved in, how he liked his new neighbors; and he had answered, "Just fine—no wild parties." Dr. Buchstein, by the way, is a brain surgeon, handy had we ever needed a house call.

One day shortly after my arrival in Minneapolis I had a call from one Jack Oberreuter, who had seen my picture in the paper and who had been a near classmate of mine at Creighton in Omaha. Jack mentioned that he and his family lived on the other side of the lake. "Sorry," I told him. "We don't speak to people on the other side of the lake." But we did, and the Oberreuters and I became good friends.

But if there is a deliberate, cultivated pride in one's own lake district in Minneapolis, it's nothing compared with the rivalry between the twin cities Minneapolis and St. Paul. Since I lived in Minneapolis, I may have some slight prejudice myself, but I prefer to consider my attitude one of objective truth. At one time, I understand that the two cities were supposed to have been joined into one with the common name of Minnehaha, a rather common name around that territory—Minnie for Minneapolis and ha-ha for St. Paul. The river, they'll tell you, doesn't completely divide the two cities—culture does. And you interpret that theory according to which city you live in. One of the people I played handball with a few times, Carl Witham, was the only man ever offered a free St. Paul T-shirt if he'd wear it playing in the Minneapolis Athletic Club. Oh yes, the offer came from members of the Minneapolis Athletic Club. I hasten to add that I found St. Paul people warm and friendly; and I've met not a few St. Paul expatriates, such as Father John McAnulty, S.J., who managed to overcome their previous environment to a high degree.

Minneapolis, besides the work of writing, meant a lot of new friends. It meant doing quite a number of TV shows I enjoyed immensely. It meant the Minneapolis Athletic Club and handball camaraderie. How tremendous it is to go along a street or up

106

In Minneapolis everybody talks to everybody.

and down in an elevator or into a store and to be able to talk or
joke with people immediately—something I have never experienced
so generally elsewhere. (Just the other day I heard a California
sports announcer say that Minneapolis had to be the friendliest
city in the league, so I guess I'm not the only one to have noticed!)
If you think I loved the place and still miss it, I did and I do. And
just why they can come up with a lovely song about San Francisco
and the blooper they did for a greater city like Minneapolis, I don't
know.
    Some memorable characters went through or stayed in the
Minneapolis Jesuit Residence. Brother Lee McNamee, then
business manager of the Jesuit Mission office, is by no means the
least memorable. On weekends when we had no cook in the place,
Brother Lee and I (mostly he) would take over the cooking. Our
most unforgettable triumph was the two ducks we marinated in wine
until they revived, came upstairs, and stamped through the rec room.
    Father Tom O'Connor was our superior in Minneapolis, and a

great one. I had thought—probably with the narrow, yet completely confident judgment of the immature—that he had been a bit too much as superior in our previous two encounters: at Florissant when I had first entered the Society and he was assistant to the Master of Novices, and at St. Mary's when I was a theologian and Father Tom was Rector. In Minneapolis the situation was different; and so, undoubtedly, was I. No one could have surpassed his great kindness and thoughtfulness for us in those years. He could, I'm convinced, have been elected mayor of the city any day, or perhaps manager of the Twins. A great athlete himself, he took all the sports pretty seriously.

Near the end of our time in Minneapolis, things must have been especially hard for Tom, since he knew the house was to be sold and he thought the sale was a mistake. He was also beginning to acquire a few ailments. Later on, Father Tom accompanied a group to Ireland, which he had never seen. He said Mass for the group, I understand, on their arrival that August 27, went to bed and died that night, his fiftieth anniversary as a Jesuit.

We had a few ships which passed through Minneapolis, sometimes in the night and sometimes over the course of a year or so. One such boarder coined a phrase (in which some of the more regular members of our community took a fiendish sort of delight) introducing me, when showing some friends through the house, as *our other writer* even though he had forgotten my name.

There were lots and lots of visitors, many of them from the missions, so that we were able to keep a pretty good world view of things.

The main writing goal I had set myself at this time was putting together a four-year, high-school religion course. This meant a re-study of everything I had ever learned or thought I had learned, chiefly theology and philosophy and anything else related to it. The first draft of this work was a four-thousand page manuscript, and the final draft eight thousand pages, so I had had to follow a fairly consistent schedule not to get discouraged and overwhelmed by the project.

There were other writing ventures at this time. In the book field the *Love and Live!* series was finished off, plus a book for parents, *What to Do Till the Psychiatrist Comes!,* plus one on Catholic apologetics as it then was, *Friends, Romans, Protestants.* Quite a few articles and some short stories were done, and for three years I did the syndicated column "Working To Beat Hell!" And so as at St. Louis, the years at Minneapolis were productive and enjoyable.

We got word, one otherwise fine Minneapolis day that the

Jesuit Residence was going to be sold. I can't say this made most of us jump up and down for joy. At any rate the selling of the house produced a number of displaced persons, including one misplaced writer. The closest Jesuit "house of writers" was Canisius House in Chicago. Since, however, there is usually a waiting-list for Canisius House and since my writing was turning to fiction and, hopefully, towards the movies and TV, I went west.

The Lord clearly loves fools and Jesuits, even when the two coalesce in the same person, and so He let me stumble into a fine setup for a writer. When a California Province Jesuit, Father Art Rutledge, suggested I take a look at Montecito where the Society was just completing work on a new novitiate plant, I shuddered and said "No thanks," because I have this allergy thing to spending any more than the required two years in a novitiate. But I looked anyhow and found a lovely big house on a hill, overlooking both the mountains and the Pacific. It had been used as the Jesuit novitiate for a few years, and now that the finishing touches were being put on the new buildings about a half mile up the hill, it was about to be deserted even by its skeleton community of six Jesuits. For a few months from August to December we were a community of six or seven, but on December 15, 1967, I became the hermit of Montecito, with an occasional short or longer term Jesuit fellow boarder. It had been fun to live in a community. Fun or not, a writer can get more done alone—at least this writer can—but I joined the novitiate community for many meals and for an occasional spiritual conference before dinner.

I've mentioned that Minneapolis was, despite the snow, the warmest city I've lived in; and maybe that's why Santa Barbara seemed to me, at first at least and despite the lack of snow, a relatively cold town. Another reason, of course, is an obvious one—our house was outside of the city and so the nearest neighbor was out of sight. I went into Santa Barbara when I had to—to play handball, or to buy dog food or some other similar necessity of life.

California Jesuits, even when sent east of Eden, have a well-deserved reputation for friendliness and hospitality, and the small community I joined when first coming to this house confirmed that reputation. Father Karl Von der Ahe was in charge of the building of the new novitiate, and he not only did a fabulous job on this gigantic project but managed to preserve his California sense of hospitality as well, amid what must have been uncountable details and not a few headaches. Father John McAnulty, now Rector and Master of Novices there, was fabulous in his considerateness of this outsider (from the east, as Californians call places like Denver and Minneapolis) and was a good friend as well as a superior—a somewhat rare combination in our computer-controlled world. Only occasionally does Father John seem to remember his St. Paul origins and my spiritual relationship to Minneapolis. Father Bill Maring is the treasurer of the whole California Province. Although he didn't live at Montecito, he did drop in occasionally to see if he'd inadvertently left any money lying around.

But the man all of us at Montecito looked up to most was Father Ed Whelan, in his eighties and one of the youngest men I know. Father Ed has been rector of so many Jesuit houses they've lost count. The rumor is, in fact, that he would have become provincial had not everybody felt he'd have given the province away the day after his appointment.

St. Ignatius used to pray that he become inebriated with the love of Christ, and he meant exactly this—that he wanted so to love Christ that, like any genuine lover, he would throw caution to the winds in serving Christ. Ignatius believed in taking every human and prayerful means available in making decisions; but then going ahead with blind trust and faith even when the consequences seemed risky, just as long as it also seemed to be the will of God. He felt, for example, that Jesuit superiors should send their *best* men on the missions, "sacrificing" them if you will. Obviously, we haven't always done this—I went on the missions myself. Ignatius was quite capable of giving something to the poor even when the gift seemed likely to cause hardship to himself and sometimes even his fellow Jesuits. But he knew very well how Christ was liable to treat such prodigality too.

This aside on Ignatius is run in here to explain what I mean by saying that Father Ed Whelan has apparently always had this same uniquely Ignatian, or Jesuit, spirit of faith. He gives things away and he always has, and Christ always comes back with more as He always does. And as we so-called modern Jesuits seem sometimes to rely more and more on impersonal committees and their computer assistants, it's to be hoped that we can find a way of building into the computer some of this foolish faith and impractical prodigality and inebriated love. In other words, let's have all the Father Ed Whelans we can get.

During my three years in Santa Barbara, I was, perforce, 99 percent hermit, and yet I had a few other friends in the vicinity too, most of them acquired on a handball court at the Santa Barbara Y or the Los Angeles Athletic Club or at the tennis courts. Besides, I didn't remain even a 99 percent hermit, since I soon took in a permanent house guest, Sam F. (for Fanny) Spade, girl detective.

110

Sam is a German Shepherd girl, the "Sam" being part of her clever disguise. Beside being a private eye and the custodian of our house, Sam is also something of a literary critic. (At the moment in fact that I typed this passage she sat there staring at me and the typewriter with an eloquence no words could convey. So, for a while, I thought I might as well tear up this page.) Fortunately, she doesn't say much—as I recently pointed out to an oft-divorced friend who said he wished he could find a human-type female with a disposition like Sam's.

At this stage some amateur psychologist is sure to nod knowingly and mutter, "They always get that way when they live alone." The truth is, though, that I was *that way* even before I lived alone, being a great lover of any animals, especially dogs and still more especially German Shepherds. Their devotion and flattery is something both tremendous and inexplicable. I can look out my window right now at the autumn colors of Tacoma and realize that God

Sam can't spell any better than I, but she thinks she can type better.

must, indeed, be lovely to have made things like these. But I can look at Sam with her crazy antics and her blind devotion to me, and realize that only an utter fool could say that a phenomenon like Sam *just happened.* She's a living, walking, running, jumping, happily barking testimony to God.

Hollywood too became a minor part of my California life. Certainly it would be unfair of me at this point to suggest that my impressions of Hollywood are objectively and universally valid. But since they *are* my impressions just now, let's go.

The word for Hollywood, as I see it now, is "commercialism." And I know at least one very well-established writer who has hung up the whole Hollywood thing and cleared out, because he was fed up with kowtowing to the little men with briefcases who often enough know little about art but much about money. He was also tired of catering to the established genius who thinks he is buying a writer along with his scripts. Now I'm not an established Hollywood writer, but I've already encountered some of this commercialism. I did a novel that every reader, even those armadillo-souled people known as agents, liked very much. A number of real pros, in fact, were really sold on the story. But their main comment was, in essence: "Great. Wonderful. Unmarketable." The whole attitude was summed up by a reader at one studio who, when told of the general story by my then Hollywood agent, refused to read it. "It sounds," he said, "like the kind of story that wins Academy Awards, if you can get anyone to do it or even read it. Me, I won't read it."

Hollywood strikes me too, despite its protestations to the contrary, as very much a closed circle. Each producer seems to have his own coterie of people around him, so that when he chances on a story—probably one some scriptwriter has bought for peanuts—he has this scriptwriter do the script, gets another buddy to direct, a name to act, and so on. He ventures outside the safe circle only with great trepidation. He is, in fact, so committed already within this circle that he never really gets the time to step outside it. I personally know producers who are booked for years ahead.

Then there is the big-name-star syndrome. A scriptwriter friend of mine told me that he once approached a very well known producer with a novel he wanted to turn into a movie script. The producer, although also a personal friend of his, turned it down. Two years later, however, another scriptwriter who had in the meantime acquired the same novel, went to this same producer, offered to write a script from the novel—and had it accepted. And the only difference was that he also brought along a star who would work for peanuts, $400,000. The picture was almost sure to be a turkey, but there was this big name. . . .

For "Olympus" read "Hollywood."

Certainly no one can be unaware of the unique sort of deification which takes place in Hollywood. The Hollywood star is applauded and appreciated everywhere he goes—except sometimes at home, and so he often has to get a divorce to secure also the domestic applause he feels he deserves. I have, of course, met stars who don't fit this description, but clearly many of them do fit it all too well. A great doctor or teacher or carpenter can go almost anywhere and not be applauded or be in danger of having his clothes torn off as relics. But not the Hollywood star. Occasionally, on some of the interview shows for example, we get an insight into just how thoroughly some of them deserve their divine status.

But this deification of the actor has also become a thing with many of those behind the actor, and so there are other gods on Olympus—not so universally known, perhaps, but still deities. If you want to talk with some producers or even some top agents in

Hollywood, you're going to be made to acknowledge, at least implicitly, both your own humble status and the nature of the Persons you are trying to contact. I remember having an appointment with a TV producer, and I was to call to confirm it. I called. Then I called again. And again. Then I was told at exactly what time I was to call next. I called at this precise moment. "Who's calling?" the secretary asked. I told her and waited while I heard indistinct voices in the background. "He's very busy now," I finally heard, even though this had been the exact time agreed on after many efforts.

"So," I told her, "am I," just before—gently of course—hanging up.

Then there was the agent, a lady, I was supposed to meet and talk with. The same sort of thing went on. "How about lunch tomorrow?" I finally asked, after exhausting every other route.

"Oh, I can't possibly make it tomorrow, honey," I heard. "Tell you what—give me a jingle next week."

"Next week, honey," I answered, "I have no time for jingling around."

When I first orbited into Hollywood, I was introduced to a gentleman with a beard (which seems to be very nearly standard Hollywood equipment and proves something or other). Not very originally he came up with the standard Hollywood crack about a clerical collar, "Is that collar for real, or are you made up for some part?"

Being an innocent at the time and not realizing that this was only airing an old bromide, I instinctively answered, "I was wondering the same thing about that beard."

Sometimes, indeed, the Hollywood names and his or her press agent begin to believe their own verbal creations and take over not a few prerogatives of a deity. When an otherwise ordinary gal has a child out of wedlock, nobody particularly admires her for it. But when a Hollywood star manages this, her various press agents will label it as honest, freedom-loving, romantic, not noting that *his* wife or *her* ex-husband (also an "ex" when she encountered him, most likely) might argue a bit about the accuracy of some of those adjectives and add a few others of their own.

One should not, however, make the mistake of supposing that all of Hollywood's values are phony and that it has no serious aims. There *are* important questions being mulled over all the time in the film capital. Just the other day, for example, I read one such in one of the more thoughtful columnists: "Is that or isn't it Myrtle Furtil's *derrière* you see in the first frame of her upcoming movie, *Naked at Noon* (with George Bull)? Some say it is, some say it

114

isn't . . . ." When earth-shaking questions like this are pondered, there has to be depth.

In a decidedly more serious vein, from what I hear and the little I know, I suspect that the vast number of Hollywood people are warm and kind and friendly. Certainly I've seen these qualities in the few I know—on sets and in private. But the stand-outs seem to me, at this stage, very selective about those hands they reach down to clasp, and very, very conscious of others who may be sharing their own level or even attempting to climb a bit higher. Applause is at once their aim and their right.

Make no mistake about it—there are big men and women in Hollywood, great and skilled people, genuine, fabulous artists. Some of them are even close friends of mine. Henry Blanke, now retired from production, is one of them; and he's a *big*, big man even though he isn't very tall, physically. In fact, Henry feels that because he's somewhat short he must sometimes stand on the table and shout a bit to emphasize a point during an argument. Henry produced some fine shows, some of the marvelous Paul Muni pictures for example, and a gripping show called *The Treasure of Sierra Madre.* I think Henry's favorite is probably *The Nun's Story,* but I like *Treasure.*

I spent three happy years in California and only left because the house began to get too crowded for a writer to write undistractedly. Luckily, at just the right time, I chanced on an even better place to do my writing thing. And so, at present, I am resident chaplain at Marymount Military Academy in Tacoma, Washington.

Marymount is a delightful place, a military academy for boys (with about one hundred of them presently on hand, from sixth through ninth grades), run by Dominican Sisters. My official duties are light, and so most of my time is free for my writing. I have my own house, and Sam Spade has her own yard, plus plenty of space to run—for both of us. Both of us, too, are thrilled at the change of seasons, a thing we missed in California. Perpetual summer could be all right, but you can only really appreciate the summer after you've been through a bit of winter.

And there's another plus: In the years I have been more or less insulated in the writing thing, I never allowed myself to think about how much I missed the school and the kids. It's nice now to have at least some limited contact with them once more in what is obviously an excellent school run by completely dedicated and proficient people.

We Jesuits have a saying that the Lord loves fools and Jesuits. Clearly, he also loves Jesuit writers—even to the extent of providing such great places for them to write.

It used to be that scattered about in our population were a few people who had never written a book, but the number is apparently dwindling. There is, of course, still some discrepancy between the number of those who have written a book and those who have published one, but that's changing too. There isn't the slightest doubt in my mind that if Lee Harvey Oswald hadn't been scratched by Mr. Ruby, we'd have a *How It All Happened to Me* book on the market by this time, and had Ruby not also left us, we'd be blessed with a Do-It-Yourself best seller by now. Both of these, of course, would be serialized under far more descriptive titles in the big picture magazines.

Perhaps because of this widespread leaning towards authorship, my own quasi philosophy of writing might be of interest. Despite the vast number of those who try to write, one still encounters, on occasion, a certain awe towards writers and authors (a distinction comparable to that between a batter and a hitter). Autograph parties and review talks (of one's own book, of course) always bring out a few of the more ardent worshippers. Not that I deplore this entirely, especially if I chance to overhear it rather than having it thrown at me directly. But it is embarrassing, and this for one particular reason over all others—any author knows his stuff isn't that good; and even if it should be good, it's not going to be any better than the work of a mother or a teacher or a dentist or a typist, none of whom ever gets this sort of public praise. An author is almost always aware too that his final product has fallen far below his ambitions for it.

Many of the papers (especially perhaps the diocesan papers) seem incapable of headlining only an author and letting it go at that. They always make him a *noted author* just as they make anybody who has ever heard a lecture on the Bible a *scripture expert* or *noted theologian*. One trouble with this, as far as I'm concerned, is that I've been billed as a noted author since my first amateurish little article, and so there's been no opportunity for advancement.

The awesome admiration for a writer's talents are, I believe, often misplaced. Not that a great novelist (such as Graham Greene, at least as a novelist) hasn't a certain genius, but for most of us who write, the talent consists rather largely in two abilities: (1) the ability to sit for long hours, working a thing out painstakingly, going over and over it until he's sick of it; and (2) the ability (or stubbornness) to override the fear of making mistakes or becoming a target of criticism in public. It is, I'm convinced, this latter characteristic which often stops the genius or the expert from

116

writing, apart of course from the fact that he's sometimes far too occupied with criticizing what's being written by others to do anything of his own.

The important point here, however, is that the ordinary author (whatever *that* is) needs only one king-sized talent—the ability to sit for long periods.

But if a writer has his admirers, even a few who admire him as a writer far beyond his merits, there are also those for whom a writer and his alleged talents are simply blah. Anybody, they are certain, could write if he wanted to waste the time. Sometimes you run into these retiring sages directly, but more often you only hear of them, probably because like the avowed expert, they're very busy elsewhere.

Quite often some pastor or other would call the Minneapolis house asking if we could spare him a man to help out at his parish over the weekends. Often enough someone was available, but invariably when he wasn't, the next question was sure to be: What about that guy who's just writing? This, in fact, got to be a standard joke, at least to all but one of our inmates. Father probably just wouldn't have believed that I usually started writing on Saturday and Sunday mornings even earlier than on other days—about 6 A.M.—and that a knocked-out weekend could have meant as many as seventy-five pages still undone. And even if he'd believed that, he might still have wondered if those seventy-five pages thus lost were really worth preserving anyhow.

I once received a call from a lady who wanted some incidental information. I was happy to be able to help her out somewhat in the course of ten or fifteen minutes. But then just before hanging up, she blew the whole tender relationship. "I was going to call the Pastor," she said, "but I knew he'd be busy."

Within my own Order I have for the most part met with nothing but kindness and charity and the suspicion, at least, that writing can be quite some little chore, at least on some days. There have, naturally, been those who knew nothing about it—a situation that, unfortunately, doesn't always prevent a display of this precise degree of knowledge. "How," one such perceptive adult asked me when I was moved into full-time writing, "did you manage to get out of teaching?" By pure coincidence, I recall another story about this same Dale Carnegie graduate.

Before *I'll Die Laughing!* came out, the manuscript went around to quite a few readers of my own choice. I had been careful in this book to include some anecdote or other about each of my classmates and about quite a few other Jesuits as well. Among these anecdotes was one about this gentleman—a story, moreover,

117

which I considered not just mildly humorous but also complimentary or at least harmless. One of my spies, however, passed the word to me that he didn't take it this way, but was vocally pretty indignant about its inclusion. Now that sounded like a legitimate gripe to me, so I simply sent word that he and his story were being erased from the final manuscript—excised, deleted, omitted. The odd thing was that this act of humble charity seemed to annoy him more than the original story had. This offers one small clue as to why not even a nice, kindly, even-tempered writer like myself can please everybody.

I.D.L.! was far and away the best selling of my books—prior, that is, to *Living To Beat Hell!* It turned, in fact, into two things I hadn't had in mind at all—something of an ecumenical book and a vocation book. In fact, a survey taken in one province, asking the novices what had been the occasion, at least, of their interest in the Society, showed a great proportion at that time influenced by this book.

Now naturally, this fact neither disheartened nor humiliated me; and so on the occasion of a private conference with my then provincial, I had this interesting little document in my pocket—prepared to flash it at an appropriate moment, casually of course. Naturally, we got onto the subject of writing, and I mentioned that now that I had done a book on the course of training for Jesuit priests, I would like to do a similar one on the brothers. The provincial only remarked, looking out the window as I recall, "I'm not sure those books do any good"—about as efficient a "shut up, sesame" as he could have come up with. And so my survey remained forever in my pocket and the proposed book on the brothers, for now at least, in my imagination.

Today's Jesuit attitude towards writing is quite different, thank God, from what it used to be. In days hopefully gone—if I may speak like a patriarch—writing seemed often to be regarded as a harmless sort of hobby that superiors allowed subjects to indulge in, just as long as it didn't interfere with their real work. One might also write during a sabbatical or some such leave of absence, but then he would be expected to get back to work once this vacation time was over and the writing mania presumably worked out of his system.

Even to imagine an assignment to full-time writing in those days was laughable. A lot of circumstances, a lot of luck, a lot of understanding on the part of some superiors, and an infinite Providence did eventually work things out to where I was occupied with full-time free-lance writing. There are, however, still some occupational hazards. When I first met our then secretary of the

Society, Father John Correia-Afonso, he greeted me with "I heard you'd left the Society." Lord knows where such rumors start, perhaps with some wishful thinkers. Believe me, that "S.J." is the only degree I ever care to write after my name.

Sometimes too Jesuits and non-Jesuits alike, even when admitting some small validity in the writing syndrome, regard writers with some suspicion, not as creatures from Mars, perhaps, so much as creatures who *ought* to be on Mars. Sometimes, in fact, I tend to agree with them. Once, for example, I was invited to a "dinner," along with about a dozen other writers. As I looked around the room, brushing one or other of a dozen or so frolicking kittens off my shoulder now and then and righting the TV tray which had previously held my plate of lasagna, I thought to myself, "What a collection of characters!" The next thought in the series came spontaneously: "What am *I* doing here?" And the final realization came uninvited too: "They're all writers and probably all asking themselves the same question."

Even as I admit, however, that one might detect a minor eccentricity or two in a room full of writers, I'd have to say that maybe one could spot a tiny peculiarity now and then in other groups as well. I have, for example, also found myself meeting with groups of actors and groups of psychologists.

But speaking of psychologists, there is a psychology connected with writing too. And the very first psychological quirk of a writer is probably the compulsion that drives him to write. I simply can't imagine a day when I wouldn't be writing, even if busy in some other job as well. Writing is like owning a dog—you shouldn't do it if you'd like to, but only if you feel you *must.*

But there's much more psychology in the writing racket than this compulsion. Any good psychologist can tell an enormous amount about a person from what he writes, because we human beings give ourselves away with every word we utter or write. I shudder, in fact, to think of the nearly two million words in the manuscript of my religion course, because if every manuscript is a Rorschach, that course amounts to a lot of ink blots. Happily, the religion course is not fiction, and it's in the latter field that the psychologist can have a real brain-blowing field day. In fact, since I've done a great deal of psychological testing, I sometimes test myself too; and the reader may or may not be interested to know that whenever I'm deeply involved in writing fiction, my schizo scale jumps up a few notches, too. I mention this so that I can always plead to those who analyze my fiction, "That's not the real me."

There's some fascinating psychological doodling involved in looking back on the things one has written with an eye to the circumstances surrounding them at the time. No great perception seems needed to understand why a writer's first short story might be a thing on how his mother and father had met—unless, of course, he had fashionably hated both instead of being straight enough to love them. Nor does it require a genius to figure out why a first-year theologian, heady with his sudden understanding of what the centuries had missed, would write what he considered theology. The connections here are obvious.

Not so obvious, perhaps, is the psychology behind my first published book; a murder mystery called *Happy Holiday!* and published under the pen name I used on fiction for years, Thaddeus O'Finn. Now certainly every writer of fiction has to make use of characters he has known or seen—or at least composites of same—together with whatever additions and subtractions his imagination will suggest. But he doesn't always do this consciously, and neither did I. Some of my readers of that species which always insists on seeing real people in fiction have told me that they fancied they saw some members of the theology faculty then teaching us at St. Mary's, Kansas, in some of my victims and the other *personae* of the book. This came, of course, as a complete surprise to me, and if there is any objective truth in it, the explanations can only lie in some deeply hidden psychological compulsion.

The psychological implications inherent in the title of my next published book *I'll Die Laughing!* are a bit easier for me to detect—and admit—largely because they're completely unsubtle. This book was outlined while I was taking a year's vacation in a hospital. That explains the title. The fact that I had only recently completed the Jesuit course of training explains the compulsions leading to the book itself. The next book *Smile at Your Own Risk!* which concerned teaching, was done when I was once more up to here in that occupation. Nothing very complicated about that. The teen books, the *Love and Live!* trilogy (*Learn a Little!, Yearn a Little!, Burn a Little!*) plus countless articles for teens and a book *Backstage Missionary* on the greatest worker for teens I have known, Father Dan Lord, came at a time when my world was wall-to-wall teen-agers There can't be any deep psychological secret to my attempting a high-school religion course—anyone who had done any writing and had tried to teach religion would have attempted the same thing. In fact, some who were neither writers nor teachers have tried it too sometimes with an amazing degree of success.

Even the desire to write fiction betrays a certain psychology of the would-be author. So I need say nothing of my leanings towards this field. Since, however, I'm baring my psychology here and promising the reader still more shocking revelations when he reads the stuff, I might as well mention a thing which originally came as something of a surprise to me, but which I've now accepted and coexist with. Among other defects I have as a writer (which is, incredible enough, only a small proportion of those I have in other categories), I'm a loner. Except for some partial collaborating on a play or two, I've turned out to be the most utter failure at collaboration. This may be because I've become accustomed to thinking best with a typewriter, or it may be sheer bullheadedness and independence. Whatever its reason, I realize that this fatal flaw may well keep me from ever doing anything worthwhile in the movie and television industry where collaboration, the experts will tell you, is of the essence.

Titles too give some clue to a writer's psychology as well as to his sense of salesmanship. And since I shudder at the thought of the psychological implications of my own titles, I'll only list a few of them here and let the amateur-psychologist reader have a field day:

> *Happy Holiday!*
> *I'll Die Laughing!*
> *Smile at Your Own Risk!*
> *What To Do Till the Psychiatrist Comes!*
> *What Not to Do on a Date*
> *Become Little Children—Are You Kidding?*
> *Getting a Kick Out of Life!*
> *Working to Beat Hell!*

One thing that strikes me immediately is all those exclamation marks! Incidentally, if you think you can discern some psychological quirk in an author's using a title like *Working to Beat Hell!* what about an editor who changes it to *Striving to Gain Heaven?* No kidding—there was one.

It's hard to imagine anyone serious about his writing who doesn't also look at its marketability. And since there are three necessary evils here which are intimately related to each other—marketability, criticism, and censorship—we'll take a look at all of them more or less together.

It's quite true that some genuinely good stuff is simply unmarketable. On the other hand, for a writer—especially a beginner—to think that what he writes is always great even when it's universally rejected, is suspect at the very least. I doubt if anyone can rival my own stacks of rejection slips; but the constant flow of this variety of junk mail has never discouraged me for long, although periodically it still can do so briefly. But the fact is too that if one gets *only* rejections, he still shouldn't give up—not at all—but he ought to examine his writing (and, incidentally, the markets) very, very critically. In my own case, I feel that three or four of my unpublished short stories (two of which won literary awards) are far better than any of those I've had published. On the other hand, I can see why no one accepted the other rejects, whose number is far out of sight. I can also see that there may be many reasons for the rejection of even a good story—the publication's lack of a sufficiently large or appreciative audience for a particular type of story; their appeal, perhaps, being to an entirely different public; the pressure of magazine advertisers (who don't ordinarily want anything in a magazine which might antagonize their prospective clients); and so on.

But apart from exceptions like these, I feel that in general if a thing is good enough it *will* sell. If an author never sells, he's doing something not quite right or omitting some essential—even if it's only that he's not studying the markets well enough. It *is* a broad market.

When it comes to constructive criticism, one's friends or associates or both (and, of course, primarily oneself) are often the worst judges of marketability. At one time, for example, I had two book manuscripts ready for publication— *Call Me Joe!* and *I'll Die Laughing!* Almost everyone who read both manuscripts was sure the former would be a great smash and the latter—well, forget it. Naturally, things went just the opposite: the first barely squeaked by, while the second became the best seller I've had—so far.

Nor are criticisms from non-friends and/or non-associates always valid either. There is, in fact, a type of non-professional criticism any writer has to learn to ignore—or else forget about being a writer. Criticism is going to come to anyone making a public splash. In fact, I feel sure that many a potential writer won't write because of this very fear of criticism. It could be that they themselves have been so critical of other writers that they can't seem to come up with the perfect word or expression or solution. I am, of course, talking here about people who *could* write and who do have something to say, but who will not. There's also that large group of would-be authors who can't write, some of whom don't allow even this to deter them and some of whom are even published on occasion.

When it comes to the priest and/or religious-writer, there is, I believe, another reason why some who could and perhaps should do so will not write—and that's the fear of that form of criticism called censorship. (To be quite honest, I know many Jesuits who could write far better than I, but who will not, because they have not

122

yet acquired the very first requisite of a writer, the ability to sit for long periods.) Often enough, the fear of censorship is a groundless fear, although even the fact that it exists can be some-thing of a hurdle. Sometimes it definitely *is* a valid fear. And yet, groundless or valid, this fear shouldn't stop a real writer, someone determined to say something and to make use of his talent, no matter what its limitations nor how vulnerable to criticism he makes himself. In other words, he considers his purposes worth the price he has to pay to achieve it. It's a little like the priesthood: If you think it worthwhile you have to pay the price, instead of spending your whole priestly life griping about it or fearing its consequences.

The field of criticism seems much ˙ke today's field of theology—everybody is a critic or a theologian by divine right or at least intuition, aided sometimes by extensive research into some headlines, a few issues of *Time*, or maybe even one or two abstruse lectures. And so criticism has never surprised me in this racket.

It isn't the censor that bugs you; it's his shadow.

Some of it I have considered ridiculous (especially when it comes from a non-reader), while some has been helpful. Some of it has even been interesting. The several grudging critics of *I.D.L.!* in fact, seemed to have one quality in common: no appreciation of my attempts at humor. They remind me of one of the nineteen publishers who had refused the manuscript and who had sent me a note saying, "You have no more sense of humor than I have, so you shouldn't try to be funny." As I recall, I sent him copies of many of the book's early royalty reports, which were substantial and which seemed to indicate that the book had obviously fooled a lot of people into thinking it was somewhat humorous. And if the book wasn't humorous, *that* is.

My fellow Jesuits, in their almost instinctive charity, gave me all the breaks in their reviews. Only one mystery still puzzles me in this area—a periodical run by a few Jesuits, one that claimed it reviewed all the best current books, never reviewed or even mentioned the book, even in those months when it was atop the best-seller list published in this magazine's pages. At the time, I found this surprising and puzzling. Somewhere in between, I found it humorous. At the moment, I find it satisfying.

Another bit of criticism I once found interesting was one from an editor who didn't know I was a Jesuit and who sent back a short story manuscript with the comment that I was "as anti-clerical as [the writers] Harry Sylvester or J.F. Powers," a crack J. F. and I, at least, got quite a kick out of.

Since much of my writing has been aimed at the contemporary teen-ager or his parents, its language has been theirs too as well as mine. I've no ambition to be a Shakespeare, an Erle Stanley Gardner, or anyone else who clearly writes for posterity. And so I find the sometime criticism of reviewers and censors—"The author's use of slang is unfortunate, because these expressions change so much"— just so much hooey. (Now there's a word that has endured, as have some of its less polite synonyms.) Who cares whether it lasts or not? And who wants to be published only posthumously? And so I consider it more my bag to write in my own contemporary language, such as it is, for my contemporaries, such as *they* are.

But one can't really talk about criticism without getting into that great subject of endless dialog on the part of high-school debaters on rainy days when the teacher is out of material— censorship.

I've no intention here of scratching deep into the general subject of censorship, since that would require a whole book and still wouldn't solve the problem. And so I'll leave the whole subject with only one or two remarks: First, I feel that to argue against any and all censorship is ridiculous, as ridiculous as having no traffic laws or laws against murder or rape or any other species of harm. Where harm can come to a person, there are all sorts of people (and moral *persons*) with responsibilities—the State, the Church, parents, teachers, counselors, what have you. True, to detect a possible moral or social injury may be more difficult than trying to prevent traffic homicides, but the responsibility remains—particularly since moral and social injuries can be more critical to their victim than physical ones.

The second abstract principle I would express is that as a religious, I've taken on a bit more responsibility to endure censorship than have others, because no matter what my own or anyone else's disclaimers say, my writing in some way or other reflects on the Society of which I am a member. For a Jesuit to take the law into his own hands, to encourage the violation of just laws, and then to say, "I'm acting as an individual and not as a Jesuit," is as unrealistic as saying, "My hand did it, but *I* didn't." Unless I can hide successfully and completely behind a pen name—and, in a sense, even then—I don't see how I can claim not to be writing as a Jesuit. Certainly, it's pretty generally understood that what one Jesuit writes is not necessarily what all, or sometimes even any, other Jesuits would have written or agreed with. But this doesn't mean that I, with that S.J. on the book, am dissociated from the Society.

In general then, I believe in censorship—annoying and frustrating and hampering as it sometimes may be. I feel that the system can undergo great improvements—some of which it *is* undergoing. I am, for example, particularly bugged by the fact that "the bad guys" publish anything they darn well please without censorship, but if I want to answer them, my efforts have to be approved by someone who may not know anything about the subject at all, or even by one of *their* friends—who, as censor, has the power of suppressing what *I* write. I particularly dislike the idea of writing for a censor instead of for the public I'm trying to reach, because in that case I'm only publishing his thoughts with my name signed to it. Nor do I chortle with glee when a censor forbids publication because he doesn't like what is laughingly referred to as my style. I'm particularly leery of censors when it comes to fiction, because while everyone is an authority in this field, he may not be an objective authority.

I have a Jesuit friend who is a proficient, often-published writer and who, besides, has something to say. He once did an article on which he had spent a great deal of time in research and documentation. One of his censors rejected the whole thing with only three words: "This isn't true." The fact that the paper was finally published is immaterial. What is frightening is the fact that a censor, who knew nothing about the subject, could have the power to kill the article and the fact that his killing it cost the author a month of annoying fighting to get it resurrected. (Some time ago, I ran into a similar case—where a Jesuit wrote an article in support of Pope Paul's *Humanae Vitae* and had a censor refuse his permission to publish it. And again, he had to go through the annoyance of fighting to get his work through—a ridiculous turn of events.)

I suppose my most interesting brush with censorship came when *I'll Die Laughing!* was banned in one entire country by a superior who, it turned out, had never seen nor asked to see so much as a single page of the manuscript.

Although I've sometimes been annoyed by them, I've never really had any earth-shaking difficulty with censors. The fact is that I've been helped by censors immeasurably on more than one occasion. On my religion books, for example, I had two censors who were well-known theologians. One of these men did me the enormous favor of writing eighteen single-spaced pages of suggestions, most of them scriptural, on how the books could be improved. It would have taken me months to research all the Scriptures he gave me, and so the help he gave was tremendous.

The other censor, however, wrote half a page in which he said that several things in the books worried him, gave perhaps two nit-picking examples (neither of which worried *me*), and closed it off with a very grudging and doubtful approval for publication. He didn't help me in the slightest. Censors, like real human beings, vary.

There *are*, then, hangups in the whole censorship process. And the great difficulty at the moment is that the Society, so concerned with hangups which concern more men than a relatively few writers, seems to be doing very little on the subject. But if there are hangups, there are also (as I have tried to point out) advantages, and I'm simply not in favor of the whole thing's being abolished—particularly for beginners. But having said that, I feel too that I owe censors the same courtesy my critics owe me—some positive suggestions.

Get the subjectivity out of censorship; make it looser for published and proven writers; make its acceptance, at least, voluntary where that seems reasonable, instead of investing a censor with absolute power—and we will have more effective and less worrisome handicapping censorship. The fact is that I've always sought much more censorship than I've had to, but the very fact of my choosing it has kept me from writing for these censors instead of for the public I'm supposed to be writing for. Sometimes

126

an author wishes to answer something he has seen in print, an answer which calls for great speed if it is to be effective. Sometimes, too, the chosen censor may not agree with his answer. And some provision should be made for this, always, of course, provided an author can be considered competer and sane in the area in which he writes.

When it comes to fiction, I simply can't see that censorship for a published and proven author is either necessary or valid. On the other hand, for the unpublished and unproven author to decry any censorship is about as logical as a child demanding that his parents allow him to say or do anything he pleases. One could, even in fiction (which is a form of truth), find the most blatant untruths and lack of self-discipline.

But on this subject of censorship, all I want to do here is indicate my awareness of both its benefits and drawbacks, and to make a few minimal suggestions.

You can't discuss the whole subject of marketability and criticism and censorship without saying something about the guy who, as he'll keep reminding you, takes all the risks—the publisher. Now as the reader well knows by this time, any sort of criticism is alien to this kindly old author's nature. But I do have a thing or two to say about publishers anyhow.

Your heart does bleed for an occasional publisher when you listen to his troubles, and especially when he tells you about all he's doing for you and your books—always, seemingly, at great sacrifice to himself. As time goes on, however, especially as he begins to bleed a bit himself, the author begins to ration his sympathy somewhat. One's first contract is a big thrill, of course; so big that he's likely not to read the small print. On his second contract, he'll read this first. Apart in fact from my very first contract, I can't recall very many which were not returned to the publisher unsigned, at least once, because of some unagreeable or even disagreeable clause or other. Even at that, the final contract has often been less than perfect for this author.

The publisher's great argument for his own large percentages is always that it's his investment and that he takes the financial risk. This is, of course, true, but some publishers seem to forget a few of the "risks" the author takes. To give but one small example: My religion series cost me six years of my life, three thousand dollars in typing fees, a smaller amount in paper and supplies, and a very sizeable amount in books for research. And yet no provision was made for these expenses in my contract, nor did I ever get the idea the publishers even recognized their existence or their importance. As a matter of fact when it came to the teachers' manuals for this series, the publisher even tried to shift this cost onto the author—an act which appalled me for sheer chintziness more than any other in all my publishing experience. To this day I find it incredible—except that it did happen.

There's a bit of phonyness in this business—something which should surprise no one since there's bound to be some phonyness in *any* business. I'm told, for example, that a great (in the financial sense only) best seller of some years back became a best seller with the help of a lot of chicanery—all the publicity which could be con-trived (literally) on the work as a "dirty book," frequent public condemnation of the author and relatives by alleged establishment squares and finally, paying out a tremendous amount of money to individual "buyers," just to go and buy the book and so keep it out of print and atop the best-seller list.

Foreign publishers are something else again; and after the initial advance royalty from any foreign publisher, I've never heard from one a second time. They could have sold no books or a million—there's just no way of telling. Too, I occasionally come across copies of books and pamphlets of mine published abroad in places I've never sold them.

Then there was the book I contracted to do for a publisher—reluctantly, I might add, for several reasons. I worked very hard on that book and submitted everything as it was finished to the publisher. Each outline and each chapter was approved and accepted right up to the end. I was sitting back counting prospective royalties and waiting for publication when I got a letter informing me that a senior editor had just returned from Europe or Russia or somewhere and insisted that the whole book be done over—completely. Contract meant nothing. Agreement meant nothing. Ethics meant nothing. Had I been a layman, I would have kept the advance and let this publisher try to get it. But as a religious, I preferred not to make waves. But then, perhaps, they realized that this would be the case.

But the hardest facet of some publishers' personalities for an author to understand is their sometime attitude towards publicity. It's almost as though once the book is published, it's locked up in a warehouse and surrounded by armed guards just in case anybody should hear of the book and try to buy it. There are a few unique attempts at advertising, many of them seemingly useless. It's hard for me to figure, for example, how anybody could order books via a direct mail pitch which lists—and says little or nothing about—forty or fifty books on completely different themes. Then there's the system—which might be called the vicious circle method—of advertising only already successful books. All of which contradicts the financial principle that you have to spend money to make money.

Some publishers give you the idea they'd prefer not to sell your book.

Perhaps if some of the publishers didn't continue to tell an author they're straining so hard to bring his books before the public eye, he wouldn't mind so much. Some years ago I visited a southern city to give a series of talks and retreats. It was my custom in those days, before I found out it didn't do any good, to give my itinerary to the publisher so that he'd alert the eager natives and they'd mill around in a near-riot attitude, clamoring to buy my books. On this occasion, I was told to be sure to visit a local book store and tell the lady in charge who I was. "She'll really roll out the red carpet for you," I was assured. "She's a great plugger of your books." So I called the lady, my toes wriggling in anticipation of that carpet, and my empty wallet ready for the fat royalties.

I find the sound of southern voices no less charming today than I ever did, and this lady's accent over the phone was no exception. I must have been greeted with a dozen variations on

"Welcome to Our Town," the very first of which made me begin
to feel welcome enough. But that was it. There didn't turn out
to be any of the old give-till-it-hurts bit connected with the hospitality, nor, in fact, any give at all. All I got was "Y'all come in and
autograph some of your books sometime. The customers like that."

Now that I look back on the incident, I don't know what I
really expected, but I suppose I had anticipated some sort of small
autograph party at the store, at least, or maybe a free Seven-Up.
What I got was the loss of half a day autographing books and some
small talk about the city's fine restaurants, with no visible book
sales or promotion. (It should be made clear that in many cities
talk about food is never really small talk.) Nor did I see any red
carpet.

Even when one makes allowances for an author's prejudice in
behalf of his own books, he can see how utterly frustrating it must
be to encounter again and again a complete blank as far as publicity
is concerned. This may be especially true in my own case in years
past, when much of my writing was for teens and most of my travels
were for speaking at teen conventions. It was a pretty harrowing experience to go place after place and find absolutely no advance or
any other kind of publicity on my books—books written for this
specific audience. At the moment, fortunately, I have the good
fortune to be doing business with two very good publishers, Crowell-
Collier (MacMillan) and on this book, Prentice-Hall. Unlike some of
my previous publishers, these people seem anxious to bring books to
the attention of those for whom they are written.

Then there were those great books I had which came out in
the autumn and were allowed to go out of print over the Christmas
season of their first year—which shouldn't be too bad a time to sell
books. There were the textbooks which came out right after school
started. There were . . . oh, forget it!

Many publishers have what they call an Author's Service, and,
in general it fills a real need. I don't particularly appreciate it when
they try to sell your own books back to you, but otherwise they do
a pretty good service for an author. Sometimes, no doubt, in the
press of more important properties than authors, publishers and
their Author's Services don't come up with 100 percent efficiency.
I can best illustrate this sometime exposure of feet of clay by an
actual happening in my life as an author. Since I have a large fat
folder of correspondence on this one incident, I'll condense it here
and, of course, change the names to protect the guilty. It all began
quite innocently, when I wrote to the publisher in an attempt to get
fifty copies of my own book. Let's call this one *How to Ask for
Directions* since that's not its title, and call its publisher I.M. Schnook,

Inc., since that's not his name. The publisher's first reply went like this (notice the dates, too):

April 5, 1962

Dear Father McGloin:

We have no account accommodations for authors, however [sic], whenever you wish copies of the book, send the order to my attention with a check attached . . . . May I ask that you do that for the 50 copies that you requested in this letter?

Sincerely,

Henry Armstrong
Vice President
Schnook, Inc.

April 9, 1962

Dear Mr. Armstrong,

I am enclosing a check for _____ for which I wish you would please send me fifty (50) copies of my book, *How to Ask for Directions.* . . .

There were several little bits of decreasingly good-natured correspondence at this point, but unfortunately I didn't realize at the time that they'd turn out to be worth saving. The next exchange I have on record here is this one, dated almost a year later:

Dear Mr. Armstrong,

Will you please check your records once more to see what could have happened to my various requests that 50 copies of my book, *How to Ask for Directions,* be shipped to me?

(At this point, the letter gives something of a summary of the correspondence on this to date.)

I did not yet receive these books. . . .

131

I got this back:

> In order to expedite the handling of correspondence we are using this form.

> March 11, 1963

> Dear Sir:

> Sorry I don't know why your book is not listed in the fall 1962 catalogue. Please write to the editorial department for information.

> Very truly yours,
> Jane Jackson

And this:

> Dear Reader:

> We are sorry but the title(s) you have chosen are not available for the reasons indicated.

> OUT OF PRINT

> For prompt action be sure to return this letter in the postage-paid envelope enclosed; it has been coded for special handling.

> Sincerely yours,
> Schnook, Inc.

> March 17, 1963

> Dear Schnook, Inc.,

> I'm returning to you 50 copies of Helen Guernsey's *Sex and the Adolescent Girl*, which must have come to me by mistake, since I did not order them. To keep things clear, I have an order there for 50 copies of *How to Ask for Directions*, my own book. This order has, in fact, been there for some time, and it was accompanied by my check for _____ in payment. I'd appreciate your untangling things and getting these books to me.

At this point there's another lacuna in my records, since I apparently had to return the letter referred to here. It had been addressed to a Miss Gloria Marin at, of all places, Jesuit Residence in Minneapolis, and it had been signed by Jane Jackson. Since I had just been addressed as Miss Marin, I saw no reason to recognize Miss Jackson's sex either.

Miss Jane Jackson
Schnook, Inc.

Dear George,

I get some interesting letters, but this one is downright fascinating. I suspect that Miss Marin has an equally intriguing letter addressed to kindly old Father McGloin. Happy Lent.

April 12, 1963

Dear Mr. Armstrong,

I don't know quite how to approach this any more, since I have been writing about it off and on for some time . . . but I still have not received my order for 50 copies of my book, *How to Ask for Directions*. Some weeks back, I did receive 50 copies of some other book, which I returned with a letter to the order department. However, no signs of the *How to Ask for Directions* book as yet.

I would certainly appreciate your looking into this and trying to get the books sent to me as soon as possible . Perhaps I am making use of the wrong order methods. Is there some other way I should be ordering instead of by sending the money and order directly to you? I believe this was the way you told me to do it originally. Thank you for your attention.

May 17, 1963

Dear Fr. McGloin:

A batch of correspondence concerning your order for 50 copies of XY 208, *How to Ask for Directions*, and subsequent troubles, has landed on my desk. What seems to have happened is this:

We received your order with your check, and the order was put through. The books were sent, but evidently, the package carried only your address and not your name; and, when they reached Jesuit Residence, someone there returned them. They consequently arrived back at our shipping room, and since we had no evidence of an invoice, which is not made out in sending books ordered with cash on order, the Credit Department was puzzled and sent you a form in order to get information with which to credit your claim properly. You returned this sheet filled out with your own statement of understandable puzzlement.

I am asking our Mail Service Department to put through at once another shipment of 50 copies, and I am advising the Credit Department to disregard the claim for credit and simply consider the matter closed and have the books returned to stock.

Sincerely,

Ralph Schnook, Jr.,
President, Schnook, Inc.

October 16, 1963

Dear Mr. Schnook,

I enclose a note from the Credit Department . . . . it looks from here like it would be simpler all round if you would explain the situation to this department rather than my corresponding with them and thus starting another round robin. . . .

Apparently (although I do not have the records on hand) I was instructed to stop payment on the original check. Apparently too this produced a bill from the publisher.

October 17, 1963

Dear Father McGloin:

I don't understand how the mess came about, but after receiving your letter this morning, I raised "holy hell." As a result they found your previous order filed away and unacted on. I have told them to tear it up and to forget about the check on which you stopped payment as per our instructions.... I just hope there won't be any further mess.

Ralph Schnook, Jr.

October 21, 1963

Dear Father McGloin:

I understand there is an order in process for 50 copies of *How to Ask for Directions*.
Per your request of Mr. Ralph Schnook, I am returning your check No. 983, on which you stopped payment. The order for 50 copies will be billed to you on open account and you can pay upon receipt of merchandise and accompanying bill.

Sincerely yours,
Henry Armstrong

October 25, 1963

Dear Mr. Schnook,
Thank you so much for your letter, as well as for all the trouble you have gone to on this matter of the books. Incidentally, have you ever read James Thurber's essay on a similar situation, where he ended up burning copies of his books in the street?

I have changed a few details, subtracting a few which only complicated things further, but substantially this little story of instant service for authors (a year and a half in this case) is quite true. Oh yes, I finally did get the books—several hundred of them in fact.

But let us allow the publishers to lie in peace. There are a few other people, literary relatives of a writer, who are worth mentioning too. I should point out that even in my sometime hectic dealings with some publishers, at least one of the Bruce Publishing editors stands out in my esteem and affection—both as editor and friend. And this is Mr. Bernard Wirth who, like a lot of Catholics in this business, sacrificed a great deal to be there and who made his job into a vocation. Bernard was a fine editor, among many other reasons because he never confused the words editor and author. And Bruce Publishing Company lost the best when they lost him.

In my own writing avocation I've been very fortunate to have the help (on seven of the books published so far) of an excellent imaginative artist, whose work I chanced on originally by the merest accident. Don Baumgart, who is currently a junior high school principal in Greendale, Wisconsin, is a superb artist, a good friend, and a dedicated worker. We have worked together, not just on the books but on a vast number of articles, the most consistent of which were published over the course of the years in a syndicated column called "Working to Beat Hell!"

The nice part of our partnership is that Don appreciates my writing almost as much as I appreciate his illustrations. When he learns he can also write, however, I'll be all through, since I can't draw.

Another important person to a writer is his agent, and here again I've been very lucky. Howard Moorepark in New York has been my agent now for over twenty years and has done a fine job considering some of the mediocre material I've given him to work with. An agent has a pretty tough job and performs a very real set of services for a writer. My best-selling book *I'll Die Laughing!* went to nineteen publishers before it succeeded and was sold. And Howard Moorepark handled all that shuttle work, saving me all the time and trouble. Too, an agent has foreign connections which an author rarely has, and so Howard has been able to peddle some of my books and stories abroad—in Ireland, England, Italy, Germany, and Denmark, for example.

There are also, of course, bound to be typists somewhere on the fringes of a writer's life—some good, some bad, some reasonable enough, some incredibly expensive. I've encountered some good typists who were much better at copying manuscripts than at following dictation, or at least my dictation, accurately. I remember, for example, once dictating something about "the Franciscan love of holy poverty," which came out "The Franciscan love of holy property." And I've seen some weird spellings like "vulchures" for "vultures," and the line I once dictated "We encountered quite a few ferries on this trip," which came out "We encountered quite a few fairies . . . ."

In Minneapolis I ran into two incredibly efficient typists— Mrs. Margaret Lawson Forside and Mrs. Fred Berg. Both did great jobs for me, often at no little sacrifice to themselves, much of it financial. Another city holds the record so far for the other extreme, as I got taken for $1.50 a page on the first manuscript—and the last, of course—done by that typist. At that rate it would have cost me eighteen thousand dollars to have the religion manuscript typed instead of the three thousand dollars it did cost—and you have to sell a lot of books to make more than the typist does on a deal like that. Fortunately, I have since that time encountered a couple of typists who are very good—and willing to work for the relatively small fee I can almost afford.

Once when I was giving a retreat in New Orleans, a little co-ed marched into my office and asked, "Y'all care to have some help on typin' while youah heah?" I thanked her and told her I wouldn't be needing any typing since I'd be too busy with the retreat. "Oh. Well, ah don't type vehy well anyhow" was the casual reply. I only wish all of them were as honest.

Another breed the writer encounters—and this all too frequently—is the would-be writer. And if writers are characters, this species makes them seem almost normal.

Now there are would-be writers and would-be writers. We were, in fact, all would-be writers at one time, and I'd do anything possible to try to help out someone who is really interested in writing, is willing to plug away at it, has *some* tools to work with and something to say.

Too, when someone asks you to look at a manuscript that he or she has obviously worked and slaved over, you're willing and even eager to help, no matter how good or bad the manuscript might turn out to be. All too often though, the would-be writer brings you something in its virginal or pre-adolescent state, dashed down on paper, often in longhand, and never gone over again. At times like these one's patience can wear a bit thin—if indeed it was fat—especially when he remembers the twenty-plus painstaking revisions he went through on the last manuscript of his own.

I had met one such would-be writer by correspondence rather often before finally meeting him in person. At this latter meeting (in a Chicago restaurant, we'll say, because it wasn't) I noticed as I sat down that he had a drink in a stemmed glass—which was just fine, so I ordered one too. What began to concern me just a little bit, though, was that he kept tossing a little sugar into the drink now and then. Finally, I couldn't restrain my curiosity any longer. "What kind of a drink *is* that?" I asked.

"It's a martini," he told me matter-of-factly, adding a bit more sugar. "But it's awfully bitter."

My complete answer to that logical explanation was "Oh." Brilliant repartee, even if possible, didn't seem called for at the moment. But I just don't see how anyone who puts sugar in a martini could ever seriously hope to be a writer.

The main trouble with would-be writers (and, on occasion, with some writers too) is that they're like the singing star who tries to act or the actor who tries to dance. They try, all too often, to do something which just isn't their thing. I remember reading one such manuscript by a man who had spent a good portion of his adult life in prison. Actually, he had some tremendous stuff (in a paper bag, by the way, and written on paper bags, in pencil), but he had tried to make a novel of it and so had ruined it. Factually he had something, as I tried to tell him—without success, I'm afraid.

A writer, like anyone else, likes to be accepted, and one small indication of that acceptance (although not always reliable) is the fan letter. I've long ago discarded the uninteresting letters, the over-flattering ones and the diatribes—except, of course, some of the latter when they were interesting anyhow for one reason or another. I'm sure any author looks forward to his very first fan letter, and I was no exception. I still have it right here, my very first, a touching note:

> Will you please be kind enough to send me an auto-graphed complimentary copy of your book *I'll Die Laughing!* I have heard so much about it and besides it may help me very much indeed during my recovery.

There are the letters you're not quite sure of, the puzzlers:

> ... Now why don't you write one for girls? Judging by your picture you'd be happy with us as well as the boys ...

I'm just not sure whether "the boys" there is nominative or objective case. Nor am I quite sure of this one, from a reader of *Backstage Missionary*, the Father Lord book:

> ... Father Lord must have been very holy indeed to write all those books and not take any money for them for himself.

There are, of course, the critics, some of whom are quite subtle:

> ... I have just finished reading your article. I have never seen anyone so wrong in my entire life.

Sometimes they tend to take back with the right hand what

they've just given with the left. I have here before me a letter from a fellow Jesuit complimenting me on *I'll Die Laughing!*—in the first line, that is, and then going on for a full page of what we always call well-meant criticism. To switch the tables and be unfair to a critic, one of the suggestions offered here was that in the next edition I use a better title—something more like *You'd Be Surprised* or *What Millions Don't Know*. Neither of these titles got through to me, any more than the editorial change from "Working to Beat Hell!" to "Striving to Gain Heaven" grabbed me. At any rate after a full page of criticism, this letter ended on the same kindly note on which it had begun:

> . . . Anyway, God bless you with good health and leisure enough to turn out more books.

Then there was the honest young character whose teacher apparently had "requested" that he write:

> Our sister read your book *Backstage Missionary* and our sister asked us to write a letter to you about it. I am sorry but I didn't like it.

Then there are the extremes of praise and non-praise in the fans:

> Your style ripples along like a trout stream over sunlit gravel bars. May the V-2 rocket of your success continue to climb into the ionosphere of achievement.

If I ever imagined myself in that ionosphere, there were always those ready to pull me back to reality:

> Thank you for writing your trilogy *Love and Live!* I suspect that, if pressed, you could have written it in better English.

And speaking of better English, there was the German Jesuit, then studying the English language, who wrote a letter of inquiry:

> . . . There is one expression you used which I cannot quite grasp . . . "There is always the boy, too, who has *a chip on his shoulder*." And likewise: "The alert teacher will know . . . when to knock him out

from *under the chip.*" I'd be grateful to you if you could explain to me the meaning of "chip" in this context.

This I did. In fact, I did a lot more for this inquirer, giving him a preview of the future and further educating him in the wonders of the English language. I mentioned that I was thinking of turning out a trilogy of books called *Hip or Drip, Cool or Cube, Saint or Square* (the original, and I think, better titles of the *Love and Live!* series). His reply was, I think, at least interesting:

> You explained my language difficulty very well and I certainly have learned something more about the enormous variability of your language. I only fear I will never be able to get behind all those "tricks" of a language which is constantly "on the move" and creates daily new words and idioms.

Naturally when you write a book about the Jesuits, there are going to be a few Jesuits at least who will think they've found something to argue with. I had mentioned in *I'll Die Laughing!* that Father Gene Korth and I had established something of a record for long walks during our juniorate days by going over forty miles in one day. And from far-off Hong Kong, from far out Father Joseph M. Mallin, S.J., came the objection that he had:

> ... totted up near the forty-mile mark on several occasions and once we did a forty-seven mile hike, of which thirteen miles was over a low ridge of mountains and boggy land. . . . I am certain of our hike as Fr. Gill was very put out that I would not make the maps say we had done the round fifty. I measured the run on every map I could lay hands on and got the forty-seven.

Actually, *I* measured it and got thirty-seven, since it was only three miles over that low ridge of mountains and boggy land.

But of all the fan letters, those from the kids are usually the most interesting because the most unpredictable. There was the letter that went on about how much its writer wanted to be a priest. Like this:

> To be honest with you, the main reason I took your book out of the library was cause I thought it was a

140

joke book.   For you see, I usually don't read books like yours. I usually read sport stories or war stories. All my life I have dreamed about becoming a priest but I guess it's impossible. . . . I have one big fault that will prevent me from becoming a priest. I have an older brother that is always in trouble and who sometimes gets me in trouble. He taught me how to climb roofs and steal apples and smoke. I don't especially care about smoking. . . . There's a Jesuit convent or house about 9 blocks from my house . . .

The mystery of that "one big fault" was solved in the second P.S. of the letter; "P.S.#2: I'm a girl." Too bad. She'd have made a great one.

Then there are the diplomatic types:

Sister is starting another book today but I doubt if it will be half as good. I am in the seventh grade this year. I hope to be in the eighth grade next year.

Or:

I don't think I could write a book. Sometimes it is even hard for me to write a letter. I'm sure it was fun and easy for you to write *that* book.

Or:

It really must be great to have a sense of humor and put it down in writing. All I wish is for the priests in our parish to have a sense of humor.

One can see the future English major in some letters too:

I like the book very much. The part I like best was that the first of his teaching when he prepared for his England class and found out later that he had to teach a different.

Some of the kids are already clearly masters of the graceful ending:

I wrote this letter because I want to tell you how much I enjoyed the book. I had to ask Sister if it was

> true or not because I was not sure. And I hope you
> write more books like that. Well, I have to go now.

But I'm not ridiculing the fan letter so much as enjoying it. In general, these letters come from thoughtful people, who are doing me a great favor, one I appreciate very much. In those long periods when the mail brings only rejections, an encouraging note or letter helps out of all proportion.

There's another aspect of the fan letter not to be overlooked either. Some such letters are important, not so much to the hero addressed as to the fan who writes. There *are* people who, either because of their temperament or their circumstances or both, are unable to seek help face to face with some would-be counselor. And so they write. In fact, sometimes they tear your heart out. Usually too, they make you feel about one centimeter tall, as they tell you that something you have written has helped them. It's as though you had been able to get a smile out of Jean-Paul Sartre.

I can't even begin to estimate the number of friends I've been blessed with through my writing and their correspondence with me because of it. Most of them have remained friends by correspondence only, but I've met many of them eventually too. When I was in Santa Barbara, one such friend dropped by and so reminded me of how we had met through correspondence. Among the letters I received following the publication of *I'll Die Laughing!,* there were two which I somehow mixed up in my mind—one from a Richard O'Shaughnessy in California and another from a young guy in Wisconsin. Richard mentioned to me that he was in the seminary, would soon be ordained, and that his fellow seminarians sometimes accused him of being a Jesuit spy because he read and pushed my books. Certain things the other correspondent said made me think that either he too was in the seminary at the time, or should be.

Both of these correspondents surprised me, each in a different way. I never knew until his ordination invitation came that Richard O'Shaughnessy was being ordained an *Episcopalian* priest. And the other correspondent whose vocation I felt I was nursing along at the time wrote me one bright day, "I'm coming to see you as soon as I get sprung out of here." He did this, a delightful ex (I hope) con-artist of about forty-five winters. But then so many things he had said about the pen had seemed like the old seminary days . . . .

One congratulatory letter from a Jesuit Father General stands out in my mind, too, for its beginning: *Non possum non gratulari* . . . . There's something not really overly enthusiastic in this otherwise very fine Latin expression, which translates literally: "I am unable not to congratulate you. . . ." Like the title of this book, this

142

expression is open to any number of different interpretations. I took it to mean that the book had been so good that he was simply forced to congratulate me. Some of my friends, however, told me that he only meant that he had to congratulate me because that was part of his job, and he had to send out this formula for every print job that came into his office, no matter how lousy it might be.

There are letters one can never forget—from terminal patients, from religious and ex-religious, from servicemen and peace-corps workers and missionaries, from kids with problems which some adults (in their absorption in their own, often lesser problems) have forgotten about. At this moment one letter from a teen-aged girl stands out as "typical" of the unassuming courage of the young. This girl had volunteered for a year's work among the poor in Brazil, and she had written me asking for any possible help I could offer in her teaching and other work with the little kids. This high-school sophomore asked me to pray that her mother would allow her to stay on another year after the one she had promised. Delightfully and typically she asked in the final sentence that I pray for her too, because while she wanted to do all she could for the poor in Brazil, as she put it, she also "liked rock candy" and needed all the prayers she could get. And I knew very well indeed what she meant by rock candy. She made the adult who rationalizes his way out of his problems instead of facing them seem like an infant.

When you look at the whole picture of a writing avocation, you see a mixture of advantages and disadvantages—much as one would notice, undoubtedly, in any job. On some days it's fun to write. On others that first sheet of white paper in the typewriter is absolutely terrifying—or perhaps revolting is a better word. On some days and particularly in some forms of writing, you can overcome this revulsion by a bit of forcing. On other days, forget it—the more you force the worse it gets, and you'd have to throw out what you'd write in that sort of mood anyhow.

In my own case there seem to be two principal occupational hangups: insomnia and solitude. Both are worth enduring for the sake of the writing, but both *are,* periodically at least, annoying. I've been a lousy sleeper for years anyhow, and it always gets proportionately worse as I get involved in what I write—particularly when it's fiction. Long ago in fact, I reconciled myself to the fact that when I am doing fiction, the sleep is just not going to be rated excellent.

Some years back, when a wayward tuberculosis bug found a home with me, I was driven from Denver to the hospital in Colorado Springs by a couple of Jesuit friends. At this late date I can say here that news of the disease was quite a blow. I had always been active physically and every other way, and so could hardly have been expected to relish the prospect of a year or more in bed. It is, however, a part of my philosophy of life (which is a high-sounding name for some common sense, I hope, and faith) to compromise with the inevitable. This is not only because it does no good to act otherwise, but because I've learned—apart from the many times someone else told me—that the dear Lord always has something in mind for us in these seeming trials. And so, to the sympathy of my two friends en route to my imprisonment, I simply said, "It isn't so bad. It'll give me a chance to get some rest."

That, you have to admit, wasn't a bad try. But imagine my utter horror and speechlessness when one of my friends, far from famous for his own furious activity, nodded and said, "It's lucky you have a temperament that can look forward to that. *I* sure couldn't stand being inactive that long."

I tell you this tear-jerking story as a parallel. So many people, noting my solitary life as a writer, seem to be saying, "It's lucky you have the temperament for solitude." The truth is, though, that if ever there was a social animal, it is old J.T. Mick-Jee. And the only motive which can make me put up with being alone is the greater good I can see in writing and, in turn, the fact that real writing demands this solitude. It's purely a means to an end. Nothing more.

But these are some of the smaller than life things which make the life of a writer less than perfect, too minor even to merit a healthy gripe. Some days, in fact, the very drawbacks are welcomed. I doubt if there's any man or woman, married or unmarried, who has not, on occasion at least, envied the kind of solitude I have most of the time and enjoy a good portion of the time.

Besides, the many fringe benefits of the writing racket far outweigh any drawbacks. No matter what one's sense of vocation, he has to find *some* enjoyment in what he does, and I can't imagine a writer who never enjoys his work. Apart from those days when that blank sheet of paper looks like far too great a challenge, there's the thrill of getting an abstract truth into some sort of concrete understandability; the joy of turning out a lively, interesting paragraph, of feeling that you'd put some thought of yours in such a way that others will understand it and perhaps even see some truth in it. There's the thrill of presenting new insights or of entertaining or of putting across a whole new truth to some reader or other. There's the great satisfaction in seeing something finally published—not that you're ever completely satisfied with it or that you'll even read it for that matter. But you feel at least that you've drifted near the horizons of creation.

I find this satisfaction, if I'm not too exhausted, in any completed work—with the sense of accomplishment perhaps being greatest in the theological field, but the sense of creativity coming through essentially more in the field of fiction. Within this latter field the highest sense of creativity seems to me to come in watching a play or show one has fashioned and directed finally coming together into a unit, even when that wholeness had been only vaguely envisioned in the writing. One such experience stands out in my own mind over all the others. This particular play had been the usual mess such things are—with all the writing and scratching, rewriting, rehearsing and patching, and bending lines and scenes and actors to fit each other. And always, there had been only a sense of this line or that, this scene or that, or even only a tiny segment of a scene—in other words, the usual bit-by-bit work of play production. Suddenly though, as I sat alone and silent one night in the back row of the theater to watch the play without interruption and with some trepidation, it all came together; and I was appalled, unable even to believe that I had had anything to do with it. I think I knew a little then—much as a child with a shovel and a heap of sand senses the thrill of fashioning some *thing*—why God, who *is* Love, creates. There's some unutterable connection between creativity and love; and since it is unutterable, I can hardly attempt to utter it here. And if our little attempts at creation are only a shadow of love, then . . . , maybe too, creation is worth its inevitable frustrations and even suffering.

There are other, perhaps more practical advantages to the life of a writer. He has to work hard—for one big reason because he can't forget his writing and turn it off as one can many other tasks. Still, his schedule *is* pleasantly adaptable with regard to both time and place. If I get terribly tired, I can spend some time daydreaming of future books and even starting some notes on them rather than hacking away at the present one, knowing that when the fatigue passes, I'll be able to make up for this time out. If I need a break—by way of handball or tennis for example—I can knock off about any time for a couple of hours, shifting my work schedule to some other time of that day or the next. I can accept speaking assignments I would never have been able to work into a teaching schedule—and then make up for that time off later on by a bit of double overtime on the writing. And often enough, I can think out a chapter or an article or story en route to a speaking job. The writer's office is pretty much where he is, and he doesn't have to punch a timeclock in any certain office building to do his job. In fact, everything a writer does, everything he's exposed to, every person he sees or knows or reads about, every place he goes or hears about—all this contributes to his job and his craft, if of course, he really is a writer. All of which is to say that I *like* to write. There are things I like better, but I don't think there's any job I'd feel as compelled to do as the job of writing.

I don't have to look back on this chapter, or the others for that matter, to realize that the personal pronoun "I" has been showing at every turn. But there's no getting away from it apparently, as I'm only trying to show what the life of one Jesuit has been—under the illusion perhaps that it might be of interest to someone. My life has not been the same as every Jesuit's; nor has it, I suppose, been typical. And so the pronoun, the big "I," has had to be here. (I tried "the author" and it didn't sound right coming from me—not that it sounded as revolting as the editorial "we," but pretty darned near it.)

I don't feel that anything I've done so far has been exceptionally good even when it was exceptional in some other sense. And while I've written here of my own experience as a teacher, a guy who is interested in youth, and a writer, I know all too well that I'm not a very good teacher or youth director or writer in the relative scale. Not only have I always encountered essentially greater people in these fields, but I have met those who would be far, far better than myself at these jobs if they would only put their far superior talents to them. If something I've had to say here will only goad one of the latter species into action, the unpardonable echoing of "I" should become semi-tolerable.

CHAPTER
SIX

*"Just
talk about
anything..."*

At the time *I'll Die Laughing!* was written, it was easy enough to describe the more or less typical training a Jesuit ◇ ◇ ◇ went through. It was a bit simpler then, too, to come up with some sort of general list of Jesuit ministries. Varied as their activities were even in those antediluvian days, one would still run into a Jesuit or two teaching in a Jesuit school or on the missions or giving retreats and so on.

Jesuits are, of course, still doing the two things which were their original things, working in the mission field and educating. But there are greater numbers of Jesuits operating today in other areas as well—working at other professions, doing research, teaching or administering in non-Jesuit schools, doing inner-city work in and out of the parish setting, and so on. Some are even just writing.

And so while some years back I would have admitted that my present life isn't exactly typically Jesuit, today it seems at least as typical as the life of those of my fellow Jesuits who are currently locatable and identifiable. We are all—to reuse the happy technical term of the experts—super-hyphenated. But doctor or lawyer or parole officer or writer, a Jesuit still precedes his hyphens with the word "Jesuit," and a Jesuit priest puts *these* two words first. And so since I'm not a writer-priest, but a Jesuit-priest-writer, most of my activities outside of writing are a priest's activities. It is, in fact, my aim and hope that every activity of mine be done *as* a Jesuit priest.

Certainly no one would ask me anywhere to speak if I weren't a Jesuit priest, but I am and they do. And so my next hyphen tacks on the word "speaker," for better or worse. Just blow in my ear and I'll go anywhere to speak—to youth conventions, dinners, breakfasts, P.T.A. meetings, to audiences of one or a thousand. I suppose the most frequent talks I give come under the heading of "retreats."

Most people today are familiar with the term "retreat," with non-Catholics learning more about it even while some Catholics tend to get it confused with something else. In general it's a period—usually about three days or a weekend—when a person steps aside from the rush of daily living to take a panoramic look at the whole situation. The retreat director—or retreat master as he's traditionally and often inaccurately called—is supposed to present the retreatants with ideas to think about in some sort of logical and psychological order. Between these talks, or "conferences," the retreatants try to mull these things over and pray about them, each one in his own uniquely personal way.

There doesn't seem to be any limit on the characteristics of retreatants. I've tried to give retreats to the young and old, male and female types, Catholic and non-Catholic, the hurt and the protected, delinquents and pre-delinquents, and this pretty much all over the country. Certainly no one who has been involved in many retreats could ever presume—as I've heard some knowledgeable non-retreat-givers presuming—that only the pious make retreats.

I am, in fact, convinced that one gets closer to reality in the counseling session of a retreat than almost anywhere else. In fact, this retreat counseling (which often enough isn't much more than patient listening) is of help not just to the counseled but to the counselor as well. For one thing, it gives him a pretty good barometer of how the retreat is going. And it also keeps him a realist in the constant realization that there are vast problems bugging these people he's trying to direct. And here in this situation they are utterly, completely honest. It isn't a bad experience either for a retreat master to come face to face with a degree of heroism that makes him blush when he considers his own lack of same. Perhaps even the allegedly modern priest—sneering at the piety of "just good Catholics" or of those little old ladies with their rosaries— could learn something from the little old lady who, out of a love for Christ, takes the down-and-out into her home and feeds them, never content unless she's sheltering at least a foreign student or two. And the teen-ager, courageous enough to fight his problems instead of rationalizing them away, can also be startling, inspiring— and embarrassing. At least he's trying, falling sometimes perhaps, but having the great courage to scramble up and try again. And that beats rationalizations by about 100 percent.

I once did a book for parents called *What To Do Till the Psychiatrist Comes!,* and I made the suggestion in this book that one of the best means of becoming better parents would be to make an annual retreat. One reviewer of the book, undoubtedly from his long experience in this field or some other, scoffed at this suggestion as naive. This accusation has often echoed in my mind—especially when I've encountered those who knew that the retreat was helping to save their souls and their sanity.

Clearly, there can be great satisfaction in directing retreats. Clearly too, they're fatiguing and a lot of work—intensive, uninterrupted work. And so—because of the work angle alone—there are other varieties of talk which are more enjoyable to a guy who likes to talk more than he likes to work.

150

If one is available as a speaker—no matter, apparently, how good or bad a speaker—he soon finds himself talking to every sort of audience, on every imaginable variety of occasion and a few others. He also finds himself apprehensive of the way some of the requests for his speaking services are worded. The fact that those who are assigned to get speakers *are* assigned rather than being volunteers could have something to do with this. Maybe one of the most startling approaches, until you get used to it at least, is the "We're desperate—we tried and tried, and just couldn't get anyone else" bit. This is the direct opposite of the flattery approach which is more like, "We've heard so much about you and your work, Father McTavish."

I always ask what subject a group wants me to talk about, and occasionally I've received some pleasingly precise answers. But I'm afraid the most common answer has been, "Oh, just talk about anything—I'm sure you'll be interesting." This can be literally translated into "Well, we *have* to have a speaker to fill in the program. So just go along for about a half hour."

But no matter what the approach, just as I like to write, so I also—in quite a different way—like to speak. There is, in fact, a degree of contact where the spoken word is concerned which is essentially greater, more exciting, and more satisfactory than the written word. Maybe it's comparable to acting in front of a live audience or in front of only a camera. You can sense reactions immediately. You can switch the emphasis and even the approach as you go, in an attempt to better the effect. And just as I find speaking enjoyable, I also enjoy almost any audience. The reader will probably have guessed, however, that most of the time, my audience has been teen-agers, and I wouldn't have it any other way. I've been fortunate the last few years in being asked to speak to about two CYO conventions of young people each year, an experience that always sends me back to my hermitage with renewed vigor and enthusiasm for writing—and, of course, with some new ideas on what to write and how to approach it realistically. I'm the opposite, in other words, of Phyllis McGinley's St. Anthony who found wrestling with the Devil in his hermitage "quite a relief" after trying "to come to grips with the souls of men."

But then I suspect that Anthony and I differ in a few other minor ways too, like his being one of the Friars Minor and a saint. I admit to sharing his sentiment on some rare occasions, but never after a youth convention—at least not after one I didn't have to organize.

The kids at these conventions are fabulous, and I've seen a good geographical cross section of them by now. Young people seem to differ in various parts of the country in externals—with some of them superficially more sophisticated, or slower to warm up to a stranger, than others. Don't get me wrong; the kids are essentially the same anywhere you find them, and so are their warmth and friendliness. But in some places it takes longer to get at it, to get beneath the veneers they have laid on or their parents and teachers have led them into. Once you get beneath this surface, you find the same tremendous kid. Unfortunately, too many people judge only the externals, not bothering to try to see what is underneath.

If I may use the word "typical," I think I'd consider as typical the kids in Texarkana, about five hundred of them, who waited patiently while I came in very, very late with the help of one of the great unscheduled airlines in the country. They listened even more patiently (from about 10-11 P.M.) as I talked with them about what God was trying to tell us about Himself in the Scriptures. How odd, I can hear some neo-apostle say, that he'd dream they'd be interested in God. He probably didn't even mention "involvement" and "commitment." I didn't either.

Another favorite audience of mine—for different reasons—has been the Communion breakfast group, where the whole family is in attendance, so that you're faced with an audience ranging in age from two to about 102. This is a great challenge, and it's interesting to notice if you're going over or failing with each segment—something they let you know quite clearly, each in his own way.

So far, I've been asked only once to be a toastmaster. Since this was a first, and undoubtedly a last, I was a little more nervous than usual. But it seemed to come off pretty well. In fact, I was quite happy with my performance when, after the breakfast and speeches, I stepped down from the platform to mingle democratically with the common people. The first peasant I met was dressed in a tux and looked very prominent. I was quite happy when he stuck out his hand to say "hello," and I waited in some anticipation of his coming up with a few compliments on the toastmastering bit.

"Don't they teach you people anything in the seminary about public speaking?" was his opening compliment. I laughed, confident he was being satirical. But he wasn't, and for fifteen minutes I listened to a critique of this would-be toastmaster that was utterly devastating. In fact, fifteen minutes clearly weren't going to be nearly enough to exhaust the list of my errors. For one thing, I had stood flat-footed, and any member of the toastmasters' club knows perfectly well that the feet are always to be placed at angles, with the right a bit ahead of the left. Luckily, some lady came by at one of the few pauses for breath, and asked "May I see you later?"

"How about right now?" I asked.

One thing that always helps to make a speaking assignment interesting is the introduction one gets. I have yet to encounter a dull one, even though most of them sound like the obituary of some more famous, or at least wealthier, relative; and you catch yourself looking around to see whom they're talking about, and wondering if they've forgotten that they had asked *you* to speak. Sometimes the compliments lose some of their force, however, when the MC after all his glowing words, forgets your name. And then there was the lady who concluded her introduction by mentioning that they had intended giving a copy of my book for a door prize, but added, "We were unable to buy a copy of the book, so we're giving a potted plant instead. I give you Father McGloin."

So many weird things happen to a speaker that he begins to live with them to the extent of considering them normal. I used to be shook, for example, when I was in Denver, at always seeing a mortician friend in the audience, either taking tickets or just listening with what seemed professional attention. I've had huge venetian blinds fall down while I was speaking, babies wailing, police sirens screaming nearby, people wandering in—obviously looking for some other room. I've had waiters serving and cleaning up the tables and conversing noisily while I spoke, and the high-school band waiting impatiently nearby to hurtle off into their next selection. But I've always enjoyed it, and no matter what the situation, have never quite despaired.

One late afternoon as I spoke to about two hundred girls, it seemed to me that my audience was gradually but surely fading from sight. They were too, and by the end of the talk, to them I is only a voice coming out of the darkness. Later on I found out at the sister who would normally have turned on the lights was, the time, hopelessly locked in the choir loft.

That wasn't nearly as sensational, though, as the time I was eaking from a stage and the one in charge of lights hit the wrong tton. We had light all right—all the different colors in succession, that I went from purple to green to red and back again. I can rdly resist mentioning that this was the only time I can remember hen some of my stories were blue.

Another form of public speaking I've enjoyed has been on TV d radio shows. Such appearances are invaluable to a writer, but ey're fun even apart from that practical consideration. During the years in Denver most of the shows I did were either with teens or about them, and of all these shows, the ending of one in particular stands out in my mind. We had a panel of teens discussing their parents on a previous show, and so we gave the parents equal time at the earliest opportunity. Among the parents on the panel was a great friend, Mike DeFrancia, whom I've mentioned before. Mike, tough as he is physically, was pretty frightened in front of those cameras, and so some of his answers weren't what you'd call lengthy. Near the end of the show I asked him if he'd ever gotten this one from his kids: "Everybody else is doing it—why can't I?"

And he came up with one of his longer sentences. "Yeh," he said, "I get it all right."

"Do you," I asked, "have an answer for it?"

"Yeh," he answered in a burst of wordiness, "I do."

"What *is* the answer?" I persisted, noticing that we had only ten seconds to wind up the show.

Now what Mike meant to give me was a darn good answer—that just because someone else was letting his kids run the risk of going to hell was no sign his were going to. But wary as he was of the camera, it came out a bit different and, I think, a lot more to the point.

"They can all," he said grandly, "go to hell."

In Minneapolis when *What To Do Till the Psychiatrist Comes!* hit the stands before the publisher tried to supress it, I did an interview show on the book. Since I had never appeared on that channel before nor even seen this particular show, I was quite anxious to meet and talk with the moderator a bit before we got started, just to see how it was going to work. But another of the guests, a man who wrote about birds, monopolized all her time and I couldn't break in. When there was an opening, he started talking to me until someone else had the lady's ear. I thought I showed admirable patience until in speaking of his bird book, he looked at me and asked "And do you also watch our little feathered friends?"

Now, I guess I admire birds as much as the next guy, but someone had just put a bird feeder in our yard and we were currently being besieged by every sparrow and pigeon east of Capistrano. So almost without thinking I told him, "No, we're far too busy trying to get rid of the damned things."

During the years in Minneapolis I was fortunate enough to be a regular guest on the Jane Johnston show, a noon time interview show. Jane is great at her job, smooth and unaffected, undoubtedly because she is a genuine, unaffected person in real life, despite a few trials which would have embittered someone else. These were good shows, I think, and most enjoyable. Occasionally in fact, the staff and I plotted a show that Jane knew nothing about until she saw it in action. One such show stands out in my mind especially over the others, and so I'll attempt to sketch it here. It was a cartoon show basically, with the cartoons done by Don

Jane spends a lot of time and study in carefully selecting the guest for each show. (Each of these characters *did* appear on the show, even the little Viking, who was flashed on the screen one day when the announcer said "And Jane's guest today is Father McGloin.")

Jane then contacts the guest and, invariably, is greeted with an enthusiasm matching her own.

Guests are told to be present at 11:30 A.M. in order to prepare for the show.

The light men get their equipment ready. .

Cameras are prepared. . .

The guest is fitted with his microphone. (By pure coincidence, the mike cord this day *did* turn out to be too short.)

The star polishes up. . .

(This drawing is from a photograph of "the star" which was also used on the show—often, in fact.)

The treasure-chest is readied . . .

(This was a give-away show "Dialing for Dollars" and the potential winner's name was drawn from this box.)

Sometimes the potential winner doesn't fully appreciate his opportunity.

The crew functions like a well-oiled machine, always keeping the transitions smooth.

Everyone on the show is always on the lookout for new objects to be cleaned by the sponsor's product.

Once the show gets under way, Jane gives the guest the floor and never interrupts. (An old joke among those of us who were on the show, one which in fact inspired this show—at which Jane had promised to say absolutely nothing, for a change.)

Finally, the show came to a smooth conclusion.

Invariably, there is great rejoicing, especially on the part of the producer, that another great show has been presented.

Baumgart, and I gave here only the essence of the accompanying comments.

This was a fun show and was well-received. I still have an audio tape of it, and Jane, as close to completely true to her word as could be expected, said very little. But on the audio tape you can hear some mysterious lady with a tremendous sustained belly laugh, which could hardly have been Jane Johnston since she is far too dignified for that.

There's a practical angle which any speaker, no matter what his apostolic zeal, has to think of, especially when he has pretty much to support himself—and that's the matter of getting paid at least tokenly. After all, he's giving his time (quite a bit more than most people realize, perhaps) and some of his energy to this task. At least his expenses ought to be taken care of. In the days when I was running an organization which periodically required the services of outside speakers, it was always a point of honor of ours to pay these speakers whatever we could. It might not have been much sometimes, but at least it covered their expenses.

I'm not in the same league as the lecturer who once read an old, often-used paper of his to an audience for several thousand dollars; and so I've pretty well run the gamut of payment for talks, from nothing (a far too frequent happening) on up. I've received exorbitant fees for retreats and practically nothing for them, considering the time and work and sometimes travel expenses involved. Some years back, heady from having received well over a thousand dollars for a retreat, I went east for another retreat, fully expecting that no one would ever dare to go below a thousand dollars for my services again. After giving a retreat and another couple of talks and running a panel and a few other things, I was given the prodigal total sum of twenty-five dollars—for a trip which had cost me $250 in travel expenses alone. This sort of thing isn't calculated to make even the most spiritual-minded religious superior jump up and down with joy and encourage his subject to seek a return engagement.

Actually, you find the situation in this field much like in any other—those with very little consider it a privilege to have you, while the loaded seem to think it's *your* privilege and that this is compensation enough for your trouble. That's a general statement, and like all such, has great exceptions, but in general, it's all too true. In my own case I've almost always been treated most gener-ously—probably because I'm a little people's speaker and not programmed for big shots. Then there was the time I refused to accept a check from a far from wealthy parish. They insisted, however, until I did accept it. Then it bounced.

162

CHAPTER SEVEN

*Half the fun's
in getting there—
sometimes*

One of the very pleasant aspects of my rather atypical life
and a thing which is helpful to the writing, too, is the
◇◇◇ traveling I do. I won't say "have to do" (or, as one
Jesuit put it, "Superiors have sent me to Europe three times now")
because I usually enjoy it. Strangely—or not so strangely—I find a
relative lack of demands on my presence in the places I've lived. No
man, I guess, is a prophet in his own country, not even in Council
Bluffs, Iowa. I have, however, enjoyed every place I've stayed for
any length of time—with Denver and Minneapolis standing out—but
I'm not so sure that the place itself means nearly as much as what
you're doing and the people you come to know in the process.
And so it seems to me that one's work and outlook can ordinarily
overcome almost any geographical failure, maybe even. . . . Then
again, maybe not.

There has, of course, been purpose in almost all this traveling.
The usual reason has been for retreats and other talks. Occasionally,
at least until the last several years, the reason has been some meeting
or convention or other. And sometimes when I can work it in, the
travel has been for kicks, although most of the time I've been able
to combine the latter purpose with business or vice versa.

As for conventions, I'm sure that some of them are very
profitable—not just for the host but even for some of those in
attendance. But certainly there has to come a saturation point to
attendance at even the useful conventions—a time for converting
their potential accomplishments into actuality.

When I was beginning to work out the high-school religion
course, I took in every related convention and gathering that seemed
both worthwhile and reachable. It would, in fact, be quite easy to
be still running around to such conventions and gatherings and so
to be still preparing to write. I haven't the slightest doubt, in fact,
that somewhere there exists a dedicated conventioneer with a potential religion book in his head, one far superior to my actual one.
On the other hand, I too have innumerable potential books in my
mind which are far superior to my actual works.

Traveling is always interesting even when it's wearying, and
even though—as is invariably the case—you're happy to get home
again. In fact, I feel that the latter feeling is one of the great
therapeutic effects of travel.

I've tried every available way of getting there by now—bus,
train, plane, car, and cattle and river boat. I'd rank my top
preferences as driving or train travel, but the time element usually

forbids both, and so I've had to become a bit of a jet-Jeb. In many ways one could stratify society by its modes of travel—as the various terminals tell you only too well. Until a priest, resplendent and conspicuous in Roman collar, has sat in a bus terminal in some dinky little town waiting for a 2 A.M. bus, he can't really understand bus travel or bus travelers. Just when you begin to muse that half the fun is *not* in getting there, you see a mother with two or three small children patiently waiting in a nearby seat. That is, you see her if you can shake the town drunk long enough to see anyone.

Some trips go smoothly. Others don't. There can be snafus no matter how you go—flat tires, planes that won't fly, bad weather. Sometimes you feel as though there's a conspiracy to keep you from getting somewhere. En route to Texarkana not long ago, I was routed via San Antonio and Dallas. In San Antonio I had the usual reunion with old friends Fathers Mullally and Stuebben, and so was pretty late in sacking in that night—something which is so rare with me as to be just about non-existent. And so I was completely exhausted the next day, the only bright prospect being that I was due in Texarkana at noon and so could try to get some rest before my scheduled talk that evening. But then the conspiracy began.

The first plane was late—plenty late—getting out of San Antonio. Not only did I miss the Dallas connection, but this meant about an eight-hour stopover in that exciting city. The Dallas air terminal, however, has a nice balcony section with auditorium seats facing the field, and that looked like an inviting spot for catching some sleep. So up I went, paid my dime, donned the dark glasses, and prepared to doze off in the quiet, semi-deserted balcony. I didn't even get both eyes fully closed, how-ever, when what must have been three hundred young children came trooping in, climbing over the seats and running up and down the aisles, while their three or four teachers pointed out the airplanes and other cultural attractions of the Dallas airport to them.

The next installment in this sad serial found me taking off to a motel where I hoped to get a room and some sleep. Naturally, the room had a neighboring garage and a drippy faucet which kept me awake, and when it came time to get back to the airport, I couldn't get a cab. Since I soon got a bit desperate, I stepped into a nearby bar, announced my plight, and found a kind volunteer to drive me to the airport. I wasn't really surprised when his car wouldn't start, but finally it did and we made it—just in time to be told that the plane would be another hour late. That plane proceeded through the most violent storm I've ever flown through (I later discovered that another airline lost a plane nearby in that one), a situation not helped any by the old war dog next to me who told story after story about all the plane crashes he knew of. As I've mentioned elsewhere, the five hundred teens I talked to that night were magnificent in their toleration of the tired traveler attempting to speak.

Driving is for me the fun way to travel, and I enjoy just about everything involved: the solitude and relaxation away from the phone, typewriter, and mail box; the scenery and—ordinarily—the small restaurants along the way. It's my usual practice when driving long distances, to start out about 5 A.M. right after Mass, drive until about 9:30, and then stop for breakfast. In this way you feel like you've cut off a big slice of the day's distance by breakfast time. And the people you meet in the restaurants are always interesting. In fact, it's too darned bad that because of freeways and big money and such, the small restaurant is fading from the scene, since it's not only friendly and warm but the food is usually better and warmer too. Ordinarily, you either bring your friends and friendliness into the big restaurant with you, or you don't encounter them at all. I'm a good competitor at breakfast, but I remember a chuck-wagon breakfast in Texas that not even I could finish. It was billed, innocently enough, as "sausage patty between two pancakes, plus scrambled eggs and potatoes." And it was just that—on a platter too, with two 8-inch pancakes sandwiching the "sausage patty" (the same size) plus a stack of hash-brown potatoes. I think it cost eighty cents and I wish I'd gotten a doggie bag. At any rate, as we build our big chrome country with its stainless steel restaurants, we may discover that you can't make a heart out of this—or any—material.

It's probably because of the years of community living that I still find very simple departures from that sort of life enjoyable and relaxing. Just to get a motel room, eat in a restaurant, relax and watch TV all alone, without any risk of the phone's ringing with another problem for you to listen to—this can be great on occasion. When I drove to California from Minneapolis, I was able to do this a couple of times—except for those places where I was able to stay at a friendly convent or at a Jesuit house. On that particular trip I found myself within striking distance of my ultimate destination in the late afternoon of July 31, the feast day of the founder of the Society of Jesus, St. Ignatius. By pushing I could have made Santa Barbara by about 9 P.M., but just as I was figuring this out, a brand new Howard Johnson loomed on the horizon, beckoning to me one final, lone splurge in honor of

Ignatius. My well-trained car turned in and soon I had registered, enjoyed a cool shower after the hot drive across the desert, donned a fresh sport shirt, and dropped into the air-conditioned new bar-grill for a cool rum collins prior to dinner—all in honor of St. Ignatius, of course. It was most relaxing.

You can't, however, get ahead of St. Ignatius, especially when you think you've temporarily created a moratorium on the old responsibilities. It was about 5 P.M., the place was new, and so business was very slack, until finally only the bartender and I survived. So what happened? Instead of playing his traditional role and staying behind the bar to listen to the troubles of his customers, he came and sat down at my table and for an hour and a half told me about *his* troubles. Not that I resented the time so spent—I didn't. But it hadn't been *my* plan. And I could well imagine Ignatius smugly chuckling, much as Vince Lombardi must often have grinned when catching one of his boys trying to break training.

A lot of the enjoyment of travel is, however—at least for the loner—mostly in the people one meets. It seems to me there has been a not-so-subtle change in travelers and commuters in our country since about the time of World War II. I had been taught, for example—and when the use of reason finally did arrive, I bought the teaching—that a man, no matter what his age, was supposed to be courteous to women travelers at all times, no matter what *their* age. And so I had always stepped aside to let any female types into the train or bus, or whatever it was, first, and I always gave up my own seat for them on city buses and so on. But it seems to me that during and following World War II and still today, the lady commuter and lady traveler in general, perhaps sensing and proving her equality with men, began to imitate the most boorish of male types—shoving others aside, often enough with her more than ample shover, pushing others around in a bus and so on. We have become, I feel, in many ways the rudest society in history, as can be witnessed at any speech of any politician or public figure—and this is only one manifestation of it. Just how much politness women like this deserve from men, I don't know. I do know that I will step aside for them to get in first, but it's not so much from politness any more as from the fear of being trampled or brush-blocked. And I still stand up and give them my place on a crowded bus too, but it's more because they're just about in my lap anyhow. And as I smile and get no thanks for it, how could they possibly know that I'm thinking, "This isn't for your sake, Lady, but because Christ said, 'What you did to one of these, the least of my brethren, you did to me.' And, baby, are you ever 'the least'!"

Some of the ladies use whatever unique talents they have to hint that they'd like to take over your seat.

I remember one train ride in particular where two well-past-middle-age ladies had used their peculiar talents to muscle by me on boarding the train, even though there was plenty of room. They ended up seated right in front of me, and as time went on they cackled and guffawed and talked simultaneously at one another and at the world in general. Finally, incredibly, they seemed to wear out—or, far more likely, run out of ideas—and gradually lapse into silence.

Not far behind me was a black lady with her two small children, and when the noise ahead subsided I could hear her soft cultured voice as she read to her children. Now and then one of the youngsters would ask "How would you say that in German?" and she'd tell him. Or the other child would ask "How would you say that in French?" and she'd answer that. Sure enough, from the seat ahead of me I soon heard the voice of culture: "I wish she'd keep quiet and not disturb the rest of us." Fortunately probably, I kept my mouth shut for a change, and also probably fortunately, from then on, so did they.

Occasionally you find yourself surrounded by a merry band of fellow travelers who are going somewhere together—like the Ladies Bowling Club I encountered en route to some cultural happening in San Antonio. Some such groups make one's trip all the more enjoyable. Others only succeed in embarrassing everyone else on the plane or bus or whatever it is. The lady bowlers were somewhere in between, although the vote of the stewardess near the end of that flight was not this tolerant.

This particular trip stands out in my mind, however, for another incident. Some years before when I was going to San Antonio, my two crazy clerical friends, Fathers Stuebben and Mullally, had prepared a welcoming ceremony, complete with parade and band and speeches and dignitaries, for my arrival. And so when I stepped from the plane this time, I wasn't really surprised to find an enormous, cheering crowd facing up at me, the police keeping them in line. I looked around, spotted my two friends in the crowd and waved appreciatively, if modestly, as they grinned and waved back and cheered. Just then though, I was hustled the rest of the way down the gangplank, as some obscure entertainer, one Bob Hope, was about to de-plane behind me. I guess a few of the people were there to see him too.

No one who travels at all these days—except, of course, congressmen and others on fat expense accounts—can be unaware of the enormous cost, especially in some cities, of a place to sleep. Ordinarily in my own travels I like to stay in a Jesuit house. Often enough though, the nearest Jesuit house may be too far away; or it may be crowded; or, as a matter of cold fact, it may cost you more than a decent hotel would anyhow.

After several trips to New York where I stayed at both Jesuit houses and hotels, I got fed up with paying as much for one night's sleep as I'd lay out for a week's meals. And so on one such trip I got smart and asked the cab driver if he'd bring me to a reasonable hotel near midtown. This he did with no hesitation at all, apparently since he often ran into the same request. In retrospect I suspect, too, that he just might have gotten maybe 10 percent for his trouble. So he took me to a hotel. The lobby looked better than the outside, which isn't saying a thing, but I figured the rooms were probably very nice. While I was registering at the desk, a man came up to me—pretty seedy-looking but not particularly caring since he was also loaded. " . . . Hey," he began politely " . . . 'r you 'n Augustinian priest?"

"No," I told him, "I'm a Jesuit."

A big grin, I think, split his face, as he stuck out his hand somewhere to my right, then to my left, before I was able to catch it and shake it. "Small world" he went on happily, "Small world. A Jesuit! 'n I'm a graduate of Canisius."

"I'd recognize our alumni anywhere, " I told him.

"But hey," he went on, loud enough partially to awaken some of the other lobby dwellers, as I headed for the elevator, "what're *you* doing in a dump like this?"

I should have caught on then, but I still thought it would be okay. I asked about a TV set and was told, pretty evasively, "They were ordered three or four months ago. Should be here by now." But I didn't really need to worry—there was a radio, about a 1927 cabinet model, with a large gold plaque on it: "This radio put here with the compliments of the management for your enjoyment." Naturally, it didn't work.

The lamp shade was unique also—palimpsested with innumerable newspapers until it had become far too thick for its 60-watt bulb. The window was broken out, and since it was midwinter, I spent half the night at Radio City Music Hall as much to stay warm as long as possible as to enjoy the show. I did manage to get to sleep only to be awakened by the phone—which did work all too well—with "This is your 5 A.M. call." I wondered who in that place would have requested a 5 A.M. call.

When I phoned the people I was to see and told them where I was staying, I got a moment of rather eloquent silence and then "There?" followed by what censors call an uncomplimentary description of the place, inelegant but accurate. To do it justice, the place did have two virtues: It *was* clean and it was cheap, relatively clean and absolutely cheap. I stayed there the couple nights I was in New York anyhow, at least when there was nowhere else to close up, even though I wouldn't do so again. I guess the thing that made me most thoughtful, as I left after paying my bill, was that they had given me a "clergy rate."

My next time into New York I tried another hotel, also "reasonable," but a step up, anyhow, from this Jesuit alumni hangout. When you came into the minimum room at this newest try at a hotel, you had to move in slowly or you'd crash into the opposite wall and you couldn't open the bathroom door until you had closed the door of the room itself—sort of like a roomette on the Pullman. The walls were paper thin, and I admitted shortly after 1 A.M. that I'd have to go somewhere else if I was going to sleep at all, due largely to the collegians' party next door—both ways next door. So I did what I should have done in the first place—called the New York Athletic Club and asked if they had a room; then took off, stopping only momentarily to wish a cheery good-bye and congratulations on their consideration and maturity to my good neighbors. I had the satisfaction of detecting a note of some wonder in the eyes of these intellectuals at seeing a priest suddenly appear in their room at 2 A.M. and then disappear just as abruptly.

Since that time, I've always, when I could, stayed at athletic clubs. They're reasonable, clean, and often homelike—a welcome atmosphere to a traveler. I suppose the alleged inner-city apostle would chide me for not sleeping on a park bench; but when I travel I have work to do, and the one thing essential to my getting any work done at all is sleep. Food I can sometimes do without. But not sleep. Not if I'm going to read that fine print in the contract.

There's another reason, of course, I like to go to the athletic clubs—I can play handball there. And this always makes a trip more pleasant.

Despite these ups and downs in the room-and-board department, however, I suppose I've stayed most often in Jesuit houses. And as in most other experiences, my emotions here are mixed. As Jesuits we were always taught—when criticizing a speech, say—to come up with something nice first, if possible, and then with that huge introductory word "but," launch into the criticism. Here, however, I'll reverse that process.

When it comes to hospitality, it would be a vast mistake to make any sweeping statements, since this virtue differs so much from place to place. Many Jesuit houses are so hospitable that you run into someone who even acts glad to see you on occasion. In other places a blank stare comes to seem warm to you. I once sat across from two prominent Jesuits at one of our greater universities at lunch for about fifteen minutes while they conversed with each other at length, never bothering to say "Hello," much less anything else, to this visiting dignitary. Of course they did have important business to discuss, and then too, I had seen them fairly recently, so I guess they figured there was no use in spoiling me by overdoing the welcome bit. After all, why waste time saying "hello" to a guy you've seen only six or seven years ago?

Then there was my triumphant arrival in Miami from British Honduras, where I had served as an heroic missionary for three years. I came into Miami on St. Ignatius Day, prepared for the big hello, tried every door and doorbell at the Gesu parish house there, and couldn't get anywhere. (By this time the reader is going to decide, as I did long ago, that things happen to me on St. Ignatius day, probably as a reminder both of Ignatius' sense of humor and his refusal to baby people.) As I was leaving, wondering just where I *would* go in a city I knew nothing of, I

172

chanced on three men wearing black trousers (which, at that time, meant either clergy or skid row), who turned out to be a Monsignor, a Benedictine, and a Franciscan. They had been invited to the residence to drink a toast in honor of St. Ignatius, and so I, follower of Ignatius through both sweet and bitters, joined them long enough to get past the door without incident, accepting a drink proffered by an anonymous hand as I entered. About half an hour later when I asked if I might have a room for the night, someone actually asked me my name, so I could see that the old southern and Jesuit hospitality was begining to show itself and would undoubtedly soon run hog-wild. Sure enough, I did get a room there that night.

It would be an injustice to narrate this sort of thing and tag it "inhospitality." It isn't really that at all so much as taking one's welcome for granted. And while large Jesuit communities seem to bubble over with all the cordiality of a room full of computers, they sometimes warm up a bit when fed the right cards.

Sometimes too the inhospitality you imagine comes not so much from any real coldness as from shyness or quaintness. The latest instance of this that sticks in my mind at the moment was the Jesuit chaplain in a convent who, when I began to talk with him about mutual acquaintances and such, calmly took a portable radio from somewhere in the room, turned it on, and said "I always listen to music during lunch." *That* has to be quaintness. In fact, it better be. Whatever it is, it's quite a blow to a guy who, sometimes at least, gets paid for talking to people.

But it wouldn't be cricket superficially to call these isolated instances inhospitality, and it would be a far greater mistake to generalize on them. Indeed, the only reason I include them here at all is that they seem humorous to me, largely because they're extremely rare exceptions to the rule. If they weren't rare, they certainly wouldn't be funny. Luckily they're both.

In a less humorous vein, though, I do feel that there is sometimes one reason, at least, why a Jesuit can feel not unwelcome exactly, but simply not part of the family in that house. And this villain goes under the title of *per diem*, which means simply that a visiting Jesuit usually pays a daily board-and-room fee to the house he visits.

I think that by now I've heard (often, in fact) all the arguments in favor of the per diem bit, and they all come down to something called practicality, which is a synonym for money. Now I don't like to belittle money, but the whole thing can get a bit ridiculous sometimes in a spiritual organization, with Peter paying Paul and then Paul paying Peter. The trouble is, I am told, that even a spiritually geared organization is composed of human beings who have to eat periodically.

But the pro per diem argument usually goes like this: Some houses get so many visitors that they simply must charge visiting Jesuits, or they'd go broke. Then, of course, since men from other houses (which presumably are not overrun with visitors for one suspicious reason or another) are paying these rentals, these houses in turn try to get some of the stuff back if *they* ever have visitors. And so the heat goes on.

Now I have no intention of trying to refute this argument, because I'm afraid it can't be answered, at least not entirely. Besides, I think it's probably, essentially at least, correct. I've resented the custom on occasion when, for example, I've had to pay five to ten a day for the attempt to sleep in a student dorm between factious crowds of shouting collegians—sometimes known as students, or, more often today, intellectuals—as I dreamed, in those intermittent minutes of dozing, about a quiet comfortable hotel somewhere.

And yet despite this sort of bilking by the holy rule, it's still true that there are houses with so many visitors that they simply must charge a per diem or suffer disproportionately. That fact remains even in an age when we talk so incessantly about love and about how love is shown in giving and all that jazz. So much depends on *who's* giving.

Justified as it may sometimes be though, I'm still stubbornly convinced that the very existence of a per diem can help to bring on a coldness in both visitors and visited. It can make all the difference between being tolerated and being welcomed. One is simply not met at many Jesuit doors and welcomed by some kindly, Christlike Jesuit, nor probably by any Jesuit at all. Instead if no one forgot he was coming, he finds at the switchboard or on the bulletin board a key with his assigned room number, and if he's lucky, some explanation of the house's geography and schedule. He might even find a cheery mimeographed word "Welcome," or in an especially needy house with a low incidence of visitors and a high per diem, *Venit hospes, venit Christus,* "a guest comes, Christ comes."

The implication in that pious little sentiment is, of course: We're going to treat any guest as we would Christ. I once heard of a Jesuit who visited a house displaying this slogan, who apparently, however, still got a very cold reception. And so when he left, he dropped the printed form in the minister's mail box with his own scriptural addition to the maxim, *Crucifige eum,* "Crucify Him."

174

Clearly, I dislike the per diem bit—a dislike squared once when I was caught in the awkward position of paying two per diems at once. There is too a rule in the Society that if it's possible, one should stay at a Jesuit house in the cities he visits. It's my personal feeling, however (subject to correction by almost anyone but house treasurers), that while there is such a rule, the per diem charge neutralizes it, since I can't believe that St. Ignatius would command me to support another Jesuit house when I could get cheaper, and often more satisfactory, lodging elsewhere. And so in some cities at least, I usually check into the current per diem and then call a friend in the hotel business who undercuts this rate for me. After all, even Mary and Joseph looked at an inn first before heading for the stable. I am happy to report that at this writing at least one province of the Society of Jesus is considering dropping the per diem bit. Even though this is presently only for the members of its own province, this seems a step in the right direction. While charity is supposed to begin at home, it can be hoped that it may some day no longer end there.

When all is said and done, I much prefer to stay at Jesuit houses, largely because I *am* a Jesuit and the individual Jesuit one meets is a friend and a brother and acts like one. Never, in fact, do I feel nearly as relaxed as when staying in a Jesuit house. In many houses almost everyone makes you feel this way. In others, it's often only a few, as the others go their busy way, preaching love, no doubt, elsewhere.

I'm thrilled by travel, as I think is obvious, and—not so obviously—I also learn something from it. I suppose I'll always love the midwest and north best, but I've enjoyed each coast, and have enjoyed the New England autumn almost as much as the Missouri fall when the oak trees are red. I liked California also, but I'm too turned on by seasonal changes ever to go hog-wild over it, and so the Tacoma-Seattle weather already has me hooked. I was thrilled by the historical sites of New England—around Concord for example—because despite her historical and contemporary faults, I dearly love this country and I think there are more things to be proud of in America than ashamed of. America has her loveliness, and it's up to us to make her still lovelier.

I've loved the American cities, at least in my superficial view in brief visits, and I've been excited by New York and Los Angeles and San Francisco. There's a soft spot in my heart for Denver and San Antonio and Boston. Maybe only in New Orleans could one see a duckling paddling along the street like a dog after his master. In Chicago—at least when I come in by train—I always say Mass at St. Peter's in the Loop, where the hospitable Franciscans

If you can't outtalk a panhandler, the next best plan is to outrun him.

have always been such tremendous hosts. Between the Union Depot and St. Peter's is, however, a real sucker row; and a priest always seems the favorite target of the professional panhandler. Of late I've learned how to counteract this; and so despite the way it may look, instead of walking to St. Peter's and back, I run it. Most of the panhandlers can't keep up and still manage to carry on an intelligent conversation.

San Antonio is always fun, and its Hemisfair made it still more so. There was even a Texas Cultural Center—how about *that*? I saw an excellent film on prejudice at the United States Pavilion there, and still remember overhearing the remark of one San Antonian as we left the theater, "It sho hadda be a comminist who wrote that un." To be quite fair to the man, we *were* some yards at the time from the Texas Cultural Center.

Certain impressions of other places stand out in my mind: the dead seriousness of the hooked little gamblers at Reno, their expressionless faces not quite masking their near desperation as they fed nickles into the slots; the Del Webbe Towne House in Fresno, where Dale Seiders, then the manager, gave me royal treatment along with the royal suite; the charm of New Orleans together with the ugly memory of some New Orleans women,

176

some time back, screaming with ugly frightening viciousness at those who were bringing children to newly integrated schools.

New Orleans, in fact, stands out in my mind for many reasons, most of them pleasant—with the exception of one of the most frustrating, and yet one of the funniest, experiences I ever had. This particular visit there was marked by something of a reunion with an old friend, Pat Pelzer and his wife, Ann. Like most reunions of this sort, this one bore some of the characteristics of a minor celebration, and we did have a pretty fair time. The only difficulty was that amid the genteel festivities of that evening I lost my wallet somewhere or other—or someone lifted it, which comes to the same thing.

Now this put me on something of a spot, not because of the money in the wallet which naturally wasn't much. But there were a couple of credit cards there, and most important of all, my driver's license. I had driven across the country in the car of another friend, Jack Cusack from Roswell, New Mexico, and since I had to drive back to Roswell soon, a driver's license seemed darn near of the essence.

With complete confidence, a sentiment immediately shattered, I went successively to city, county, state officials and lawyers. There was, all told me matter of factly, nothing they could do, for instance, about issuing a temporary license. "What," I asked, "if I get picked up without a license?" All the answers boiled down to a polite form of "Tough."

There were only a few days to fool with, so I called Minneapolis, and the license bureau there sent me, special delivery, a license application. This might have worked, except that just as I was ready to mail it back, I noticed at the bottom of the form: "We are not allowed to mail a license out of the state." A further check on this by phone proved it to be all too true. Finally, I had the filled-in form notarized and carried it along in the hope that there might be some legal loophole (which every official assured me there wasn't), should I get stopped and asked for my license.

Looking back on the situation, however, I'm not sure that would have worked either. I said Mass about 4:30 A.M. and then took off for San Antonio and Roswell about 5 A.M. So there I was (a) in a borrowed car (b) without a driver's license (c) unshaven, since it was so early (d) in old driving clothes (e) with the smell of wine on my breath from Mass and (f) with a revolver in my luggage—a thing I sometimes used to bring along on longer trips just for a little target practice. The accumulated impression these things might have given didn't really hit me until I came abruptly onto a road block just outside of New Orleans and was, happily, waved on by a state patrolman. It would, I'm sure, have been an interesting interview, like maybe: "I'm a priest."

"Sure you are."

And then my schedule, at least, would undoubtedly have suffered.

I've hardly ever had a travel schedule go far wrong, even though there have been some delays and some very close calls. On one of my trips through Denver, I had the pleasure of having dinner with a good friend, Ed Simones. Ed was at that time manager of the Oxford Hotel, which had long been favored particularly by salesmen since it was near the railroad station in a day when there were still moving passenger trains. And since the station was so close, I didn't pay much attention to the time until I realized that my train should be just about ready to blast off.

And so with a hurried good-bye I rushed out the door and started running the very dark two blocks to the station. Immediately ahead of me as I ran, however, was a blonde young lady. She turned around, took one look at someone in black, passing under a street lamp and gaining on her in the dark, in what is not Denver's best neighborhood—and ran. So I shrugged helplessly at Ed, who was watching and laughing from the door, and walked the rest of the way. I still wonder if that poor girl had been brought up on some of the stories about Catholics which non-Catholics used to hear at a kindly mother's knee, or whether she was only a Catholic ahead of her time.

But if I've come close to missing a train or bus on occasion, I actually did once miss the whole town where I was to speak— Taylorville, Illinois, I think it was—and I drove right by it before doubling back to try to find it.

But I've been going on here solely about business trips for giving retreats or other talks or just migrating to a new home somewhere. Since such trips are a break in themselves, I've relatively seldom ever taken other trips, or formal vacations.

There are, of course, notable exceptions to that assertion— both ways, since not all business trips are either enjoyable or relaxing, and on the other hand, since there has been some travel which is not fileable under the title "business trip."

I find that I'm by no means alone in not taking advantage of the places I've been. I've met many a New Yorker who seldom goes to the theater, lots of St. Louisans who never visit their zoo, and some people in St. Mary's, Kansas, who never bother to watch the trains go by. During my years in Denver there never seemed to be time to take advantage of the marvelous scenery to be seen on short or longer trips out of the city, and I managed to get to our lovely villa at Fraser, Colorado, for exactly two hours on only one occasion in ten years. When I lived on Lake Harriet in Minneapolis, I guess I went swimming there only on an average of once every couple of weeks in the summers. And I'm kicking myself now for both omissions. On the other hand, I'm still doing it—while in California, I never got to Cucamonga or even Disneyland.

During those six years in Minneapolis, however, I was smart enough to take off periodically and drive for a whole day, just when stir-happiness was beginning to set in. There were some quite beautiful trips in that country, within striking distance in almost any direction. I'm sure California, too, had some lovely drives, but it seemed mostly freeway as far as I was concerned. I did manage, however, to get out on one short trip—to Sequoia and Yosemite, breathtaking places which make you hungry for more. Sam Spade, German Shepherd, was especially enthralled with the magnificent redwoods, looking at me and seeming to say in awe, "Now *there's* what I call a tree."

But the most enjoyable trips I've ever had have been the several drives I've been lucky enough to take to the south—once all the way to British Honduras and a few times to Mexico City. To say all one should about these trips would produce a travelogue. So we'll have to be content with a few of the highlights. Even those few highlights, however, will require a section of their own. If any place in the world deserves a chapter of its own, it has to be Mexico.

CHAPTER
EIGHT

All *the fun's*
in getting there,
amigo

It was Denver and midwinter and the streets were filled with snow, when some of us were sitting around talking about ◈ ◈ how nice it must be to be able to take off for Miami Beach or some such land of allegedly perpetual sunshine for at least part of the winter. For most of the people in that group Miami Beach was about the same distance as the moon, and they could have afforded one just as easily as the other.

"Why talk about Miami Beach?" I asked, without thinking much about it. "Why not take a trip to British Honduras? It has everything Miami Beach has except the plush accomodations—same sandflies, mosquitoes, beaches, fish, ocean, and warm climate." It seemed an innocent enough little conversation, but after a few days we were surprised to find ourselves trying to figure out how we would really make the trip. And—for an even greater surprise—make it we did.

Naturally, the primary and essential consideration had to be dirty old money. And so planes and ships were out, and cars were in. Clearly too, our aim had to be to get out of the United States (which meant largely Texas in this case) and into Mexico as quickly as possible. It costs far too much to live along the road in the United States, with hotels and motels doing their bit to share the traveler's wealth. Besides, Mexico was new to all of us and there was always something novel and interesting (although not always completely pleasant, such as the poverty in northern Mexico) around every turn in the road.

With planning, we made the trip for about five dollars a day apiece for everything that year—gas, lodging, food, the works—except, of course, for one item whose cost can never be predicted, souvenirs. Don and Gloria Baumgart, for example, restrained themselves heroically until we hit a little village called Cholula, at which point they tried their best to blow their then life savings in one shop. (Actually, Cholula may still be about the best place to buy things Mexican—where else can you get champagne at three bottles for twenty-four cents , for example, and still be able to enjoy drinking it?) I feel sure that such a trip can still be done at about $7.50 per day without too much trouble but, of course, without too many Henry VIII type feast days either.

My own expenses ran a bit higher that those of the others at first, because of the higher cost to someone addicted to single rooms. But this soon equalized itself, as on subsequent trips most motel owners wouldn't take my money, and neither did the Jesuit houses

Tourists have been known to lose some of their sanity in some Mexican shops.

which put up with me. I found some irony in this latter kindness, since some of these Mexican communities looked like they could have used that per diem almost as much, say, as some of the slightly more elaborate houses in the United States.

The first thing that might be suspected by anyone except the very naive traveler (or the parasitic type which is worse) is that such trips call for a bit of planning—more, at least, than is required (or was before the day of the hijacker) for only hopping on a non-stop plane going in the right direction. As one might also suspect, these plans always undergo a lot of changes—enough sometimes, in fact, to become unrecognizable—before the trip is completed. On our first trip, for example, not a single one of the original group which had discussed it, and had agreed that they were going along, actually went—except, of course, for kindly old Father. Twenty people might be signed up for a trip one day, and the next day (even if that "next day" happened to be the very eve of departure) you might find yourself with one or two fellow travelers, and minus a few wheels, which was even more serious.

This sort of fiasco, with its consequent waste of time, makes you seriously determine never to fool around with planning another such trip—until you see how very much worth all the trouble it was, both for yourself and for the others who finally go along. And so you do it all again, willing to put up with the frustrations and wasted motions and sometime baffling acts of God and men you know you are going to run into.

All the trips have been fun, and all for different reasons. And while it was also enjoyable—and left kindly old Father with less baby-sitting chores en route—to travel with just one companion on two occasions, the group trips were by far the most kicks. Apart from other reasons, such as the invariably delightful personalities of the travelers, with a good-sized group you can alternate cars and so also companions now and then. Usually too, you can even make friends out of some previous strangers.

Plans included things like getting the wheels, sometimes walkie-talkies between cars, and Styrofoam iceboxes. We always planned on picnic lunches en route, making sure we had a good restaurant and motel (with, when possible, a swimming pool) waiting for us each night. After the first trip I always wrote ahead to reserve the night accommodations.

That first year Don Baumgart's wife, Gloria, suddenly developed gallbladder trouble, and decided with the help of her doctor the night before we were to depart that she couldn't go. Gloria's very next decision was, however, that no mere gallbladder was going to cause her to miss such a trip, and so she and Don both showed up in Denver, raring to go and carrying a case of baby food for Gloria's delicate gallbladder condition. We carried that whole case all the way to British Honduras and back untouched, as Gloria discovered that a little tequila helped her to handle any food at all, even though she did turn in her gallbladder once home again.

Travel in other countries is exciting—for one reason because it differs so much from travel at home. In British Honduras, for example, our group traveled the hundred miles from Corozal (in the northern part of the colony) to Belize (the capital) by bus. Since I'd previously spent three years in British Honduras, the bus trip was old stuff to me but not so to the rest of our group. It was only an often repainted school bus and it required two drivers, not because of any union regulations but because it was a lot safer to have someone stand in the open doorway, watching for trucks hurtling towards us around the blind curves of the one-lane road.

The bus trip was a little different from those in the United States in other respects too. When we got to Orange Walk, for instance, I asked the driver if he'd wait around a few minutes while I went over and visited at the parish house with Father Phil

Pick. And wait he did—with all his passengers—for a half hour.
When we got to Belize too, my group was a bit surprised to see the
bus not following any set route, but taking each passenger to the
door of his home instead. That needn't have surprised anyone; it
happens in Mexico too. A nun friend told me that she and a
companion once took a city bus in Guadalajara and that they and
the others on the bus, including the driver, got talking about the
church she was going to. Soon the driver, bus, and passengers
were accompanying them, far from the designated route, to visit
this church.

Don Baumgart is still sorry his camera wasn't all set to go as he
rounded the corner of the bus at Orange Walk and saw a fellow
traveler of ours and myself "assisting" a lady through the back door.
It was a high door, and she must have weighed close to 250 pounds,
so there was really only one practical way to hoist her in, with one
of us working each side.

Mexico demands that if you come into the country with a car,
you're darn well not going out without it, or else you're going to
leave it in the tender care of the government. And so when we
left Mexico for British Honduras by air (it was four days by car,
an hour or two by air), we stashed our cars with the government

Without a derrick, you use whatever tools are at hand.

at Villa Hermosa. The trouble was that when we returned later on to pick up the cars, a clerk had apparently lost all record of them. From this whole incident I remember most vividly a little jefe with dark, dark, eyes, sitting calmly at his desk laying his .45 on the top, and calmly telling the clerk to "find it." He found it all right.

Mexican pilots, we discovered, are about like Mexican drivers— they enjoy what they're doing, do it well, and have absolutely no fear, a virtue not always completely shared by those they serve or compete with. As we ate breakfast in a motel restaurant in Chetumal looking out at a tropical downpour, one of the teen-agers in the group wondered aloud if we'd be able to fly out that day for Villa Hermosa. The captain of our DC-3 was eating breakfast at the next table, and his answer was typical even if a bit surprising at the time, *Como no?* "Why not?" We flew all right, and when we visited the cockpit en route we saw only a relaxed, happy pilot, his feet comfortably raised while his fingers drummed time with some music coming over the radio.

On this same trip (by the way, our first), the most sensational and beautiful drive of all was from Mexico City to Tamazunchale (which we in the States tend to call Thomas-and-Charlie) through the Sierra Madres. You really feel like you're on top of the world especially since instead of guard rails, the Mexicans prefer to erect a little shrine in honor of the last poor guy who plunged over the edge. Actually, this sort of reminder seems far more effective than guard rails anyhow.

It's always seemed to me that the simplest forms of enjoyment are the best, especially where one has to work a little at it himself instead of having it all presented to him. That's probably one reason our budgeted driving trips have been so much fun. On that first trip, for example, at our last Texas stop, San Angelo, we stopped at a very nice-looking motel and immediately confirmed the suspicion that it would cost far too much for our budget. Right across the street, however, we saw a pretty ancient, weed-surrounded motel, one that *did* fit the budget. We also discovered a huge public swimming pool nearby. So we had a much-needed swim, then bought the makings and had a beer and sandwich dinner in the front yard of our cheap motel. And that evening stands out, with its conversation and picnic atmosphere, as one of the most enjoyable of any trip.

The next morning we went to the Franciscan "church" (an auditorium actually, since their new church was still being built at that time) for Mass. A sung Mass was in progress, and a Franciscan priest was off to the side, playing the organ and singing out the responses of the Mass. He turned out to be an old friend,

Father Fidelis, who had been of great help to me at some of our youth congresses. As we headed for what passed for a sacristy, he recognized me and alternated his conversation with the Mass responses, saying "Hi, Joe," and then singing as he shook hands, *"Et cum spiritu tuo."* He arranged things in the sacristy for me to say Mass at a side altar, pausing every now and then to rush to the door and sing out another *"Et cum spiritu tuo,"* or whatever response seemed a good one out there at the time.

Later on, it was San Antonio that was to become the spot I liked best in Texas. It's sort of an oasis in a desert spotted with oil wells, and it isn't made of chrome as some large Texas cities are. If one is to appreciate fully and enjoy the hospitality of Fathers Stuebben (a native) and Mullally (a transplant and currently retransplanted in Miami) in San Antonio, he has to observe certain rituals. There is dinner at the Red Barn, with a birthday party for someone in the group, no matter when his birthday might be. One must also stand reverently before the Alamo in the wee hours and sing or at least listen to "The Eyes of Texas Are Upon You," suspecting that this is, indeed, literally true and refraining from repeating the old rumor that had there been a back door in the Alamo, there might not even *be* a Texas today. On the other hand, for the hospitality of these two, the price is right.

Not all Texas towns are this warm—at least on the part of those not yet of a completely ecumenical mind. When we stopped at a gas station in one small village, and I asked the attendant if he knew anything about the Catholic church up the street (which obviously had no resident pastor), the only answer I got was a grumbled "All I know is not many people would go there." As I recall, I told him I was a Catholic priest and I'd just love to go there, but this brought on no great burst of that vaunted southern courtesy either. Later on, in that same town I found out that the motel manageress wouldn't rent her rooms to a priest. Fortunately, the motel owner across the street was not only willing to take in this paying pariah, but also helped me locate the sacristan of the church so I could say Mass there the next morning. This latter tracking down entailed a chain of about a dozen phone calls, each one to someone who knew someone else who might know someone who knew how to get into the church. We finally made it.

Incidentally, since we were afraid that the first motel might be the only one available, the rest of the group, since it contained no priests, stayed there. And they were not too surprised when paying their bill, to find that the personable charmer who ran the establishment wanted to sell them the motel instead of only renting them rooms. "Business picks up a lot," she assured them, "at jubilee time"—whenever and whatever *that* was.

On that first trip, at least, I always went to a church to say Mass, and this was interesting and enjoyable, especially in Mexico where we always ran into some wonderful people and some unique churches. Subsequently though, I got permission to say Mass in any appropriate place, and so I began to do so in suitable rooms of the motels or hotels along the way. One big reason for this was the time-and-comfort element, since saying Mass in a church meant hunting up both church and pastor when we got into a town, and so blowing a few hours just when we were pretty dirty and tired and needed mainly a swim and some refreshment. More importantly, it meant getting a much later start the next morning, and we had found that the earlier we started and the less we had to hurry, the more pleasant the day's drive was likely to be.

But there's still another reason I prefer to say Mass somewhere in the motel or hotel—the fact that we often found more than our group at Mass there, some of the motel staff, for example, and sometimes others we had met. It was good too for Mexicans to see our groups' devotion to the Mass, since many in that country, so rich in its own religious values, have come to look on the United States as an atheistic, pagan, materialistic country without any spiritual or religious values of its own.

I've always realized that God loves fools and Jesuits, especially maybe when the two coalesce in one person, and on all these trips this convenient fact became more apparent than ever. The aged Chevy I drove on that first trip steamed along beautifully until its old battery, by this time pretty well homogenized with the motor, konked out completely. So there we were in a small village at the bottom of the Gulf of Mexico surrounded by jungle, and with no battery. Without much hope of anything I took a walk down one of the few streets of the town, and after about half a block and around a corner, ran into one of the biggest battery stores I've ever seen. I'm not sure whether it's still there, or had only appeared for the occasion.

Most non-visitors to Mexico know for certain that the Mexican tourist, especially one crazy enough to drive it, is going to have to rough it—either living in tents or campers, or running the risk of disease or at least some embarrassing discomfort. The truth is, though, that with a little planning and a modicum of experience, one encounters in Mexico the most comfortable lodgings, sometimes, in fact, even near-elegant—at least to one who had been used to living a charmed life in the old Regis faculty firetrap in Denver. We found, actually, not only good lodgings, but two elements often lacking in our country's inns—reasonable rates and a warm, sincere sense of hospitality. With the great influx of tourists into Mexico and their often obvious throwing around of more money than many Mexicans get their hands on in a lifetime, it's neither surprising nor unreasonable that prices are constantly going up along the more-traveled routes. But Mexican travel is still much less costly than that in the United States and almost always less impersonal.

It's impossible to mention all the individual motels and hotels visited in Mexico, but at least two of them stand out. When driving down from the midwest, we almost always stopped at Saltillo and at the Estrella Motel in that city. This is not the Biltmore or the Ritz, but it's certainly nice and comfortable with adequate, clean rooms and a very nice restaurant. The hospitality here is of the same sort that one meets throughout Mexico, and it usually comes as quite a surprise to the new tourist. One evening when the Hale family and I were having dinner here, Joe's wife, Hazel, in an unguarded moment, looked the other way long enough for me to steal her drink without her immediately missing it. But the waiter noticed it and in a moment was at her side with another drink "on the house." It's pretty hard to get ahead of people whose humor and hospitality come up with things like that, so suddenly and spontaneously. Besides, ever since my first stop at the Estrella, the owner, Señora Maria Concepión Gonzalez de R., has never charged me a cent, although on more than one occasion I've tried to pay. And the cost to my paying companions has always been most reasonable.

On our first trip, among many lesser blessings, we ran into one outstanding stroke of what most people call luck. I'd checked out the guide books, both American and Mexican, and had a pretty good idea of where we'd try to stop along the way and at what motels. Without really knowing anything about one town along the way, San Luis Potosi, we planned on one night there too. And *that* was a lucky break in itself, since not too many tourists used to stop there in those years, preferring to go on to Mexico City which is only about five hours driving time farther south. In checking out the motels in this city, I had come across one which sounded great in the *Guia,* or Mexican guide book:

> 25 rooms with bath. Minimum charge for single room $1.20 (15 pesos). Minimum charge for double room $2.00. European plan. Patio for receptions, dances and pilgrimages (tours). Pool. Gardens. Garage.

Now that sounds great—impossible to beat, in fact, especially at those prices. So when we got to the edge of town, we asked a young guy on a bicycle if he would tell us where this hotel was. He'd do more than that, he said, he'd take us there. And so he did, although by hindsight he did seem to have a rather amused look on his face. He took off on his bicycle, looking back occasionally and grinning, to see if we were keeping up. It may sound ridiculous to wonder if a car could keep up with a bicycle, but we clocked him at upwards of 35 m.p.h. through the streets. Finally we came to the motel and with something of an exaggerated grand gesture, he pointed to it. *"He aquí,"* Here it is!"

There it was all right, in all its splendor. It had absolutely everything that the guide book had described—more than that, in fact, since it had magnificent high-ceilinged rooms and a lovely old beauty. But it also had wall-to-wall cobwebs, lots of weeds, and everything that goes with a place that had become an authentic ancient ruin.

The young guy laughed and told us he'd now take us to a real motel, one, in fact, he happened to work for. Just then, however, I remembered that a missionary friend had once told me that when he was driving to British Honduras, he had once stayed at a motel called the Tuna, in this city, and so I asked our current "guide" about this one. He was a bit reluctant on the Tuna—understandably, since he worked for another hotel—but he took us there anyhow, only about two blocks away.

The Tuna has, in fact, become my favorite place in Mexico. It's a beautiful motel with lovely grounds and a fine swimming pool, the whole thing kept up immaculately. Guillermo Reyesgomez, the owner, has become a good friend, as has Javier Olivares, his manager. In fact, the entire motel staff is a group of friends, and coming to the Tuna is really like coming home, with all of them clearly happy to see this traveler and his friends once more. As at the Estrella, my bill at the Tuna has always been marked *cortesía*, which is a far more friendly and significant way of saying "on the house." Since that first seemingly accidental stop, we have always stayed at the Tuna—on the way down to Mexico City *and* on the way back, and usually for a few days instead of the usual one-night stands customary for us in other places en route. Once we hit the Tuna, our group invariably decides from the vast scope of their new experience that really nothing in the rest of Mexico could equal this, "so why don't we just stay here?" But Mexico City has its own charm, and so we always pull up the new roots and go on.

In Mexico City itself you don't find many motels, but there seem an infinite number and variety of hotels. In general, the AAA gives good advice on these and you can be pretty sure that if AAA recommends them, they're good. On the other hand, there are also plenty of good hotels that AAA doesn't list, for one reason or other, and we've found them perfectly satisfactory and comfortable, clean and enjoyable—and sometimes more fun. The ladies on our trips never fail to be charmed when elevator operators lead them out of an elevator at their floor, stand aside and bow. You can't buy that kind of courtesy in the United States no matter what you pay for a hotel room. And if I had a wife, I'd never spoil her by bringing her to Mexico either.

Everybody, especially one who has eaten a few cans of alleged tamales, likes to discuss Mexican food. And the one term you always hear in connection with it is "hot," or in more rarified cultural pockets "highly seasoned." The truth is, though, that Mexican food has to be as varied as any in the world. Some of it's hot all right—the tears I've shed into a bowl of unsuspicious seeming soup on occasion can vouch for that.

But the fact is that you can have food about as highly or lowly seasoned as you wish in Mexico, and in general, Mexican food in Mexico isn't nearly as hot as what is billed as Mexican food in the United States. It's still an excellent idea, though, to get into the Mexican diet gradually. For myself the best method seems to be to stick with fowl of some sort at first, usually chicken or turkey, and then start building up the temperature gradually. It may be, in fact, that the way Mexican cooks do fowl, especially turkey, can't be matched anywhere, and they can glamorize that gawky old bird beyond recognition. One should probably go a bit slow on the fruit at first too, even though the tendency, since it is so great, is to overdo it right away. I had come to love mangoes, for example, when in British Honduras, and so on my first trips to Mexico probably went at them a bit too enthusiastically at first, not realizing that I wasn't used to them any more. Subsequently I went slower.

Little Sheila Hale was barely saved from a horrible fate one evening in a Mexico City restaurant. She had ordered soup, and in bringing on the preliminaries, the waiter placed one plate which resembled soup near Sheila. Her mother kept urging her to "eat your soup," but she just continued to stare at it warily until her mother insisted. Father Ruiz' casual voice stopped her spoon in midair: "I wouldn't eat that if I were you." It was pure *chile salsa*— and we would have undoubtedly have had to call at least the Fire Department.

By the way, there is *chile* and chili, the former meaning only "pepper" to a Mexican, and the latter usually meaning nothing to him. Chili con carne is a Texan dish, and you just don't find it in Mexico.

Eating can sometimes be a novel experience.

As one would suspect, Mexico's seafood is fabulous. One night at Sanborn's Restaurant in Mexico City I had some shrimp which I thought the best I've ever eaten. But Luis Carrera's wife, Ana Elena, looked at it scornfully, pointing out that it was "not gulf shrimp." It still tasted like the best shrimp I'd ever had, until we had some gulf shrimp at Luis Carrera's house a couple of days later. Ana Elena had, of course, been right.

You also encounter some foods in Mexico which you don't ordinarily run into much at home—such as the octopus I finally tried and liked. Mexicans are adventurous people, in their food tastes as well as other ways, and so they like to try new things. Silvio Margain and his wonderful wife, Sarita, always order different meals in restaurants and then trade half way through the meal. But then sharing in every way is so habitual with these two people that this isn't surprising.

But if one is smart to get at the Mexican food gradually and not overdo it at first, he has to be still more careful with the water. He's not just asking for trouble but will need a first-class miracle to avoid it if he ever drinks unpurified water out of the tap. On the the other hand, there's no need to use this water, since all the restaurants and motels bring purified water to your room. The

193

trouble is that a tourist will sometimes forget, swallow some shower water, brush his teeth out of the tap, or drink part of the swimming pool. And away we go!

Not only is purified water readily available everywhere, but there are plenty of even better substitutes obtainable as well. Mexico puts out a variety of really great beers, my own preference being XXX (a dark beer made by Superior) and Bohemia (a good light beer). They also make some fine wines and champagnes. In the harder booze department Mexican bartenders come up with some marvelous drinks—tequila sours and margaritas and *berthes* and the brandy and rum drinks—which are not just cheaper than these same drinks in the United States, but essentially better. One of the young fellow travelers on our first trip started the custom of having a glass of Mexican champagne served to everyone on our last night in Mexico City—a reasonable and memorable drink. Actually, I have no way of comparing this with other champagnes, since it's the only one I've ever had, (I almost got to taste some once in St. Louis at the old *Queen's Work*, but somebody gave that bottle the last rites before it reached my end of the table.)

In general food, like most other things, is quite reasonable in Mexico. One can, of course, really blow a bundle on a meal if he goes to the right (or wrong) restaurant, but he needn't do that of course. Mexican restaurants are always fun, because you run into the same hospitality here that you see everywhere else in the country. Sanborn's is a nice place to eat, and you can get Mexican food there, but the Sanborn restaurants are not really Mexican. Even by American standards, they're usually crowded and rushed. One of my favorite restaurants was the Fonda Santa Anita, a small one off the beaten track rather than their larger restaurant, although this one too is great in *its* own way. Once when I was at this small restaurant, shortly after the Christmas season, I admired the Christmas decorations, still up, and the head waiter began to take some of them down and to give them to me. This too is a typical Mexican reaction. (Incidently, the thing billed as the Fonda Santa Anita at San Antonio's Hemisfair seemed to have had nothing in common with the Mexican restaurants but some of the superficial appearances and the name.)

But we not only brought tourists to Mexico—we also ran into them. When I first wandered through Mexico in 1943 on the way to British Honduras, there seemed to be innumerable tourists who easily qualified as "ugly Americans, " but fortunately one seldom encounters this breed in its raw form any more. When you do happen to run into one such, he's certainly recognizable, largely because you can *hear* him so well. I walked into the office at the Tuna once when my friend Javier Olivarez, the manager, was talking on the phone. I knew enough Spanish to know that he was simply doodling away some time with some girl on the other end of the line, but his expression was all business, and I soon dis‑ covered why, as he'd say a few words and then wink at me. On my side of the desk was a tourist who kept insisting that Javier drop his phone conversation immediately and change his travelers' checks for him. But Javier would only pause long enough to say, "Please, a very important business conversation," wink at me, and then continue to josh the other party. And he talked just as long as the tourist pushed. When the man finally became silent and waited, Javier immediately gave him his attention. The sad part is that the guy seemingly didn't learn what he should have from this.

Something ultimate, I think, in the tourist mentality was unwittingly illustrated for me not long ago by someone who said that he always tried to talk Spanish when he went to Mexico, "because otherwise they think they're as good as you are."

Fortunately, on our own trips we never had the misfortune of having this type of tourist along, and the few little misunder‑ standings we had were negligible. We all tried to talk Spanish as we went, not for any phony reasons, but out of respect for a Spanish-speaking people and for ourselves. And no matter how we groped about in the language, the Mexican was always courteous and gracious, appreciating our stumbling attempts, never—as I'm sure many an American in the States might have done were the situation reversed—laughing at our efforts. My own slaughtering of the Spanish language was, in fact, praised so sincerely and so often by the Mexicans as "beautiful Castillian" that I began to buy the politeness as truth, calling the attention of my teen-aged com‑ panions on that trip to the linguist who was their leader. That is, I boasted along this line until the night we were coming into Veracruz through that tropical sheet of water we call a driving rain. I stuck my head out the window to ask a gas-station attendant, "*Donde está el camino a Veracruz?*" And he answered with no change of expression, "I do not speak Eengleesh."

Don Baumgart picked up the language rather quickly, if some‑ what limitedly. Early on the trip he had learned the word for "please," and a little later, for "butter," respectively *por favor* and *mantequilla*. Not much to go on, perhaps, in lengthier conver‑

sations, but since Don has always believed in using to the full whatever gifts God has given him, we found ourselves with stacks of butter on the table at every restaurant we went into as he practiced his entire vocabulary incessantly. We were, in fact, fortunate that he hadn't learned the word for "cow" or something that would have been equally awkward to have around during dinner.

But perhaps our most dedicated linguist was Joe Hale, a Denver policeman at that time, who was never afraid to stick his neck out with his own attempts at Spanish. The nice part of Joe's efforts—apart from the courteous gesture of the effort itself—was that he always spoke with utter confidence, unhesitatingly, and, often enough, so that even those in the next state could hear and learn.

It's hard to remember all of Joe's best tries, but certainly one of his most effective was when a headwaiter placed a tequilla sour in front of him and Joe smiled at this tough-looking gentleman with complete confidence and said *"Gracias señorita."* He may have topped this later on when he wanted some coffee, asked me the word for it, and called for *café,* then turned to me and asked, "How do you say 'cream'?"

"Con crema," I told him, not bothering to add, "That means 'with cream.'"

The next thing I heard was Joe calling across the room to the waiter, "And bring some of that corn cream."

But if Joe was a fearless linguist, it was his wife, Hazel, who once used almost her entire Spanish vocabulary most effectively. I was stopped in the city for (1) running a red light, and (2) not having a front license plate—an item that no New Mexico cars have but all Mexican cars must have. My biggest mistake on this occasion was in talking Spanish to the policeman who, not quite logically, noted, "If you know our language, you should know our laws too."

By way of a footnote, I never made that mistake again when stopped by a policeman, but always responded with a puzzled look, a helpless shrug, and "I do not understand Spanish." Soon enough, I'd be waved on with his own helpless shrug, and *"Ay, turista."* I should explain that the big reason they kept stopping me when they saw no front license plate is that in Mexico City when there is a traffic offense, the policeman doesn't take your driver's license, but your car's license plate—which is, after all, a lot more effective and revealing loss than that of one's driver's license.

At any rate, on this occasion, I'm pretty sure I had to endure something of a bawling out. You're never sure in such a case, since as soon as a Mexican hears you use a few words of

Spanish, he presumes until proven otherwise that you know the whole language, even when spoken at incredibly high speed. Finally, this friendly fuzz let me off the hook and walked back to the Hale car, which Hazel was driving and which had also run the red light right behind me to avoid getting lost. I was horrified when Hazel, who probably hadn't heard and certainly hadn't understood a word up front, smiled her nicest smile and said happily, "*Gracias.*" For a moment the policeman hesitated, just not sure, then gestured helplessly and seemed to be mumbling something to himself (or perhaps praying) as he went back to his traffic post and waved us on.

Once you've been any distance into Mexico, you begin to get a little—and often more than a little—tired of the clichés many of your fellow countrymen use and re-use in teaching you something about Mexico and her people. Mexicans are superstitious, you're told, and backward; and the whole country is characterized by only great wealth and great poverty with nothing in between. Above all, many a busy or even not so busy North American likes to think of Mexico as the land of *mañana,* by which he means that it's a lazy country with lazy people.

It shouldn't take more than one short visit to Mexico City, by a normal person at least, to dispel the *mañana* idea—at least in the form most citizens of the United States interpret it. Relatively few of us, for example, leave our homes at the crack of dawn, work until dark cutting cane or at some such undemanding job, and come home only when there just isn't enough light to work by—and this, day after day after day. Not many of us, either, can surpass the energy of the Mexican businessman or professional. On the other hand, not many Mexicans seem to work up a set of ulcers through their jobs either. It seems to me that two things may help to account for this disgraceful rejection of the U.S. businessman's badge of success: their warm spirit of hospitality which allows them genuinely to relax in the company of friends or acquaintances without worrying about all the work that's piling up, and the *true* spirit of *mañana,* which only means that if it's impossible to do something today, you aren't going to get it done by worrying about it either. And so the Mexican American, unlike the U.S. American who tends to stew and worry over the things he can't do today anyhow (especially when he's still trying to get today's job done), is much more at peace. Certainly one reason for this is because, besides having a certain amount of trust in his own ability and yet with the humility to acknowledge his own limitations, the Mexican also has the good sense and faith to have a lot of trust in God, who takes care of *mañana* until it becomes today, and pitches in even then. In general too, the Mexican understands that material things simply aren't worth ulcers anyhow. And so when he relaxes, he really does—and takes his time at dinner, for example.

The Mexican works hard all day—and a long day it is, usually uninterrupted by that fabled subject of U.S. conversation, the *siesta*—and finally, when dinner time comes, usually around 9 or 9:30 P.M., he relaxes. He doesn't want anyone rushing him at that time, whether he's at home or in a restaurant. Or sometimes, his "siesta" *will* be his dinner time at about 2 P.M., and then he'll take only a light supper after work about 9:30.

This unhurrying spirit around a Mexican restaurant seems one of the hardest things for us in the States to get used to. My friend Joe Hale, for example, being a Denver cop, had had to work very hard all his life to make a living, taking on not a few extra jobs to make ends meet. It wasn't surprising, then, that when we went to Mexico, Joe was a bit uptight at first, and so in the first Mexican restaurant we tried, in Chihuahua, he found the leisurely service just about intolerable. Even when I asked him, "But Joe, where are you rushing off to?" he didn't fully relax, although about a week later he was taking it easy with the best of us experts in the art of relaxation.

I should add another newsworthy item about Joe and Chihuahua. At the time of this trip the police scandals in Denver were going strong, and about eighty Denver policemen were spending their newly found spare time in the pen at Canyon City, where they had been assigned for their efficiency in knocking over supermarket safes and similar extracurriculars. Like the other honest cops in Denver (the overwhelming majority of course), Joe had taken quite a beating, and of course it was hard to resist asking him why one of Denver's most honest cops was heading for Mexico.

Now in some parts of Mexico, because of the still all too well remembered persecution days, you find church tabernacles seemingly secured by combination safes, and in Chihuahua, confronted with such a safe, I couldn't seem to get the tabernacle open at Communion time. So I called up my server, Joe's son Vernon, and told him, "You'd better call your dad—we need a pro on this one." Joe wanted to know after Mass what had been so funny, but we didn't hurry to tell him. This was partly because earlier he had thought it hilarious when he'd asked the parish priest if he was a Jesuit and the man had replied, with great originality, "No, *señor*, I am a Catholic." Very funny.

198

On a later trip one of my unrelated namesakes, the eminent Father John McGloin, S.J., of the University of San Francisco, was my only companion. Now John is an historian and a darned good one at that, so he read a lot of history aloud to me during our trip, thus managing to miss many of the sights along the way. When we got to Queretero, John was most anxious to see if some historical personage or other was buried there, and so he asked the Franciscan brother on the premises of the church where we said Mass about this.

"Ah, *sí,*" the brother assured John. "He is here."

"Could I see his grave?" John persisted, with that thoroughness unique to the Ph.D.

Como no? Brother answered with a shrug, as he led us to a hole in the ground about thirty feet deep. Down the ladder we went and watched as the brother opened the bottom drawer of what seemed to be an ordinary old wooden dresser. "He is in here," he told us, pointing to the drawer. He might have been at that, since there seemed to be about six assorted skeletons in the drawer.

The only other small-group-of-two trip which I made was with one John Erger out of Denver, currently a young bachelor and always a great friend. One January I wound up a retreat in San Antonio at about 3 P.M., and by 6 P.M. John and I were eating dinner in Nueva Laredo, en route to Mexico City. That whole trip was magnificent—especially perhaps because of a reunion with one Juan Valero, a great friend who put us up for a time. On the way home we stopped in San Antonio and once more encountered that unique hospitality of Fathers Larry Stuebben and John Mullally. We had come a far piece that day, and so we were dirty, not to mention tired and hungry and thirsty. As was their pious custom, the two padres had an adequate assortment of booze available, and they encouraged John, who drinks very seldom and very little, to have a martini as he showered. When John emerged from the shower, refreshed materially and spiritually within and without, all he said was, "You Texans really know how to take a shower"—a statement, I feel, that ought to go down in history with "Remember the Alamo."

Teen-agers always add so much to such trips as ours that I've become reluctant to go without some of them along. But if a youngster's good spirits are obvious, it's equally apparent how he feels when he gets a bit under the weather. On that first trip we did quite well for the most part, but almost everyone did feel the gentle touch of Montezuma's Revenge, or *turista* as Mexicans refer to the occupational hazard—which is, more bluntly and technically, a form of dysentery. One of the most heart-rending pictures I've ever seen was Jim Doyle in a back corner of the car, glumly strumming a banjo he had bought in Villa Hermosa and didn't know how to play, a faraway look in his eye as he no doubt dreamed of giving a banjo concert at Carnegie Hall while enjoying the best of good health and vitality. Later on Jim (no doubt experiencing both the exhilaration and the fatigue which follows one's recovery from M.R.), when we arrived at a motel in Chetumal, walked right into the swimming pool, clothes, shoes and all—and then spent the next half hour looking for his glasses at the bottom of the pool.

When you talk to many U.S. citizens about Mexico, you get that knowing "I've been there" of the closed mind, the clear implications being that they want no more of it since they know it's a dump. And invariably, you'll find that if they've been there at all, they've been only as far as some border town and they're judging not just the entire big country by these holes but the entire populace as well. Even here, I suspect that the stories are often pepped up substantially, as so many male types usually start off with how often they were propositioned in the streets of these towns. Quite frankly, I doubt if even the propositioners found the narrators of these exciting luscious tales quite *that* consistently attractive.

To judge Mexico by the border towns and to judge their people by those one encounters there, would be about the same as judging the entire United States by those same border towns, on our side of the Rio Grande, and judging our entire populace by those one runs into there. And if the Mexican side of the border town is sometimes at least partially crummy, it's most often the ugly U.S. American with his ugly U.S. American dollar which has made it that way.

The border towns I've seen to date (Matamoros, Nueva Laredo, Piedras Negras, Juarez, Mexicali, and Tijuana) are definitely *not* the gold coast of either the United States or Mexico. And I couldn't swear that these towns are 100 percent free of the sad ancient human tragedy of prostitution, perhaps not, in fact, any more free of it than Chicago or Omaha or New York or even Decatur, Illinois. And there are other cities here in the North with which they couldn't even come close to competing.

On the other hand despite some of their ugliness, even these border towns have some beautiful homes and motels and restaurants and many, many completely lovely people. But of course one has to take the trouble to look for them instead of noticing only the pitiful moral slum he's been told to expect, and searching for story material which will be interesting to the boys in the bar back home.

Everyone going to Mexico for the first time seems to think he's leaving civilization for an Amazon-like jungle or Sahara-like desert or a combination of both. One year, in fact, two teen-aged boys who went along with us were looking forward to the trip with some eagerness but also with some mixture of reluctance because, as they put it, it meant no more dates for three weeks. When we got to the home at which these brave kids were to be billeted, however, the first thing they noticed—and no one could help but notice—were the three young girls of the family all dressed up and waiting to go out to a party. Now for certain obvious reasons I wouldn't dare to say in print that Mexican girls and women are the loveliest in that part of the world I've seen to date. But lovely they are, and they have an inner vivacious-ness and spontaneity and non-sophistication which add im-measurably to this whole impression of beauty.

And so my teen-aged friends simply stared—or gaped—and wondered where their education had fallen short. The girls asked me almost immediately if the boys might accompany them to the party that night. I told them, regretfully, that it would have been perfectly all right with me but that the boys had told me they weren't going to have any dates for three weeks, so they obviously didn't want to go. The guys didn't know a lot of Spanish at that time (as one of them put it proudly, he was a straight "D" student in Spanish), but they knew enough to realize when they were being sold out. They did go to that party, of course—and to many others.

New travelers to Mexico may know little or nothing of the place or the people, but this never seems to dim their certainty that the only capable professional people—like mechanics, for instance, and doctors—have to be living in the United States. At the first Mexican service station we stopped at on one trip, when the attendant started to lift the hood, the car owner stopped him. Something went wrong under the hood later on anyhow, but he still wouldn't allow it to be checked. It certainly looked at least suspicious when his car always had to be started by opening the hood and jumping the motor with a key, and the Mexicans in the vicinity always watched this ritual with an amused look. But still no Mexican mechanic was allowed to examine the hallowed interior of this heap. I still wonder what he was hiding in there besides a simple short circuit.

My own experience with Mexican mechanics has, in fact, been much happier than with U.S. dealers—although, to be fair,

I've had to deal much oftener with the latter. I remember my four trips to a California dealer to get a set of defective lifters replaced, and I never met a Mexican mechanic yet who was *that* slow to catch on to what was wrong the first time through the fourth, even though I told him what it was, with accelerating emphasis each time. On the other hand, I also remember having the clutch on our car go out in Laredo on one occasion just as we pulled into customs on the way home; going to the U.S. dealer's there and getting no satisfaction; and finally encountering a Mexican mechanic who made me the part I needed for about $1.50.

I remember something else about that occasion too. It was about 99 degrees in the shade in Laredo that day, and since we were pushing to get to San Antonio, I ran the mile or so to the car dealer's while my companion, Father John McGloin, religiously guarded the car and said his breviary—in the shade. Then I ran back a mile or so to a small shop, where I was lucky enough to encounter the Mexican mechanic who did the job for us. After all this when we were seemingly set to go, Father John, piously closing his breviary, remarked that he was quite warm and hungry and suggested we have a sandwich and beer before driving on to face the ordeal of the Alamo. So we got a couple of sandwiches and beers to go and took off, my temperature at as high a level as my patience was low. And as we pulled out of that shady spot, I asked John if he would please pour me a beer while I drove—which he cheerfully did, missing the dixie cup however as the car jolted, and pouring most of the beer in my lap. And yet, despite minor mishaps like this, it really was a great trip—and, for many other reasons, unforgettable.

Maybe the most ingenuous and comprehensive indirect description of the *a priori* United States knowledge of Mexicans came from one of my fellow travelers, who on our arrival in Mexico City looked around in wonder and exclaimed in all sincerity, "Why Father, they don't even *look* like Mexicans."

Even in the border towns there is so much to notice if only one bothers to look. We saw the mud and dust of Piedras Negras when we went through customs there—that was all too obvious. But there was something much more important to see there too, if one would only look. In the dirty little customs shed, the desk and chairs heavy with dust (quite unavoidably so because of the constant traffic on the roads which then—and usually for that matter—were being repaired), a short gray-haired official was idly and routinely reading my visa when he came across the word *sacerdote,* "priest."

Immediately he picked up a feather duster which must have still boasted all of four or five scraggly feathers, dusted off

202

part of a chair, and asked me politely and with tremendous, innate dignity to be seated. That single gesture had more courtliness and affection in it, amid the dust and rubble and dirt, than any number of bows or curtsies in a regal court could ever have had. It is, after all, easy to seem regal and polite in a nice clean handsomely accoutered and polished palace. But here it was the deeper courtesy of the mind and heart which transfigured the surroundings. And that's the way it ought to be—with courtesy enriching and beautifying one's surroundings, instead of having one's surroundings shame him into some sort of hypocritical courtesy.

I've invariably seen an amusing, ironical contradiction in some of my fellow travelers' strenuous objections to tipping Mexican customs men, scorning it as that dirty word, "bribery." And yet, they'll tip any and every waiter in the United States exorbitantly (the percentage depending on who the witnesses are) when he hasn't really done anything to earn the tip at all—and this, often enough, because they're afraid through human respect not to. I have no hesitation at all in paying a few *pesos* to the people around Mexican customs, not as any bribe, but for the help they can usually give—especially in the timesaving category. When we were traveling with seven people—including four bags and all their baggage—in one station wagon, it would at the very least have been inconvenient and time-consuming to have to unload all the stuff and carry it to the customs house for inspection. And the few *pesos* we contributed to the cause of avoiding this—I think it must have come to a total of perhaps 48 cents U.S.—probably saved us, and them, over an hour. Besides as far as I know, there wasn't a single hot item in all that luggage.

Most Mexican customs men like to get U.S. cigarettes, and what's so terrible about that? If they want to get cancer, why not go American? The joke is that they probably trade them off anyhow, since once one gets used to the much stronger Mexican cigarettes, he hasn't any taste for the U.S. brands.

There are a few little tricks one should be aware of for driving in Mexico—just as there are in any place in the world, the United States and our cities included. I have driven at night on the Mexican highways, but I prefer not to. For one thing, the cattle like to get on the roads and stretch out at night, and it can be startling suddenly to come on a sleeping four-legged jackass unless you're ready for it. Even in the daytime, although one needn't worry much about other traffic, he does have to keep an eye out for the burros and cattle who know very well that the road is primarily theirs and that cars are only tolerated. On our first trip as four cows strolled leisurely across the road in front of us while we slowed up and waited more or less patiently, Brian Kimmel, I think it was, casually remarked, "Well, I guess *that* bridge game's over."

Trucks in Mexico don't usually dim their lights when they see you coming at them, but they do turn them out. In fact, this is supposed to be something of a signal if you're approaching a bridge or a narrow stretch of road, since the first one to douse his lights has the right of way across the bridge. It's nice to know this, when all of a sudden the lights coming at you disappear, especially if you want to survive.

But if highway driving in the country of Mexico has its little idiosyncrasies and minor perils, city driving is something else again— with Mexico City combining all possible driving phenomena into one great mass of what seems, at first anyhow, almost movement for its own sake. One's first driving experience in this city could at least make him think about a possible heart attack, but once you get used to it, it becomes a sort of fun game—or so at any rate it has always seemed to me. (After all, I had driven a bus in St. Louis, Missouri, for three years, and that prepares its rare survivor for almost anything anywhere.) Mexican drivers go fast; no one can dispute that. And they usually seem to stop fast too, or perhaps more accurately, they have to. But you soon find out that they're *good* drivers, and that one reason they have as few accidents as they do (especially considering the state of some of the equipment they're using) is that they really enjoy driving and so they give their entire attention to it—except, of course, while they're waiting for a signal to change, at which time they invariably catch up on their reading.

Mexican drivers are generally calm and philosophical about the sometime poor state of their equipment. Father Ruiz and I once drove up behind a taxicab in the city, a little car with the motor in the back; the only relatively unusual thing about this one being that it was on fire. As we pulled up alongside, I pointed out to the driver in my flawless Spanish that his cab was on fire. With no hint of any surprise or shock and with no particular haste either, he smiled as he thanked us and got out, pulled an old, blackened throw rug out of the back seat, and proceeded to beat out the fire. Then he threw his fire extinguisher into the back seat, got back in, waved in gratitude and drove off. Apparently this happened often, but it was really nothing to get excited about, since he was always ready for it and had that rug along.

But if it's fun to drive in Mexico City, it's an uninhibited riot to ride those roller coasters off their tracks, the cabs and buses. At least one class of bus seems always to have a suspicious number of bumps on it, and when *you're* driving, you soon learn to use this sort of bus, as Mexican drivers always do, to run interference for you across intersections.

The one impression you seem to get from Mexico City traffic is that at a given signal everyone in the eastern part of the city heads for the west and everyone in the west goes east. Then at night they all come back again. It's lovely to watch the traffic at night, especially perhaps along Reforma Street, and it's about as much fun trying to walk, run, and dodge your way across the street at that time as it would be to find yourself the only human being in a ring full of playful bulls.

Even when you try to avoid the travelogue tag, there are little impressions of Mexico you can't bypass: the unique market at San Luis Potosi, its streets made of tile; Cholula, the town of 365 churches, now off the beaten tourist track and so a great place to visit and to buy things Mexican; the beautiful town of Cordoba with its unassuming hospitality, and the lovely Catholic Church there literally filled with fresh flowers every day; Tamazunchale where I talked to the lady manager in halting Spanish for about ten minutes, only to hear her turn to a helper and tell him in perfect English to show me to my room; the professional guides who sometimes get a bit obnoxious in pressing their services on you; the bubbling village of San Juan del Rio which I must have driven through twenty times and which always has great crowds of people and emptying buses, streamers and mariachis—all there for the current seemingly perpetual fiesta. But after you get through listing all the scattered impressions you can, you always come back to the real reason for Mexico's charm and attractiveness— her people.

You can't get more than a few feet into Mexico before you realize that *something* is different. As you drive along the road which may not have much on either side of it by way of homes or, during some seasons, even much vegetation, you notice little touches of beauty for its own sake added here and there—trees which have clearly been planted, cacti arranged in some unique sort of way, flowers everywhere and brightly painted beehives. You'll see rock fences winding gracefully up the slopes and over the tops of hills, some of them running for miles. You'll see liter- ally hundreds of shrines and churches, large and small, everywhere; and if you get close enough you'll discover that they're always filled with fresh flowers beautifully and prodigally arranged, as if in an attempt to shower all of what one has on God's shrine to make up for what one has not. And in the cities you find similar touches of original, creative beauty in the buildings, homes, and churches. Many an architect of the United States has told me of his jealousy of the Mexican architect's freer hand in putting into a building some of the lovely things he wants to. Mexicans don't just build practically, but creatively. The beautiful hotel Camino Real in Mexico City, designed by my good friend Richard Legoretta, is a fine example of this.

Non-travelers to Mexico and those who have gotten all the way to some border or other are invariably eloquent about the terrible poverty to be found there. And poverty there is—sometimes, in fact, almost as appalling as one can find in the United States if he looks in the right direction. Not too long ago, I was listening to a lady, an artistic type, who was bewailing the poverty in Mexico and its contrast with the great wealth there. Presumably she read a lot, since she'd never been there. I mentioned somewhat hesitantly, of course, that we have a little scattered poverty in our own country too. And her answer jolted me out of any further hesitancy. "Yes, but here at least you don't have to *look* at it." It's my considered opinion, to coin a phrase, that this may well be one of the things wrong with our country—there are so many things we feel we don't have to look at.

But if there's beauty in the Mexican countryside, some of it man-arranged if not man-made, there's often a breathtaking beauty in Mexican people, men and women. Much of it is external. Much of it comes from within, from a vivaciousness, a love of life, a spontaneity and ready smile and warmth and friendliness that can make the otherwise externally ordinary person quite beautiful, and can make the already beautiful person darn near incredible. Without going into too much detail, I remember visiting one home where only one of many teen-aged daughters was home at the time to show us around. Her name was Paz and she was about fourteen at the time, but with the lovliness and poise and utterly unconscious and happy charm of a mature woman, without the sophistication or affectation of so many mature women. There was no shyness about her nor any brashness either, no phony esoteric vocabulary of teendom she felt impelled to assume, no fads to flaunt to call attention to herself. She was simply lovely and personable and bubbling with life, and sharing her love of life and of people with us, strangers as we were supposed to be and as we would have felt almost anywhere else. I personally am utterly sick of the cliche, "a beautiful person," but if there was ever a truly beautiful person in the non-cliche sense, it was Paz.

Nor is Paz any isolated phenomenon, but only one example necessarily chosen from many such. When we visited Father Wasson's orphanage in Cuernavaca, a boy about eleven or twelve years old showed us around with all the politeness and poise and none of the pretensions of so many adults, his eyes laughing and his smile contagious. But then Father Wasson's orphanage is the happiest place I've ever visited in my life anyhow.

One thing, I'm sure, which contributes to the amazing combination of youth and maturity you encounter in young and old alike in Mexico is a sense of family, which for the most part we civilized U.S. citizens have lost or even destroyed—the very sad part being that we haven't as yet even realized our suicidal crime. When you first encounter Mexican children in flocks, you begin to wonder why it is that they're so well-behaved and why they seem to show a maturity, in fact, beyond their years. Without any long philosophizing, I think I can explain this somewhat by another example, which I hope the reader will look on as not only actual but symbolic. Once while we were resting up from a hard day of relaxing at the side of the pool at the Tuna Motel, a baby, barely able to walk, came tacking across the lawn all by himself. He must have sat down pretty hard, at least five or six times as he moved towards the swimming pool, and each time he picked himself up, clearly with a philosophical attitude, and ambled on again. No one else showed. But as soon as the little guy got within range of the pool, adults seemed to come out from all over the place to protect him. When there had been no serious risk involved, he'd been allowed to go it alone. But when danger showed up, so did help. And you could write a whole philosophy of education and child rearing on that one.

Somehow or other, this affectionate sense of family seems to reach out to embrace you too, so that you find yourself treated not as only some guest, but as a friend, as a member of the family. And when the Mexican tells you *Mi casa es su casa*, he isn't just echoing a polite cliché, much as some people will say mechanically, "You must come and see us again sometime." He means it. Periodically I hear from a Mexican friend who once offered me a home in which to write—and he keeps asking when I'm going to take him up on his offer. Somehow, I was most deeply touched by the hospitality of a wonderful priest in Villa Hermosa, Father Samuel Ginore, S.J., and his two assistants at that time, Fathers Ruiz and Sanchez. It was obvious that I was given the best room in the rectory to stay in—a relatively large room, complete with mosquito net over the bed. This was, in fact, the only furniture in the room except for a little clanking electric fan of ancient vintage which I'm sure was the only one in the house too. One other detail which characterized that room was a shower in the corner—no kidding, a shower right in the bedroom. Handy.

When it comes to courtesy and generosity and thoughtfulness, nothing can possibly approach the excellence in all these lines of Father Luis Ruiz, S.J., in Mexico City. This busy man knocked himself out for us on every trip, even though he had lots of things to do elsewhere, with all the jobs that are his. But Father Ruiz is too close a friend for me to go on praising him.

When you try to characterize the Mexican people, one quality seems to stand out over all others: a love for life, a humor (not to be confused with that sometimes contrived thing, "a sense of humor") which has nothing to do with wealth or poverty, nor—as so much of our professional humor has—with putting down others by one's own attempted witticisms.

If you want to see this love of life in action, go to the Ballet Folklorico in Mexico City sometime, where both cast and audience are so appreciative of what the other is trying to say and where the show invariably ends with the cast applauding the audience. On one such visit to the Ballet I went with José Luis Perez and his lovely wife, Sophie. As usual, we struck up a conversation with the people around us, who in this case happened to include a man who pointed out his daughter to us in the chorus of the Ballet. He also mentioned that he came to every performance. Naturally, José Luis found out the daughter's name and at each encore called out "*Viva Maria Elena*" so loudly that the girl had to glance, in some embarrassment but mostly with the same good humor, towards the general direction of the shouts and her father. At the end of the performance, when we were—again as was usual—shaking hands all around, I told her father that his daughter was the most beautiful girl on the stage, and of course, I could mean it, because that she was, despite the close competition. He smiled and cried a little at the same time, no more proud of her than might have been expected of the man with the loveliest daughter in sight.

My friend José Luis, by the way, has about the same attitude at the *jai alai* game as at the Ballet. And *jai alai*, in a somewhat different way, was just as much fun—especially with him along.

At the Jesuit house I usually stayed at in Mexico City, I was going out one day when a little old Jesuit came in the door, pushing a motorcycle which he promptly rolled into a convenient closet, tipping his checkered cap to me as he made for the stairs. If you can picture a little man nearing eighty years old, wearing a checkered cap and swerving in and out of Mexico City traffic on a motorcycle, and realize besides that he's not considered unusual, then you're getting some idea of the spirit of Mexico.

But if a phenomenon like this is taken for granted and so goes relatively unnoticed by anyone but a visitor, it's the sense of humor that's at the very root of the Mexican personality—not as I've noted just a *sense* of humor, but a living humor. Often enough the Mexican has the instinctive good sense to laugh at a thing instead

208

Mexico is an octogenarian on a motorcycle.

of crying about it—which is one of the great, indispensable secrets of living life instead of enduring it, one that our own present generation of minstrels will apparently never discover, preoccupied as they are with self-pity. You don't find the Mexican, at least, even when he's as far as one can get from being a millionaire, wailing, "Yes I'm lonely, wanna die, if I ain't dead already." He lives.

The Mexican finds humor in life itself, whether he's living in poverty or wealth. He'd really dig that *Fiddler on the Roof*. He has what might be described as a pixyish sense of humor, one that bores into the ironies of life and people and yet doesn't seem to hurt. Many tourists, at least on their first visit to the Mexican markets, are surprised at the practice of haggling for everything, and many of them make the mistake, when they do get into some of the spirit of the thing, of taking the whole thing far too seriously. Since everyone knows that you're supposed to argue over price, it can't be dead serious; and once you realize this, it's a lot of friendly fun. Even with their limited Spanish, our teen-agers have always gotten into the spirit of the market and had a ball, probably because teen-agers are ordinarily able to spot a humorous situation before most adults can. At least they have this ability innately, until they get sentimentalized by the over-serious and constant dronings of self-pity usually surrounding them.

One of the young guys in our group had been arguing with a girl in the market one day about the price of a hammock, and finally, summoning about all the Spanish he had and maybe a bit more, he said, "At that price, I suppose you throw in a tree with it?" The girl thought this was hilarious enough to knock off a few more *pesos*, and in context, it wasn't all corn at that.

Once we stopped at a leather goods dealer's and went through some of the usual arguing, although not so much as we would have in the markets since it was obvious that the prices were already unbelievably low. At the end of our buying spree, such as it was, the family who owned the store invited us to have coffee and snacks with them, which we did. Then they accompanied us to the car, telling us to come again—clearly not just as customers, but as friends. You just don't hardly run into that sort of thing at the May Company or Sears or even Gimbel's.

You encounter this feeling for humor in what seem some very unlikely places. Father Ruiz was once stopped for running a red light, and he mentioned to the policeman that he didn't think the light had been red at all, but *"solamente un poco tinto,"* "just a little pink." So then they got into an argument about just *how* pink or red the light might have been.

There's a Woolworth store on Reforma in Mexico City. (Oldsters will remember that we used to call this store a dime store, a dime being a small coin that used to be negotiable but which is only useful now in some of the less fancy rest rooms and for buying the cheaper newspapers.) Along one side of this store is an export counter where one can buy anything he wishes and have it sent out as a gift, duty free. I bought a couple of those ugly little Scandinavian trolls there one day. As the salesgirl was filling out the order blank and chatting along cheerfully, I told her that the one worry I had was that these trolls seemed to resemble some friends of mine but I couldn't remember who they were and so I was afraid of insulting them. She thought this was extremely funny, stopped filling out the order, went over and huddled with a couple of other salespeople, and pretty soon we had a whole discussion group going in the store. You'll run into an attitude like this in the U.S. ten-cent store about as often as you'll find something selling for ten cents.

One night we came out of Sanborn's Restaurant to find the streets flooded up over the curbs by a sudden downpour. I watched in fascination while Father Ruiz calmly hopped onto the front step of a bus until it had brought him, nice and dry, across the street, where he jumped off and waved at me to catch the next bus across.

I was lucky enough to be able to watch the 1968 Olympic Games from Mexico City on a Mexican TV channel. Occasionally

I'd switch to a channel from the States, but it just wasn't the same. There wasn't the same spirit of fun and humor that the Mexican announcers put into the thing, nor did the Mexican broadcast constantly remind us—and constantly show portraits to prove it—that this was Chris Chumley doing us the favor of bringing us this broadcast. In a singular, unique way, the original spirit of the Olympic Games *is,* I think, the spirit, the humor of Mexico. As someone remarked when the first Mexican won a gold medal in 1968, "This is a great stadium, and well-built. But I'm not sure it can survive one more Mexican victory." This is the spirit, or should be, of the Games *and* of Mexico—try to win, sure, but it *is* a game, so treat it as such. And so in a sense, is life—the main difference being that *this* game can always be won, even when you seem to be losing.

The artistry you see at every turn of a corner in Mexico is startling at first, until again you realize that you're in the presence of a people with centuries, and not just a few years, of culture behind them. Perhaps the only other time I've sensed this existence of centuries of background and culture and politeness came when I was driving into Yosemite with Sam, my German Shepherd, then only a gangly pup. The ranger, an Indian, looked at her in admiration and remarked that with the centuries of breeding and instinct behind her she would certainly enjoy the lavish natural beauty of Yosemite. Only one who, himself, had centuries of this sense of natural beauty behind him could have said it as well, or perhaps would have said it at all.

The pyramids throughout Mexico, too, help to give you this same sense of awe in the centuries of culture—in fact, they even did this for me, a slob who never dreamed he'd have the slightest interest in "ruins." Of course, it helped to go to Teotihuacan with Silvio Margain, who either knew every stone in the pyramids there or could think fast enough to make it sound like he did.

Then there was the glassblowing factory, which looked at first like only some old garage where a bunch of mechanics were having a barbecue. But then as you watched the incredible skill of these men and the triumphant laugh with which they greeted their successful efforts, you began to realize you were seeing artists of no small stature at work. And why shouldn't an artist laugh when he's accomplished something, instead of crying crocodile tears?

The anthropological museum in Mexico City may well be the greatest thing of its kind in the world. If you run, you can get through it in several hours. The historical museum too is a most cleverly conceived setup with its circular, winding display halls, so that without ever turning a corner you suddenly find yourself out of the building, only on a lower level than the one on which you entered. And as you go, in some awe of the artistry of the displays and the carved and ceramic figures, a tape recorder gives you the history illustrated before you.

I don't know much about art, but I do know I'm hooked on the wood carvings to be found in Mexico, especially the work done by José Pinal. This man's carvings show not just a great creative artistry but the Mexican humor and humanity as well. He has, for example, a Last Supper carving, with most of the features of most of the faces rather vague. If you count heads, you'll find that there are twelve men at the table, erect, and at the very end, another poor guy who has slipped off the end and is nearing the floor, right after a money bag. And what better way could one possibly depict Judas?

My favorite single carving by Pinal is one I call the rocker madonna, which shows Mary on a rocker holding the Child above her head. Quite clearly, she's enjoying this moment of mother-hood as well she must have in reality.

But the piece of Pinal's work which shows the Mexican attitude best is, I think, a chess set, each piece a beauty and the entire set a satire on pompousness. The king and queen are *campesinos*, "poor country people." The bishop is a smiling, slightly portly poor Franciscan. The castle, or rook, is a church. All the pawns are peons, with their sombreroed heads bowed to their knees in *siesta*. And the payoff of the whole theme is the knight—a cocky-looking little burro.

No one can, however, talk about the culture and general outlook of the Mexican people without understanding something about what is, perhaps, the major element beneath it—their faith. On this subject as on so many others, one can find countless U.S. authorities, both among those who have been to a border town (or perhaps even on a conducted tour of part of Mexico) and those who haven't been even that far but who just *know* things without seeing them at firsthand. Perhaps the predominant bit of knowledge among these intuitive sages is that the Mexican faith is really only a form of superstition.

Now there *are*, of course, some practices in a Mexican's exercise of his faith which aren't exactly the same as our customs. There are even a few practices taken over from paganism. And yet, the incense we burn in this unsuperstitious country of ours, and many of the church feasts themselves began, in some respects— their dates, for example—in paganism. For the superficial visitor to Mexico to call some outer expression of faith only superstition is the rashest of judgments and is, in fact, judging another by one's own attitude—which is never safe.

One thing's for sure: our own first lady of atheism wouldn't like Mexico. She'd be tickled pink—or maybe even red—by the fact that public officials don't feel, very often at least, that they can always show their faith publicly (and that's too long and complicated a story to go into here). She'd be aghast, however, at their "hypocrisy," as they do practice their faith, in fact, much the way one Nicodemus did, and especially as they permit such vast public displays of religion everywhere in the nation, on street and highway, in town and country.

Everywhere you look in Mexico you'll see shrines and churches. The Mexican *zocalo*, or "town square," is supposed to be built so that the houses of government and finance and the house of God surround the square. Many *zocalos*, including the lovely Mexico City one, are indeed built this way with the old cathedral obvious in the whole picture of things.

If there is, however, a single church or shrine or both which seems at the very heart of the Mexican's faith, it's the shrine of Guadalupe in the northern sector of Mexico City. One can't really describe those things closest to him, and so all I can say is that this shrine has come to mean nearly as much to me as it does to the Mexican. On each trip I've said Mass at the main altar here and have never failed to be overwhelmed by the experience. For one thing, as you look up above the old altar during, say, the elevation of the Mass, there's that picture—which couldn't possibly exist, whose origin is inexplicable, which went through fire and battles and hundreds of years in the open with people touching and kissing it, which is, most appropriately, on a rough serape on which no one could possibly paint. And yet, with all these impossibilities, there it is, in all its quiet, eloquent beauty. Outside the shrine are words, in Latin, "I have not done this for any other nation," which is simply another way of saying that the dear Lord appeals to different peoples in different ways. One couldn't possibly imagine a more effective way of getting at these warm, family-minded Mexicans than through the Mother of God represented here at Guadalupe.

I once tried to explain Guadalupe to a practical atheist—by which I understand a person who *lives* as though there were no God and who at least pretends, no matter what his secret misgivings, that there is none. This man said that he couldn't, above all, understand why some Mexicans will go on their knees along the concrete front walk up to the shrine itself. Now it's hard to explain *anything* concerning faith to an alleged atheist, and I'm not sure I explained this either. But I tried to point out that the Mexican with his warmth and humanity, when he says "I love God," really means "I *love* God" with mind *and* heart; and not just, as many Americans in the States would understand, "I have an intellectual conviction that I ought to have a high regard for *ipsum esse subsistens*," a philosophical term for God. The further fact is that when you love someone with your emotions as well as with your mind, you have to try to show it somehow and you search and scrape around, sometimes desperately, for ways to do so. The gift a man gives his wife doesn't really mean too much if he only had his secretary call up and order it or if it was no sacrifice at all to him to get it. O'Henry's lovely story *The Gift of the Magi* shows how love and sacrifice go together. So when the Mexican says "I love God," he looks around for ways to prove it and to show it. And so often enough, he goes on his knees up to the shrine at Guadalupe.

But if one of a different temperament imagines that this external show of love is all there is to the Mexican's religion, he's making an enormous mistake, since the externals are only the natural manifestation of what's within a warm people. I once watched a little man, maybe thirty years old, immaculate in a white shirt and pants, a machete at his side, in the upper shrine at Guadalupe, as he pointed out to the near infant in his arms the meaning of the pictures on the walls. (The child, by the way, was sporting some nice shoes, although her father was barefoot— another clue to the Mexican sense of values.) It occurred to me that the know-it-all tourist, pausing long enough from his constant picture taking to tell this man that he was only being superstitious might not always be answered with an intellectual argument, but answered he would be.

Or perhaps the cynical tourist could watch, as we did, some sixteen thousand men walking along the highway, most of them barefoot, on an eight-day walk, or pilgrimage, to this same shrine of Guadalupe, in a driving rain much of the way. Just how one could explain this tough voluntary act of faith as superstition or how he would explain away his other, oft-voiced conviction that "the men never go to Church in Mexico," I don't know. But then, that's his problem not mine.

I also remember another touching scene of courtesy that this same mythical tourist wouldn't understand even if he did happen to notice it. A lady, holding her little child, was going on her knees towards the shrine, when another lady, a stranger to her, came along and placed her own shawl on the ground before the woman as she went, all the way up to the shrine. Think about that enough, and you discover a courtesy and faith on the part of both women that's hard to explain or emulate. It might, in fact, have taken as much humility and courtesy to accept the shawl as to offer it—and this is another bit of insight the Mexican seems born with.

But maybe with *our* peculiar temperament we can best understand the depths to which the Mexican's faith can go by some contact with the *M.F.C.*, *Mensaje de la Familia Christiana*, which is most easily translated as the Christian Family Movement and which I've mentioned elsewhere in this book.

To summarize the Mexican *M.F.C.*, I would say it's the practical working out of the high ideals of the sodality. The members bought a home in Mexico City which they've converted into a headquarters. Among other features this home had a nice swimming pool in the middle of which, on a pedestal, they placed a statue of Our Lady. This gesture alone, I think, somehow symbolizes the whole movement—this dedication of a fun thing, like a swimming pool, to something and someone essentially more important.

On one occasion I said Mass for about a hundred members of the *M.F.C.* and their families on the veranda of Ricardo Legoretta's ranch house. Since I said the Mass in my Baron Munchausen Spanish, there were a few unavoidable chuckles, but I simply told them they were excommunicated and went on (come to think of it, maybe that *wasn't* what I said). It went along pretty well anyhow, although I had so many people helping me to say that Mass, pointing to the place in the Spanish missal and so on, that I'm not sure just who was the celebrant.

But maybe I remember most easily and most often the time I said Mass at the side altar of our Jesuit Church on Enrico Martinez Street, while the Mass for the *niños* was going on at the main altar. I remember their singing and their wholehearted participation in the Mass with the help of a great fatherly priest, a real child in the right sense himself.

Some years back a crew of psychiatrists analyzed an entire Mexican village, a peasant village. Among other findings that would startle the a priori expert on Mexico, this group of experts came to this conclusion (*Atlantic Monthly,* March 1964):

> ... What these villagers express in their concept of love is the knowledge that love is not a bewitchment or a sexual attraction, but a deeply rooted trait of character, a respect for someone or an interest that is always different, depending on the person or object loved, but always essentially the same.

A young farmer, 27 years old, in this village, put it this way:

> There are many kinds of love, for a plant, for the
> land. First, there is the love of God. Second, for a
> father or mother. Love is to love a woman, the love
> that one's sons grow and develop. One has many
> loves.

Not bad for a peasant, huh? Almost as good as Antoine St. Exupéry's "To love is not to look at each other—to love is to look in the same direction."

I have gone on here at some length about Mexico, and maybe occasionally I've seemed to put down my own countrymen in comparison with the Mexican. The truth is, though, that while one likes to travel, to visit Mexico, one also loves to come home. There *is* no greater country and there are no greater people than the majority of United States Americans. But I think the Mexican has something, among his other gifts, that we once had and lost or are losing fast, something that a majority of our people still have but are often afraid to show—a simplicity or non-sophistication, with a simple love of God. And if the Mexican could sometimes use a touch of our logic and intellectuality in his faith, we could certainly use some of his genuine warm love and humor. We could, in a word, learn really to mean it when we say we love God, and this would suggest that we'd show that love a lot more genuinely in the way God has pointed out to us—in the love of our neighbor who is really everyone.

CHAPTER NINE

Priests are people— or ought to be

Lots of people can tell you that Christ turned water into wine at Cana, but not so many of them seem to know what ◈ ◈ He was doing there in the first place. They seem to find something irreverent in the very idea that He went to blasts like this wedding party—preferring, against all the facts, to imagine Him as a non-partygoer, a sanctimonious teetotaler, a social zombie drifting in and out of places instead of walking, mysterious and, above all, unsmiling. But the truth is that He *was* a partygoer and a warm personality, who was never accused by His contemporaries of being a teetotaler. And He must have had to laugh out loud with and at His twelve hearty but often bungling friends more than once.

And what about this poor man's mediator, this allegedly other Christ, the priest?

Priests are like anyone else, even though they're not like everyone else, and the word "mediator" describes that sameness and difference as well as any word could. The priest is supposed to be a mediator between God and men, and so he has to be aiming himself and helping others to aim at God. But he's still a man, so he doesn't stand on top of some celestial ladder and pull people up to his lofty level so much as put an arm around them and help them to move upwards, while he climbs too—as slowly and painfully, for the most part, as those he tries to help. And despite his own sometime slowness or stumbling or discouragement or even reluctance, it's his job always to keep climbing instead of giving up and sliding back down with the rest of the cowards.

And so the first requisite for a priest has to be a sense of balance. He can't be a real mediator at all if he takes his eyes off God nor if he mistakenly tries to dispense with his essential human personality. And since you don't usually encounter a balanced human personality without some balanced recreation, clearly the priest, like everybody else, needs some recreation and relaxation in his life. After all, we're told on the best authority that even Wisdom played around a bit ". . .then was I beside him. . .playing before him all the while, playing on the surface of his earth and I found delight in the sons of men." (Proverbs 8:30-1) But one big difference between the priest and any other man is that he's not just on call when relaxing, but he's really on duty then as well. I'm no less a priest on a plane than in the chapel, no less a priest in a restaurant than in the pulpit. A fireman isn't exactly working at his job when he plays handball (I'd rather some of them did), but a priest, absorbed in the game as he might be, is still a priest, even here.

It's the priest's job, not just to preach, but to *show* how one can achieve one's real purpose, which is God, not by neglecting material things and all life's enjoyment, but by *using* them. And the priest who can't manage this is not just failing in his job, but in segregating his priesthood from the other areas of life, he's giving a phony impression of what life, and his priesthood are all about.

Once the priest himself digs this basic fact, he needn't worry about falling into either extreme—the hermit or the compulsive social animal. The active priest (I'm not talking, of course, about the very valid, very special and very wonderful vocation of the contemplative) is just as poorly balanced when he deserves to be called a recluse as when he's playfully referred to as just one of the boys. In either case, he *is* a boy, an immature boy at that. Both extreme types, in fact, seem particularly susceptible to the "marrying priest" syndrome, one because he's finally found his dry bread diet too tasteless and the other because he'd prefer to give his full attention to the frosting on the cake.

And if a priest's job is always and everywhere, so is his identity. The priest or nun who imagines that he or she is more effective when in disguise has simply never lived as a real priest or nun—nor, perhaps, even a real human being.

Much of the time a priest's social life will take place outside his own home, which is fine. If, however, a priest feels that he can relax *only* with non-priests, it seems like something might be missing—in him, in his fellow priests, or maybe even in some of those non-priests. I've always considered it one of the great blessings of being a Jesuit that we could enjoy each other's company and relax together. And now that I look back on community life rather than living it consistently, I'm most grateful for the precious gift of those days with my fellow Jesuits.

I do think it somewhat unfortunate, though, that lay people are only rarely invited to visit priests and religious in the latter's own home. I understand perfectly well that community life has its obligations and so it has some need for privacy. But there ought to be times when people would be welcomed in a priest's home, not just for business, but socially. Of course, you can't expect them, at first at least, to come bubbling over with good spirits into an institution, a place with as homey a name as *rectory* or *presbytery* or *seminary*.

We were lucky in Minneapolis to live in a place called very simply Jesuit Residence. Certainly that wasn't any *typical* Jesuit community house, even though we did have seven or eight Jesuits in residence, the number usually varying with the dinner menu. But this was a *warm* house, and we got along pretty well. Since it was more a home than a house, it didn't have the usual religious house's "parlor" for visitors—complete with small table, one straight chair for the inmate, and another chair only a bit less straight, clearly for the visitor. In ordinary communities you'll find this parlor, often so marked lest anyone miss it, next to three or four other similar parlors, all furnished with similar gay abandon and all with a glass window, for looking out or in—I'm not sure which.

But Minneapolis was nothing like that, and so people came to see us usually for counseling of some sort or other, but often enough too, just out of friendship (which should not, of course, be divorced from counseling or ecumenism or similar relationships). Prior to Christmas one year, I seemed for the first time to notice our large picture window, about seven or eight feet square, overlooking Lake Harriet. Something seemed to snap, and suddenly this window seemed the ideal site for a nativity scene. That first attempt at artistry began in a delicate sort of way, with heavy tarpaper silhouettes and every kind of glue imaginable, even gasket glue. Naturally, this turned into something of an aesthetic mess, particularly since, whenever the sun hit the thermopane and the heat inside the room did its part, the Holy Family tended to slide around a bit. The next year, although I had never painted anything in my life, I decided to paint the scene instead in tempera. And so I discovered a hidden artistic talent—not that I could paint just anything, of course, but I could, copying slavishly, paint a nativity scene on that picture window. And so, had I been a lay artist, I could have earned enough to eat, once a year. I painted that window every Christmas Eve from then on, heady with the knowledge that I had added another hyphen to my title, a veritable clerical Grandma Moses.

In our last couple of years in Minneapolis, we combined this mammoth artistic project with a sort of informal open house and invited our friends and neighbors in to watch the artist at work. While I got out the old smock and beret and paints and set to work, Brother Lee McNamee mixed the eggnog, as only he could, with the same artistic lack of restraint so obvious, at least to the true art critic, in my painting. I believe about a hundred people must have stopped by on those Christmas Eves, although I'm not sure whether it was the eggnog or the other art work they were primarily interested in.

Not every Jesuit house has the advantage of this sort of informality and warmth. And yet I'm convinced that all that's lacking, sometimes at least, is the effort and initiative on someone's part to start something of a fire. One drawback to growing

The skilled artist can always draw a crowd.

up in a large religious community is the tendency to sit back and wait for something to be done rather than to do it oneself. And so you can find yourself in the deadly rut of a "recreation room" where the most exciting thing to do is catch an old Perry Mason show or wait for the omnipresent community lector to finish his second lap through the comic section. Of course sometimes too, there may be a superior who is anti-social—at least towards *you*. In general though, superiors are only too happy to have people in the community who will go out of their way to homey up the place, and smart and thoughtful superiors will see to it too that the members of their community won't be forced to go out of the house if they want to find any real companionship or conviviality. Many communities now offer a sort of weekly cocktail party for this purpose, but I remember one community where we were never, not once, offered a drink—officially, that is. In fact, I once went to a dentist in that town who was very fond of our then superior, noting that said superior had given him a bottle of Scotch for

222

Christmas. At least that explained where some of the stuff had gone to. He might at least have traded it for a little laughing gas.

Like everything else, booze is one of those creatures the good Lord puts before us—to use or abuse. I sincerely wish that the day were past when anyone would lift an eyebrow at a priest's taking a drink, but I'm sure it's not, since there will always be those with the uncanny charism of spotting something wrong long before it ever happens. I've known some pretty snobbish teetotalers and some charming drinkers, some obnoxious drunks and some magnificent alcoholic teetotalers. But of course balance is to be found, as usual, somewhere near the middle. I've always gotten a wry sort of charge, in fact, out of those religious bodies, clearly much more moral than Christ, who "celebrate the eucharist" with grape juice instead of wine. One presumes, of course, that he can avoid the plight of one priest-teacher who in all innocence got one too many, and his students called another priest to give him the last sacraments, thinking the poor happy guy was dying.

It seemed to me some years back that I managed to get on several planes in a row where the stewardess, coming around to ask the passengers if they'd like a cocktail, simply passed me by without asking. Now the fact is that I not only enjoy a cocktail when flying—even in a plane—but it seems to help smooth out the flight too. Or maybe it's only that the new jets are smoother than the old DC-3's I used to throw my saddle on. So I would gently and patiently remind the stewardess at the earliest graceful opportunity that this saintly-looking priest-passenger would also like a cocktail. On one flight, however, I suddenly had had enough of this being passed up when the orders for cocktails were being taken. When the stewardess asked the two super-adult ladies next to me if they'd like a pre-dinner cocktail, they not only said no but they seemed to fire the word out with some indignation. And then instead of asking this modest but expectant cleric near the window if he would like a cocktail, off the stewardess went. I looked at the two ladies in some astonishment and remarked, "She didn't ask me if *I'd* like a drink."

And one of them looked down through her bifocals at me and said righteously, "Yes, we were pretty insulted that she asked *us*."

That was the straw they talk about, and so I whistled the stewardess back and asked her to bring me a couple of martinis. I still feel that those two ladies would have liked a drink too, but they felt that in public, or perhaps in public with a priest nearby, they ought to pretend not to like the stuff. And that kind of hypocrisy, as well as all other kinds, we can do without for a lot longer.

In general, I enjoy a drink when the time is right, when it's part of the proceedings, or—in my present circumstances—when it helps to relax for an hour before dinner and think about the next book or story or article. I'm still a peasant, however, in the finer points of booze drinking, although I hope not quite to the degree I once was. Some years ago I went to Galatoire's in New Orleans with a great good friend, Father Dan O'Callaghan, S.J. As was his custom, Dan—who was really just a Brooklyn boy gone cultural—studied the wine menu with clearly great know-how and seriousness, until I asked him to the horror of both himself and the hovering waiter if we could, since this was an occasion, have some real special wine, like maybe Virginia Dare.

Then there was the lesson I'd had to learn about testing the wine when it's brought. John and Lois Doyle and I had gone to a restaurant somewhere outside Chicago; quite a plant, in fact, boasting wall-to-wall headwaiters—no braves, only chiefs. When I ordered wine—rather grandly as I thought, since I had, after all, once dined at Galatoire's—the waiter brought it, poured a tiny bit in my glass while I wasn't really looking, and stepped back. Without thinking about it much, I told him to put some more in the glass and fill the other glasses too, since we all wanted some and not in little sips. John Doyle informed me I was supposed to taste it first, however, and so another lesson in the social graces was learned. I've since been tempted, just to see what would happen, to make a face and spit the stuff out, but then I've never really wanted to go that far with a practical joke either.

It is my unconsidered opinion too that all other things being equal, it's not just permissible but even important for a priest to take a drink on occasion. At a Hollywood cocktail party I got involved in what turned out to be a rather vital conversation which had its abrupt beginning in my turning around suddenly and dipping my elbow into a lady's large old-fashioned glass. Her glance at my own drink—after a preliminary startled look at the black elbow and white collar—started a conversation which might otherwise never have been.

One year, as is my sometime custom, I gave up booze for Lent. (Lent for the uninitiated, is that time of year when Christians used to make some special sacrifices in honor of Christ's fast and cruci- fixion in their behalf. Now it's only a time bounded by Mardi Gras in New Orleans and the Easter celebrations in Fort Lauderdale.) One night during that then holy season I went to dinner with quite a number of people, with my friend Bob Swassing of Council Bluffs the host. While all the others were having a pre-dinner drink I stuck heroically and unnoticeably with cola or some such vile concoction. Later in the evening Bob said to me in effect: "You klunk. I put you across from that guy because he's never met a priest before, and he thinks they're all stiff-necked puritan types. So what do you do? You have a bottle of pop." I've been quite careful to avoid similar errors since and to make my mistakes on the side of the spirits.

When Tennessee Williams became a Catholic, the lead in a newspaper article about his conversion went like this:

> American playwright Tennessee Williams says he is "very happy" to have been converted to Roman Catholicism by the Jesuits because "Jesuits drink, laugh, and love life."

Leads being what they are, I'm sure there was a bit more to it than that, but the idea does give food—or drink—for thought. I feel that if we're to be honest in this day of medical honesty, it would be much better to see ministers pictured with a martini (which has no apparent or even suspected connection with cancer) in their hand rather than with a pipe—which is so inevitably present that it seems an official professional badge.

It's often hard to figure out the genesis of some people's idea of a priest. I've been invited to places—as often Catholic as not—where hosts seemed to think that the atmosphere had to be staged for the sake of a priest-visitor. And the one variation of this that I find particularly revolting is the contriving of an "intellectual evening." I once visited the home of some great people with a delightful bunch of kids—all of whom were bundled off to bed on my arrival. This left me, to my dismay, surrounded with college professors and their wives, with double monologues (as opposed to conversation) going on all over the place. There was a general attitude of screwing up one's eyes, thinking profoundly and with obvious pain, and coming out with some such probing question as, "Now can we really say that two and two are four?" followed by the considered, but hesitant and cautious answer from some courageous soul in this land of the giants, "I think perhaps we can."

On this occasion there wasn't really any genuinely intellectual conversation at all, but only a lot of old bromides dragged out with an air of profundity plus the introductory tag, "Let us now have an intellectual conversation"—which, to my mind, is the best way there is to prevent one. We had every cliché at large: the raised finger, the eyes squinting with the torture of intellectual effort, or the beard—maybe, above all, the beard—which precludes the necessity of acting well enough to show pain. We had expressions like: "I don't think you get my point . . . ." "Let's put it this way . . . ."

"Wait, let me develop this further . . . ." "I don't know—I'm just throwing out the question to stimulate discussion."

Fortunately I don't often get caught in such traps, since most of my friends are genuine, unpretending people without much affectation and therefore honest enough to be themselves. If they're terribly bright, they know their shortcomings all too well; and if they're just normally bright, they rejoice in this gift of God's without spraying it all over you. And if they're not in the same league with intellectual super-stars, their charm and insight put them in a still higher league.

Like everyone else, priests need the relaxation and the change that some social life can give. They need sometimes to get away from the phone and the doorbell. And there's another thing they need which not enough of them, as far as I can see, get—the release that regular, vigorous excercise can bring, the violence of that excercise depending, of course, on how much one can take and dish out.

For my own part, I've always felt the need for some fairly violent excercise and so have stuck with indoor handball throughout the past several years. It's the quickest way to get a lot of excercise and it's cheaper than breaking up furniture, a thing I tended to do sometimes in my younger days when there was no handball court available or I couldn't get at it in time.

Exercise is the prime reason for handball in my life, but it's not the only reason. There's really no better brainwasher than this game, since all one cares about for that hour or so is trying to play the game well and to knock off whoever happens to be in the vicinity at the time. I haven't the time, the money, or the desire for golf. And I gave up my favorite game, tennis, when I entered the Society of Jesus, for two reasons: (1) We weren't able then to play often enough to keep the sharpness one needs at that game, and (2) it was considered charitable to play with anyone who came along. I decided very soon that there wasn't really any charity involved in my playing with anyone that came along—on the contrary. So I quit the game. Recently I've ventured onto the tennis court again, and I find I still like the game, after this thirty-odd years' moratorium, about as much as ever. Father Dan Lord laid off booze, I'm told, for a number of years, and when he finally had a cocktail after all that time, he remarked, "It tastes just as good as it used to." And that's the way I feel about tennis—except that one's skill at this game is a bit more likely to lose its edge in the course of thirty years than is one's ability to drink.

It was, in fact, impossible ultimately to resist the tennis in California, with the courts so close and the year-round tennis

226

weather. Besides, the competition there was better—or at least more interesting—than it was when I was a novice. Sometimes, for example, I got to play with three Jesuit brothers: Brothers Charlie Onarato, Ted Rohrer, and Artie Lee the inscrutable Oriental—certainly the most awesome threesome of the tennis world. The mere sight of these formidable foes moving onto the courts could strike sheer terror into the hearts of the Montecito-Santa Barbara tennis greats.

A professional psychologist would undoubtedly have a field day observing handball and the varied personalities of its players. There's the guy who has to prove something, who may not be any great player but is grim and determined to the point of becoming so obnoxious that you can't work up any real desire to beat him. There's the old pro who "used to beat everybody." There's the joker who talks more than he plays—a risky attitude, since that ball will easily fit into even the normal mouth. There's the doubles player who keeps hitting the ball with his weak left just as you're winding up with your good right, or the doubles partner who allows you a shot only when he can't possibly get to it. There's the gazelle type who's everywhere at once, especially in the way. Most interesting of all is the type—fairly common in many sports, but really obvious in handball—who is always ailing

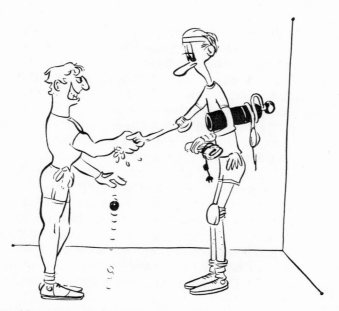

One seldom encounters a healthy handball player, at least before the game starts.

when he comes on the court. His back aches. His leg hurts. His elbow is out. He may, in fact, be bandaged from head to toe—knee bandage, elbow bandage, ankle brace; and then, of course, the sweat band and the eye protector and all that. The only thing is that once a game starts, this human wreck seems to make a miraculous and complete recovery, even though when he misses a right-handed shot, he may grasp his sore left elbow and moan heartrendingly. I once brought a fellow Jesuit to play handball at the YMCA with me—about a half-hour drive then. By the time we got on the court, I had heard so much about his current ailments that I was sobbing gently and feeling that beating him would have been about like slugging one's invalid mother. Oddly enough, his ailments didn't seem to affect his game much.

The best handball opponents are the good players who are still not convinced that this is a way of life rather than a game, and so although they play it for all it's worth, never giving an inch, the sportsmanship is clear too. When Father Walter Harris, S.J., and I first took up the game again after a long layoff for both of us, Father Walt tore a muscle near his biceps, and he was moaning about this when I asked him if he was going to keep on playing or just continue to indulge in self-pity. He growled out his choice of the former, and when I ran into a wall not too much later and smashed a toe, as I was writhing on the floor, over he came, looked down at me deadpan, and simply remarked, "I got that one."

Although handball has been great fun and recreation and exercise for me, it's had a most important by-product too—maybe more important, in fact, than the game itself—and that's the number of great friends it has given me.

Most of my handball has been in athletic clubs, with the YMCA the Santa Barbara arena. So far the clubs seem far more fun, although all quite different from one another. The Minneapolis Athletic Club pretty well spoils you because you don't realize how great, and even unique, it is until you visit the others. It's undoubtedly not fair to judge other clubs by only brief visits, but I've simply never encountered anything approaching the friendliness and enjoyment and camaraderie to be found at the M.A.C. (I've often suspected that there may be a similar spirit in the St. Paul Athletic Club, but since I lived in Minneapolis, I'm not allowed to mention it.) The Club itself, the running of the handball department, the restaurants and food and drink concessions, the sheer friendliness and courtesy of everyone involved—these just don't come any better than at the M.A.C. And if this sounds like a commercial, it's not.

The spirit of a city probably has a lot to do with the spirit of a club—at least that would pretty well explain the friendliness of, say, the Minneapolis Athletic Club and the Fresno YMCA. The latter place didn't let their courtesy interfere with their handball, however, when one Stan Mendes and I took on a couple of Fresno natives named George Takaoka and Frank Zuniga in doubles. We got beaten 21-0, before putting our whole good game together and coming back strong in the second game—to get nosed out only 21-2. Unfortunately, these two then chickened out and split up on us just when we were gaining on them.

I've mentioned that a priest is a priest twenty-four hours a day, and this holds for his social life as well as everything else, for his handball as well as for his prayer. Those who beat me seem to take a certain delight in beating a priest, and those whom I beat seem to be temporarily a little proud that a priest could do this to them. There was, in fact, a tremendous rapport at the M.A.C. where I was known as The Great White Father, and where the sometime exclamations after a bad shot were explained often enough by "He taught me all I know." One big drawback to being a priest on the handball court is that the poor shots you make are all yours, but any good one you manage is always explained away as "Somebody up there likes him," or from the more creative: "I can't beat 'em both."

But since a priest is still a priest when he's visiting a home or in a restaurant or on a handball court, quite naturally he's often called on to act like one as well. *Counseling* is really too fancy a word for the job of listening, at least in my case. But call it what you will, a priest is asked to listen and sometimes to counsel, as much through his social or athletic life as through other channels—perhaps, in fact, even more. Often enough, in fact, it's been only a chance acquaintance who has started to talk to me about something important to him—a parking attendant, or a clerk or a waiter or waitress or even someone coming over from across the room in a restaurant, someone who had been kibitzing from the gallery of a handball court, someone nearby on a bus or a train or a plane. Wherever the need has arisen, I've always been grateful to the dear Lord that I've been there when needed, when nobody more capable was available. There was that Christmas in Minneapolis when the mother-in-law of a good handball friend was dying and he couldn't find any other priest (it was around Christmas time when parish priests are at their busiest) to see her. So he had to settle for me. Had there been no priest on the handball court, this young guy—not a Catholic although his mother-in-law was—wouldn't have known where to turn. She lived only a week, and I was indeed glad I'd been around, as her heroism did more for me than I could do—except in the sacraments, of course—for her.

We used to joke a bit about being sitting ducks in Minneapolis, since there was a prominent sign over the door, "Jesuit Residence," and we were also designated as such in the phone book. One young fellow called our house simply because he "wanted to talk to a Jesuit." And many a person, only casually wandering by, turned in sometimes in near desperation to look for help. I have, in fact, many a friend today who only chanced on our house and dropped in to say, "hello."

We also used to get an occasional call—usually from phone solicitors—asking to speak with Mrs. Jesuit. It was sometimes hard to make clear that mythical lady's immediate whereabouts, at least politely.

You could probably have drawn a pretty fair cross section of humanity from those who dropped in. There was the young guy who had always felt he ought to be a Catholic and who found this the first concrete chance he'd had to talk with a priest. One evening I had a hard time keeping a straight face while a young art student, all of twenty years old, explained to me, along with his own current problem, some of the facts of life—giving me all kinds of valuable new information like "You know, some of those artists aren't always morally perfect" and "I don't want you to be shocked now, but. . . . " But maybe his crowning contribution to my education, something those who knew me would have delighted in hearing, was the admonition that I didn't have to just sit there like a kindly adviser, but should rather tell him when he said something wrong. I've never had the reputation for that degree of restraint anyhow, but he didn't know that—at least not for about two minutes. He discovered rather abruptly that he needn't have warned me in quite this way.

One of my friends who did tremendous work in the slum areas of the twin cities used to argue sometimes that only inner city work was worthwhile, since only the inhabitants of this inner city really needed help badly. And yet those who came to see us in Minneapolis were from all neighborhoods and all strata of society, and they *all* came because they needed help, sometimes desperately. Speaking hypothetically and fictionally, I can say that the young guy who comes home on Friday afternoon and finds a note with a fifty-dollar bill, "Dad and I gone for the weekend. Have fun. Mother," has to have somewhere to turn after a few such thoughtful gestures. Then there is the kid whose parents spend several months vacationing out of the country or in some remote part of it, while he stays home alone. The boy whose father sends him a prostitute on his seventeenth birthday might just need someone to talk with too, maybe even as much as someone whose father has neither the money nor the parental thoughtfulness for this sort of birthday gift.

Counseling is mostly listening, with sometimes a helpful idea offered from one's cross section of experience and from the enlightenment prayer and study might have given, or from—even though rarely—such a clear burst of inspiration that it's frightening. But there's more—a thing called involvement, in its genuine sense. The dedicated doctor certainly, try as he will to avoid it, will sometimes get involved with his patients, or *sympathetic* (in the literal sense of that term) suffering with them. The priest-counselor, too, will often—despite his efforts at objectivity, whatever that is—become so involved. He learns early, in fact, not to be too surprised when the Lord takes him up on his carelessly thrown out and completely confident offer to suffer in someone's place, and he learns too something about the mysterious suffering of the agony in the garden.

All of which is by way of saying that while such human sensitivity makes one's efforts at counseling far more significant and effective, it's not the best writing aid in the world. It isn't only that counseling takes time, often lots of it, but that the counselor-writer finds it nearly impossible to shake off its memory—at least in a hurry—and get his mind back in the writing groove. It's pretty hard, for example, to listen to seeming tragedy for an hour and then immediately try to write something supposedly comic. This becomes all the tougher when you have a genuine regard for the one you've been trying to help—which is, I find, just about always the case sooner or later.

But apart from the time and distraction elements, counseling is of course worth it all, not just for the helpful release at least that it gives the counseled, but as a great purifier, humiliator and strengthener of the counselor as well. It's pretty hard to cultivate one's own self-pity in the face of the great problems and great courage of those who come for advice. In fact, often enough you feel like getting on your knees to them.

Because of the route my own Jesuit life has gone, the counseling I've been involved in has had something of a universal nature, and I've had to try at least to be of some help to a pretty representative cross section of people. I've listened to young and old, male and female, married, unmarried and between marriages, down and out or up and in, Catholic and mostly probably non-Catholic. And with this experience behind and around me, I find some of the things said about counseling by some of our alleged authorities on the subject amusing to ridiculous to utterly revolting.

Every now and then, some eminent theologian, psychologist, and all around expert (very often a columnist in some small but "significant" paper) comes out with the certitude that no priest who is unmarried can possibly counsel those who are in the happy or occasionally unhappy state of matrimony. This self-taught, self-constituted pundit is usually seconded by all kinds of experts, with the priest who has already decided to hang it up often foremost among them. Sometimes this thesis is put in a much more homey way, one perhaps better fitted to the spirit of the whole idea. "Until you've slept with a person, you really don't know him," the expert says, with the consequent implication that you can't counsel him until then either. That would, of course, narrow down the counseling potentialities of even a married theologian-columnist—unless, of course, his or her dedication to the task really took over.

It has always seemed to me that the person who honestly (or dishonestly for that matter) believes that only the married can counsel the married would, logically, always have to seek out a doctor with his—or more often her—own current ailment, even for that occupational hazard of the married, pregnancy. What doctor could ever counsel about or prescribe for cancer or tuberculosis, then, except one who had had the disease? It seems to me, in fact, that sometimes the doctor who has not had a particular disease could be an even better judge of what should be counseled and prescribed because, for one thing, of an objectivity of judgment that might be lacking in those who had been so afflicted. Dr. Aidan Mullett, the wonderful doctor who treated me for tuberculosis, had no sympathy for my periodic urgings that I be allowed to bust out of that hospital pretty soon. His usual answer was, "You haven't even been here a year yet," a statement which came easily from a man who had, like himself, spent twelve years in bed with the disease. And I can imagine the married priest—especially after the myth of his zeal has been exploded along with a few other honeymoon illusions—telling one of his counselees, "You think *you've* got problems. Well now hear this. . . . "

It's quite true, of course, that there are people, some priests included, who really shouldn't counsel anyone, as there might

232

just be a doctor or two somewhere on a still unheard-of planet who should not prescribe for anyone's illness. It's even possible that some of those who are certain that no unmarried priest should counsel the married, might not themselves always be the perfect counselors, even married as they are. But all things being equal, the priest who has the ability (which includes humanity and detached, or unselfish, love) and works at it, should be able to counsel anyone, married or unmarried, teen or adult, even those who are of another race than his own—which brings up another logical enigma to the like-must-counsel-like blooper.

When it comes to marriage, if a priest out of his experience isn't aware of an entire cross section of hangups which help marriages to break up as well as those things which usually help to keep them going, and isn't able to counsel accordingly, he either can't have been listening much or he's a 14-karat idiot. The average married couple, in fact, has no idea of what such a cross section is like, since they ordinarily deal (and this subjectively) only with their own marriage and its seemingly unique problems. Of course, she may have an in-depth knowledge of the neighbor's marriages from information passed over the back fence or during the morning or afternoon coffee breaks. But the priest's experience knows no such limitations, and he has seen (or shortly will if he's just starting out and if, of course, he lives as a priest instead of only a strolling minstrel) every reason for heartbreak in the book and out of it. Somewhere along the way he will have seen a few remedies and solutions which have actually worked and may work again, if adapted to the unique situation which each and every case presents. He should, in fact, have a greater sense of this uniqueness than the married, since the latter tend to relate every marriage and its problems to their own.

Now admittedly, this bit about only the married counseling the married is a straw man. But it still has to be mentioned because the over-serious people who get all their theology and advice from literary and journalistic experts seem an unsmiling lot, unable to see ridiculousness where it exists. Or perhaps it's more a question of having an idea of what one wants to believe and then looking around for substantiation.

But if a priest's social life includes counseling, it also involves another sort of activity, which is usually called by the rather stuffy name of ecumenism. Just as my own social life as a priest has led to quite a lot of counseling, formal and informal, so it has necessarily, especially the last eight years or so, been an ecumenical life. I'd venture to say that nine out of ten of my friends in this time (exclusively of Jesuits who are presumably Catholic most of the time and most of the way) have been non-Catholics. (I do wish I could think of a better term, but they've not all been Protestants by any means either, so we'll stick with that one, and my non-Catholic friends can counter, when they write their next books, by calling me a non-Protestant.)

I am, in fact, convinced that the greatest, most effective ecumenism is friendship, and I feel too that the same axiom could be applied to racial as well as religious ecumenism. At least it *is* true that when we're racially or religiously *un*ecumenical, it's often because we're out of touch with one another. True, there will always be those of other races and other religions (just as there are of our own race or religion) whom we're not going to like right off, sometimes because they're postnatal drips *in se*, at other times because we're too much alike to think much of each other. But there are bound to be plenty of people too with whom we can be warm friends, and so, ecumenical. Unfortunately, the dwellers on the lunatic fringes of ecumenism have exaggerated the whole beautiful concept to the point where one might find a Catholic confessing, "I met a Protestant I didn't like," while he'd have no qualms about disliking his fellow Catholics on occasion.

In my own Jesuit life there has been a constant unassuming and unaffected two-way involvement in ecumenism, because my friends and I have invariably taken our common beliefs *and* our differences for granted, along with our friendship. And *that's* the most important item in ecumenism, that we understand what it is and what it is not—maybe especially what it's not. It seems to me too that one who, in his friendships, is constantly saying to himself, "I am now practicing ecumenism," is likely to be as phony as one who says, "Look at me—I am now practicing heroic charity."

Basically, I feel that real ecumenism is a sharing of the riches of faith God has given us, and sharing does not mean preaching or forcing one's beliefs on others so much as living them, happily and proudly, yet matter-of-factly and without self-consciousness. To speak of ecumenism as a compromise with truth is ridiculous, because not even a simple friendship can survive without truth. To bypass one of my own beliefs for a phony thing I call ecumenism is much closer to dishonesty than it is to ecumenism. If in fact the price of my friendship with someone is a compromise with the truths I believe, or a pretended belief in something I really don't believe, then there can be neither friendship nor ecumenism involved. I look forward eagerly to some of our genuine ecumenical advances—the day, for example, when I can not only share the Mass with my non-Catholic friends but when those who believe as I do in Christ's real Presence in the Eucharist can also receive Him in

Holy Communion. But I believe too that this decision is not up to me as an individual, and I'd be betraying their friendship as well as our respective beliefs if I were to go against my convictions here.

Essentially, I would say ecumenism has much to do with charity, where one's regard and friendship for another (which is, in turn, ultimately based on his love and friendship for God and which, in turn, enhances his love for God) is such that he can rejoice in their common beliefs and respect their differences. And since I didn't do anything to merit my faith in the first place, but it's completely and utterly a gift I could never deserve, there's humility involved in ecumenism also.

Friendship has played an enormous role in my Jesuit life. When *I'll Die Laughing!* was written, I had just finished the Jesuit course of study. At that time many, probably most, of at least my close friends were Jesuits, and I felt a tremendous warmth towards them. This same warmth persists, but it's much different in practice today, mainly because I haven't lived in any large Jesuit communities for a number of years. And so the Jesuit friends are at some distance—some of them, in fact, out of this world.

The mobile Jesuit has to be able to take the constant forming and breaking up of friendships with balance. It isn't so much "Love 'em and leave 'em," however, as "Learn to love 'em at a distance." All friendship, because it is a form of love and because any love but that of God is temporary, implies some suffering. And for a moving Jesuit, it implies torn up roots and sometimes open wounds. And it implies too the heartache of seemingly losing, through distance and what appears to be forgetfulness and indifference, those once considered friends. But—to sum up the philosophy of the ups and downs of friendship brilliantly and originally—that's life.

PART FOUR

CHAPTER
TEN

*This is
my country—
still*

Although *I'll Die Laughing!* appeared in the fifties, its story had begun in the mid-thirties. In that book I tried to ◈◈◈ tell something about the recipe then used for turning out Jesuits, not just in the abstract but concretely, within the setting of the America of those days and the Catholic Church. There have, quite clearly, been a few changes between 1936 and now, even between 1955 and now—some of them pretty radical, others not really as earth-shaking as billed. And just as there was a triple setting for my book—America, the Catholic Church, and the religious life—there's a similar setting for this fifteen-year-later sequel. So I'd like to say a thing or two about *then* and *now*—the America, the Church, and the religious and Jesuit life of *then* and *now*.

When I entered the Society of Jesus in 1936, we were still trying to escape from the horrors of a great depression. This was an incredible chapter of American history, and yet it needn't have been so much a tragedy as a challenge. In fact it often did lead not so much to despair as to a greater appreciation of life and a nobler struggle to maintain it. Unfeeling as it may sound to some who suffered through those years, I'm not so sure this country wouldn't be better off right now with a good depression—at least for the wealthy, since the poor always have their own—if that's what we need to unsoften us and pull us together through common sacrifice and mutual help.

A few short years later when my generation of Jesuit was studying philosophy and theology and teaching, our country was caught up in World War II. And while we had in those years the usual relatively few who preferred to go their own way and let Hitler go his, still the vast majority of Americans believed the boasted ambitions of *Mein Kampf* and knew that Adolf wasn't going to be stopped with just sweet reason and charity. For myself this was a time of some crisis, when I was undecided about whether I should stick with that promise I had made to live forever as a Jesuit, or go off and help win the war directly. Sentimentally I suppose, this problem became more acute as some of my dearest friends lost their lives in that war. Finally though, the answer seemed clear: I *had* made a promise, and it hadn't had any conditions. And if the encounter with human love couldn't invalidate that promise, then neither could a human war.

In the midst of these two great national crises, and for some time afterward, we still seemed to be guided in the main by many of the ideals on which this country was founded. In many ways,

we were a happier people then, maybe *because* of the suffering we
shared. We still had something of a sense of humor and some
pretty fair manners, two items we seem to be losing today as we
become perhaps—at least publicly—a very cold and rude people. In
the most recent political campaign no man could speak without being
interrupted or even shouted down—something which is still an
impertinence no matter who's speaking, whether it's George Wallace
or Rap Brown or even one's husband or wife. We didn't have much
of this boorishness then, just as we didn't have any collegians beating up the dean, nor "the people of God" trampling over a priest
saying Mass as they take over God's house for themselves and what
they call their consciences. We hadn't yet evolved from freedom
of speech to freedom of preventing speech. Politics were big and
brassy and sensational in those years, but they hadn't yet become
constantly threatened with violence and sudden death as a political
weapon. We had enough racial and economic inequality to cause
us serious concern then, but we still kept it pretty well buried, out
of sight. By the fifties, we had come to some agreement with
Korea and seemed ready to keep all our future wars cold. We still
acknowledged God in public, and we considered those who suggested
we stop this as part of the lunatic fringe. We appreciated our youth
as the hope of the future, without yet letting them precociously
monopolize the present.

When one looks at America today, at least superficially, he
sees a picture quite different from that of even fifteen years ago.
Politics is just as loud and flamboyant as ever—perhaps, in fact, too
big to handle—but we are uncovering all sorts of new creatures under
the rocks, or perhaps it's that we're finally beginning to look under
those rocks for the first time. We divide everyone today, quite
neatly, into liberals and conservatives, which terms become either
glorious or dirty words depending on who uses them. And the poor
guy who tries to steer a middle course, or who is truly conservative
on some issues and truly liberal on others, isn't understood in
cliches.

Most Americans today want equal opportunity for all men and
are quite willing and anxious to use all the energy, charity, and
justice they can in the pursuit of that goal. But most too, quite
understandably, resent the demands when they're not for jobs but
for gifts, and the rude disregard for reasonable laws and manners in
claiming these gifts.

Similarly, most Americans want peace in the world, but they
don't want a "peace" that's contingent on injustice and suppression
and the enslavement or even slaughter of great portions of people.
And while, like Christ, one can die for his fellowmen, still to stand

240

by and watch his fellowmen die unjustly, can be the basest cowardice often masquerading under the name *peace*. And so I resent the paper which prints only pictures of the suffering Viet Cong and never notices the suffering inflicted, and intended, by the Viet Cong. And I resent the poetical soul "seeking" peace who does so from behind a Viet Cong flag or a burning American flag or who used to chant "Ho, ho, Ho Chi Minh," as though lauding some savior of the modern world.

It is truly tremendous that we are so aware of our problems today and so cognizant of the useless horrors of war. But now that we are so alerted, it's to be hoped that America will take the right means of correcting her problems and not create new ones by turning to anarchy.

We have, in fact, a much deeper problem today that the superficial stumper for "End the war now, . . .Burn the churches, . . . Gimme, gimme, gimme" seems to understand—a problem at the very root of all the others, the secularization and materialism of our national spirit. Until *this* problem is solved—burn and steal and demonstrate and riot as we will—nothing can be solved.

Even in the last ten years or so, our country has come a long way towards the complete secularization of our society. We *talk* a lot about our belief in God, but we've allowed God to be ruled so completely out of public life that, in effect, we're denying Him. Not too long ago, for example, the army ordered its chaplains "to eliminate all reference to God and religious philosophy in lectures aimed at instilling moral responsibilities in its soldiers." This move was inspired, by the way, by the American Civil Liberties Union! Our courts decreed that a communist teacher who advocates the violent overthrow of America must be allowed to teach and receive a salary at a state university. About the same time as this decision a boy was suspended from a high school in that same state "for talking about God during his lunch hour." Whom are we kidding with that *this nation under God* stuff?

One Easter Sunday recently, I watched a number of TV shows, some of them from the Mexican channel in Tijuana. And while *this country under God* never even mentioned or suggested anything about the real Easter, at each station break, the Mexican station silently and reverently pictured a crown of thorns. Mexico, for all its official alleged opposition to religion, still hasn't restricted her faith to the cowardly silence of the individual mind.

A material-minded society, of course, never seeks beyond this material for the solution of its problems, even when it piously quotes religious clichés for what it does. And so making our judgments only in the light of material comfort and convenience, a mini-murder like abortion not only doesn't seem so bad but becomes a virtue—a favor, in fact, to the child who is murdered. Nor in the same light would it be so bad to knock off those at the other end of life either, not so much because *they* might want it as because—to be honest—they interfere with the convenience and comfort of the rest, and younger. Logically, sticking with the same class of principle, before long one can see the reasonableness of murder of those who are already born and are hale and hearty as well, but who, unfortunately, interfere in some way with one's material convenience and comfort.

Frankly, this attitude scares me to death because, more than any other item, it shows the pagan direction in which our nation and even some of those who call themselves Christian are going. I was horrified but not surprised to hear a doctor on television one day, discussing birth defects and their early detection. One could see what was coming and come it did: "And if you do detect a defect in a fetus, doctor, what then?"

The answer was more polite, but it still came simply to "Kill 'em and hurry up and do it before they get born."

And so some members of the AMA take over God's prerogative and determine who shall live and who shall not. Many a friend of mine and many a boon to mankind would never have lived at all—great men and women as they were—had the doctor, detecting some pre-natal defect, decreed their death. And don't you ever think doctors won't do just that, with graduation speakers—and unfortunately this did happen recently—telling medical graduates that the practice of abortion is tantamount to practicing the Golden Rule: Do unto others as you would have done to you. Unless, of course, the *other* here happens to be so small and helpless he can't do anything to you. This isn't any new morality at all, as we like to call it, but only the same tired old immorality seeking new ways of rationalizing itself into virtue.

A short note in the paper the other day mentioned that biological researchers have now developed a large, terribly sexy, male rat who also has the virtue of being sterile. Omitting the many other comments one could make on that "discovery" (like how do we get these rats to Harlem), one can't help but notice that this seems the American scientific ideal for men too—large, terribly sexy, and sterile.

We are, in brief, a country which takes a garrulous atheist seriously when she chides an astronaut for reading the Bible from space. We've lost the guts to acknowledge God publicly when a few loud-mouths insist we must not.

But if we're daily becoming more secular and rude and ill-mannered and even crude in public, we're doubly so in the

242

It's hard to see how God could be any more omnipresent than the crusading atheist.

theater and, increasingly, in the movies and, sooner or later of course, on TV. There's no need to go into this subject, because we're all aware of the buckets of bilge hurled at audiences today. A director recently expressed one of his serious artistic ambitions this way: "I want to commit murder on the stage, actually kill someone." (John Vaccaro, "The Moke-Eater," *Esquire*, May 1969.) The Roman Empire had a few ideas like this just before she slipped and fell too.

Among other things we have, I fear, become an effeminate society in the worst sense of that term. And I for one am sick to death of pretty, dimpled boys with long hair wailing at an adoring public such inspiring things as "Why don't we do it in the road? No one will be watching us."

We Americans have made something of a god of democracy, rather than just a way of political life. We tend to try and legalize whatever a number of people seem to be doing, even when we suspect it's all wrong and even harmful to our society.

Where there's a 5-4 vote—and we ourselves side with the fives, of course—we don't hesitate to treat the fives' opinion as infallible. Some of us would have noted, regretfully perhaps, that the vote on Calvary was overwhelmingly for crucifixion.

Maybe above all we're an immature nation, an Uncle Linus with his thumb in his mouth and his blanket at the ready—in fact, we always have been. We used to be so immature as to hide all our problems as a nation. And now that we're looking at those problems, we tend to go to one childish extreme or the other in either "solving" them or turning away. And where in a mature society youth would look to at least some adults as leaders, in our national immaturity we do just the opposite—with supposed adults latching onto all the fads of youth as their thing in this, their second childhood. Drugs never really caught on in this country until adults began to imitate a few of their children—nor did violence or public nudity (which *is* little boy, little girl stuff) or the tearing down of legitimate authority.

Looking at material America only materialistically today can be a traumatic experience—if you're an American. What I'm trying to say is that I am much less optimistic now about America's material future than I was when I wrote that book fifteen years ago. Not only do we already have much to answer for, but we keep adding on to that "much" every day. We are, in fact, doubly self-destructing today, because even those who are allegedly trying to put our forgotten ideals into practice are in reality, destroying us instead, with a big assist from those who couldn't care less about America's ideals. Potentially we *are* great. And if that potential can be realized in making the practice of our national ideals as magnificent and soaring as our moon shots, we could survive.

America's potential, in this decade of Our Lord the 1970's, is greater than ever. But we Americans do have to make a choice—and *act* on that choice—to betray our national ideals or begin to fulfill them. And among other things, that's going to require compromise and humility—the humility, say, to accept what the young have to say when they're right and the courage and charity to correct them when they're wrong. And of course, you can say the same thing about accepting or not accepting what the not-so-young have to say.

America's ideals begin with God, and to continue progressively to rule Him more and more out of even public mention is to betray those ideals. We did a better job of recognizing Him, in fact, quite naturally, when we were universally challenged than when we became lazy, selfish, and self-centered with affluence. We were, in fact, probably far better as frontiersmen than as millionaires.

Our country is founded on God, and there was never supposed to be any wall of separation between God and her, but only a wall which kept any one religion from imposing its ideas of God and His worship on the whole nation. Our Declaration of Independence wasn't any declaration of independence from God as much as an avowal of our dependence on Him.

> When in the course of human events, it becomes necessary for one people to dissolve the political bands which have connected them with another, and to assume among the powers of the earth, the separate and equal station to which the Laws of Nature and of Nature's God entitle them. . . .

And you'll remember this sentence (which would probably be banned by our vote-conscious leaders of today):

> We hold these truths to be self-evident, that all men are created equal, that they are endowed by their Creator with certain unalienable Rights, that among these are Life, Liberty, and the pursuit of Happiness. . . .

This nation of ours is *under God,* but our country is not itself God, and so it can't *give* anybody any rights, but can only recognize and protect them—and sometimes it has to reestablish them.

Near the end of the Declaration of Independence we find our founding fathers appealing to the Supreme Judge of the World for the rectitude of their intentions, and their last sentence reads:

> And for the support of this Declaration, with a firm reliance on the protection of Divine Providence, we mutually pledge to each other our Lives, our Fortunes, and our sacred Honor.

Betray that sentiment and we betray both God *and* our country. And I'd personally rather betray the kindly, tolerant public atheist whose rights and freedom we make a great show of defending, often at the cost of the rights and freedom of countless others.

The America of today is technologically far, perhaps essentially ahead of the America of the fifties when *I'll Die Laughing!* was published. And many of our hangups are merely an honesty which is beginning finally to recognize our imperfections. Now it's up to us to use our great know-how, our technology, to solve those problems—to make earth bearable as well as shooting for the moon, and to save and help and comfort rather than to kill and destroy. But when I say "rather than to kill and destroy," I'm not talking about just the killing and destruction of war, but the killing of the helpless—the infant, for example—and the old and the guy who has a heart he doesn't seem to be using well. It does no good to end formal war if we continue to kill the helpless and innocent, and technology itself will turn on us if we kill with it.

There have been some pretty good thinkers who put this fairly well—like this one for example:

> The pagan loves the earth in order to enjoy it and confine himself within it; the Christian in order to make it purer and draw from it the strength to escape from it.
> Teilhard de Chardin, *The Divine Milieu*·

But then, Father de Chardin, being a good, honest spiritual man, would be the first to tell you that he really swiped that from a GI named Ignatius, not a bad thinker himself. And I'm humbly happy to be in the company of both in this particular sentiment. This is in fact, I feel sure, the only hope for America—the use of the world rather than its deification. Practically, that comes to a voluntary return to selflessness on the part of her affluent, a rejection of self-interests on the part of her politicians, a genuine practical concern on the part of that apathetic complacent group referred to as a "silent majority," and the repudiation of the violence and insanity of a very *un*silent minority. Until these things come to pass, as I see it, we haven't a prayer.

CHAPTER
ELEVEN

*"You
are Peter"*
—still

If I've seemed pessimistic about America's material future—
unless, of course, she returns to her basic ideals—I'm
◈◈ still a complete optimist about the absolute future of
mankind, because mankind simply isn't meant for only this
material earth anyhow. Sometimes a man, especially perhaps when
he starts to fly beyond the earth, has to be reminded maybe even
by chaos that his destiny *is* another world, one to which even his
greatest possible scientific achievements can never get him by
themselves.

God gave and still gives us all the means to achieve our destiny
with Him in heaven. But we at least have to decide to *look* in that
direction and seek out Him and His heaven if we're to make it. We
have to be men of *some* will first of all and, secondly, men of *good*
will.

Without going into the apologetics of the subject, I believe
that the big means at our disposal for getting to our final destination in God is His Church.

Now when my earlier Jesuit book was written in the
fifties, the Church was essentially the same as it is today and,
in fact, as it was at the moment Christ created it. That doesn't
change. Nor will it. There have, however, been so many external
changes in Church practice that not a few people have become
confused—some to the point of thinking that there has been
some essential change and others to the extent of not knowing what to think, largely because of the confusion and contradictions they read in "the experts."

Like our country, the Church is comprised of and run by human
beings who are elevated to a pretty lofty state by their responsibility.
Unlike our country (whose founding, however, certainly involved
God's Providence), the Church is also a *super*-natural structure; the
means that God gives us, not for a material goal, but for a spiritual
goal—the only ultimate goal, in fact, that we have. But despite the
goal, the fact is that this Church, founded on some rather stumbling,
inefficient bunglers like Peter, still has men at its head also like Peter.
The further fact that these human beings do represent Christ here on
earth visibly in His Church doesn't stop them from making mistakes
in non-essentials. But it seems pretty ridiculous to me to suppose
that Christ is going to allow His representatives to lead people astray
in essentials when they act in their capacity as leaders of the Church.

Catholics either believe this or they're simply not Catholics at all, no matter what their virtues. And so it would be foolish and hypocritical as well for one who proposes to be a Catholic to brag about his belief in Christ and love for Him and then turn around and say, "But I want nothing to do with His Church. It can't tell *me* what to do." Christ didn't restrict the powers He passed on to His Church to the lacier parts of the liturgy, nor did He say anything about taking a vote on it. One wonders where this puts those who will gladly—seemingly, in fact, with near ecstasy in their own "obedience"—give their assent when Christ's human representative makes some nice relatively harmless liturgical statement, but who deny his authority when he comes out with some principle of conduct they'd rather not accept.

I couldn't really care less whether I eat fish or meat on Fridays, but in a way I feel it's too bad Catholics are no longer accurately termed mackerel snappers. The law of Friday abstinence was one of those seemingly insignificant things which was in reality of tremendous significance, because it was one of the very few things which forced Catholics directly to show their faith in the Church of Christ as the voice of Christ Himself. This law gave us one of our few chances to do something which had nothing to do directly with the natural law (such as "Thou shalt not kill"), but which proceeded from the authority Christ had entrusted to His Church. It was a test of both faith and obedience, and by no coincidence, those who failed in this little test almost invariably failed their greater tests as well.

Some years ago now, there was an ecumenical church council. It wasn't the first such, nor probably will it be the last. But like the people of every age, we looked on this one as the most significant of all, with some Year-One people imagining that it was the only one that ever accomplished anything.

Truly, Vatican II was a magnificent council, and its ideas were wonderful. Sometimes though, Vatican II gets blamed for some things it never so much as hinted at—like "celebrating the Eucharist" with cokes and hamburgers or perhaps with a ballet dancer collecting the communion breads.

To invoke Vatican II as the authority for a new morality, or the end of the established church is the sheerest journalese, an affliction, unfortunately, which provides a livelihood today for far too many people. No movie or drama critic, holding himself up as an authority on the things he himself can't do or sometimes can't even understand, can hold a candle to the theological critic, who doesn't know much of any theology, but who knows when he'd like something declared right or wrong theologically. And maybe still worse is the writer who does know some theology and who proceeds to speak and act as if he knew all of it, or at least more than those blundering idiots Christ appointed as His representatives.

In a previous day the bitterest critics of the Church stood outside and shouted obscenities at her, but today it's the little men who insist that they're still within who seem to feel it their vocation in life to tear her apart, like some precociously brattish infant in the womb. Rarely do they say quite logically, "I disagree with the Church on essentials or *an* essential, and so I'd best part company with Her." Instead they come up with that epitome of pride: "Christ's representatives in the Church disagree with me here, and so they must be wrong. And since I can't be wrong here and they obviously are, it's I, with my unquestionable charism, who must be the voice of Christ, and they who should see the light or get out."

The critics claim, in fact, a new degree of dogmatism that the Church, as such, never dreamed of. And in general this is new, since it used to be that if people disagreed essentially with the Church (or the Jesuits or the Masons or the Elks), they took off for other locales. But today's critic of the Church will deplore her "suppressing of freedom," and then never acknowledge any opinion but his own. You hear the voice of this charismatized conscience of mankind coming out with things like "*We* are going to change the Church. . . . *We* are going to change the religious orders." And what I want to know is just who are "we"? He didn't ask me about it, so "we" can't include me, ole J.T. McG., S.J., to name only one.

The very language used by some of the critics ought to be a clue to their ulterior motives, and perhaps their psyche as well. One such gentleman—so termed here because of a cultural tradition—who signed up to practice the evangelical counsels and maybe a bit of extra charity, once came up in essence with this little gem of living Christianity (although not exactly a carbon copy of "Do good to them who hate you. . ."): "As far as suffering, I think I dished out as much as I took. I still regret the few occasions on which I failed to strike back, but I may have inflicted more pain than I thought anyhow." This imitator of a Christ, who prayed "Father, forgive them" for His crucifiers, went on to say that what his religious order had done for him was certainly no better than what he had done for her. And finally, in a burst of brotherly love, he sums up his tender regard and charity for some of his brethren: "I hate them. . . ."

There's a tag on this sort of language, since tantrums, public or private, are seldom too difficult to analyze down to their psychological roots. And yet many a person, regarding the reputation and not the axes a man has to grind, will take his word as God's. I can well imagine, for example, the enthusiastic applause of "instant theologians" everywhere when Father Hans Küng, in a burst of pettishness, termed Father (now Cardinal) Jean Danielou, S.J., the grand inquisitor or some such. But Father Küng couldn't even carry Father Danielou's theological sweat socks.

Many a critic has, of course, deserted the Church—which can follow logically after innumerable illogical steps. At least by then, these people seem more consistent than those who only stay around and gripe. Many of the deserters have interesting futures too—such as the priests marrying the already oft-married, some of them even speaking eloquently of their present atheism, for a fat fee. These are the few, of course, but all the bitter critics have this in common—that they're never wrong, but it is only the Church they left or from which they still make their living which could be wrong. Come up, if you can, with a Church which will satisfy their every whim, and they'll gladly lend their prestige to it. Cut out that crucifixion, in fact, and we'd have a lot more "christians," including that great movie star speaking authoritatively on theology when he said, "A man must never have a religion he must suffer to sustain."

Throughout the years since *I'll Die Laughing!* appeared —and of course, before that time to some extent—I've noticed that an awesome number of human hangups come from a thing we used to call human respect. Briefly, this meant that if somebody else was doing a thing, you tended to feel out of place if you didn't do it also. And when the impression was somehow created that everybody, or almost everybody, was doing it, you felt like the only odd ball in a world of marbles.

And the joker in *that* deck was that the bit about everybody's doing it, was almost a complete phony, because "everybody" could usually be translated: "a few well-publicized vocalists."

Today, people *are* confused by the apparent conflict and criticism within the Church. As a matter of fact however, there always has been conflict, criticism, and consequent confusion. Belloc said it long ago when he noted that no purely human institution could have lasted a fortnight (that's two weeks to us peasants) with such very human human beings as the Church had in charge and even sometimes only in attendance.

But it's the same old story today intensified—we get the idea that the most vocal segment of society is a majority, whereas they may be only an indefatigable flock of loud-mouths. And one vast difference between today and a not-far-off yesterday is that they have a greater than ever ally: their own press. Jean Kerr said, "The snake has all the lines," and you could say today that the loud-lunged griper-bird, even outside of its cage, makes good use of that segment of the press that still prefers the sensational to the truth.

Now certainly, there's room and often need for criticism, even in an essentially spiritual structure like the Church. That criticism deserves a hearing—when it's legitimate and constructive, and not just destructive and critical of the Church essentially, nor an attempt to turn it into something it's not supposed to be. Unfortunately some parts of the press couldn't care less about the legitimacy or constructiveness of the criticism it prints. The millions of Catholics who *are* Catholics in work as well as word never get any real shake in this sort of press, but only those who have some axe to grind within the Church or who leave her. We have today the phenomenon of the sheet which is concerned solely with negative criticism of the Church it claims to be part of—so much so that all it ever prints are all the gripes and scandals and desertions of the Church, sneering at doctrine and custom as universally square and seeking to tear down the reputation of anyone who questions their ideas. They never headline the resignation of some bishop they don't like, but rather note that this "Beleaguered Bishop "Quits" or some such more eye-catching, even if less truthful, headline.

This sort of mistakenly termed Catholic press has joined some of the secular organs as the new voice of infallibility, and it's not surprising that they constantly snipe away at the representatives Christ mistakenly chose instead of them. A certain ill-concealed glee comes through these pages whenever a priest deserts his vocation, some prominent Catholic openly deserts the Church, or

253

some celebrity of stage or screen—well versed, of course, in moral theology—endorses the pill. As one columnist noted, *"Look periodically celebrates the strife within the Church."* In fact, some periodicals celebrate the strife that isn't there too—except, of course, in their imagination and, seemingly, their wishful thinking.

A short time ago, a then rather prominent ex-nun married. She married a widower. And one magazine's little note of this wedding read, substantially:

> Dottie La Rue, formerly Sister Philomena, married George Midas. She for the first time, he for the second, in a ceremony performed by a Jesuit priest.

That this marriage should get any notice at all is the first phenomenon. And the innuendoes by omission alone are almost as sinister as that bit, "by a Jesuit priest." It's hard to believe that there's even *sincere* error here.

This part of the press is on a constant lookout for a champion— preferably a bishop or someone else of some prominence—who will openly disagree with the Church. And then they make him—wrong though he may be—into a real hero, exhorting their readers to write in and send money if they can to see that their hero "gets a fair shake," and to back him "against Rome." He might have once been just a nice guy and an ordinary bishop with ordinary intelligence, maybe, with very little pastoral experience, but now, at this turn of events, he's *outstanding, a great leader,* and above all *a beautiful human being.*

All a priest really need do to become a prominent contributor to this press is leave the priesthood, marry, and then continue to give an eagerly waiting Catholic world a constant self-analysis. He can never hint that *he* might have been wrong. That's against the rules.

He can, of course, stay within the Church and gripe. This makes good copy too—not so great as if he'd take off and yell his criticism from outside, but then there are degrees of heroism.

One example which comes to mind of the communication field's sometime disregard for truth was an incident a friend of mine ran into on a southern university campus. There had been, one evening, a bit of rock-throwing, but nothing really serious, although some papers did term it a riot. The next day when my friend, a black, was sitting around talking with a few students, up came the old TV and sound trucks, and the reporters asked the students: "How about throwing a few rocks for the cameras, fellows?" Some apostolate.

254

Some frustrated Hollywood directors must have ended up as reporters.

In 1969 a story in the Santa Barbara *News-Press* revealed that at a Berkeley "people's park" demonstration, "Black Panther types" (which in this case meant black actors in black berets and black jackets) had been hired by a major Hollywood film corporation to "enliven the action." The story grew out of an investigation by the Alameda County Sheriff's office, and quoted a Black Panther official as saying the film Panthers "were obviously imposters."

It would indeed be nice to pause here for a short footnote and point out that the members of the Society of Jesus, in their press utterances, have always been completely faithful to the spirit of their order—which includes a special attitude to the Church and to the Vicar of Christ on earth. Unfortunately, there have been some Jesuits who have loused up this spirit in individual cases. The only two things I'd like to say about that unfortunate fact here is (1) a word of apology for this betrayal and (2) the plea that people remember that the public utterances of a single Jesuit or group of Jesuits, no matter what their prominence or eminence, is not necessarily the voice of the Society of Jesus. But the press keeps labeling such characters primarily as "Jesuits" or more often, "Jesuit experts" of some sort or other.

In this day of the instant theologian who has gleaned most or all of his theology from *Time* and some of the other great theological journals, it's fairly easy to find a patsy to fit any given situation. And so when Pope Paul's *Humanae Vitae* came out, the communications experts were ready and waiting to make the most of the outcry they knew would come—with their help of course. One of the networks immediately sought out for an interview a Jesuit who had long been on the fringes of his order and whose greatest current claims to fame were his completion of a sensitivity course and his growing of a beard—the latter an ability that did admittedly come as a surprise to some of us. He was introduced not as just a Jesuit, but as a prominent Jesuit theologian. And of course, as had certainly been anticipated, he mouthed all the clichés: that the Pope's encyclical wasn't to be taken seriously, that Catholics needn't obey, and all that rot. Naturally, the fact that this man was quickly informed that he should be introduced in the future as an ex-Jesuit rather than as a Jesuit didn't get nearly the coverage his original introduction as a noted Jesuit theologian had gotten. This was a case where a year of sensitivity training earned a degree in theology, instant theology—"Never was such a sudden scholar made. . . ."

Sometimes, at least where non-essentials are concerned, the press comes up with some unconscious humor that is worthy of a very conscious Bruce Marshall. When the Holy Father recently plucked a few service stripes from the likes of St. Christopher and St. Barbara, the voices of dissent were instant and—usually—hilarious. It's pretty hard to keep a straight face when you see a news photo of a bosomy Italian actress, prone on the hood of her car, a statue of Christopher discernable (if one is that interested) in the foreground, as she declares that no one, not even the Pope, can downgrade her St. Christopher, since he saved her life—if not, one might add, all her marriages. There was another regular annual churchgoer at the time, an old pug, who was equally sharp at discerning what the Pope could or could not say or do.

But enough of the tiny world of the tiny, but strident press. The truth is that the Church, despite even a sometimes erratic, sometimes traitorous, sometimes dishonest segment of the press, continues and will continue to go on, because Christ did say "I am with you all days. . . ." The Church has, after all, survived some rather huge historical catastrophes, even something as earth-shaking as a losing football season or two at Notre Dame.

When Christianity first got under way, it did quite a little bit of hiding—in the catacombs and other handy holes. From time to time throughout the centuries, as one or another emperor discovered the sport of Christian-killing, the potential victim burrowed underground. And today we are afflicted with one of the silliest expressions a grown child playing games can come up with, "the underground church"—as though those who oppose the Church had something in common with the great Christians who were willing to suffer and die for Christ, and as though there were some glamour involved in childish disobedience. It's like calling some kid smoking behind the garage the underground family. And the greatest fallacy of the whole infantile game is the implicit pretense that the Church is out to get them.

Just what inspires otherwise allegedly rational adults to play games like this is hard to figure, and each one would have to be individually psychoanalyzed if we wanted to discover motives. The whole thing isn't worth that sort of attention here. Sometimes though, both underground and surface liturgy have things in common, so let's talk liturgically for a moment.

Unfortunately, not all the liturgical orgies we're subjected to today are underground, even when the burial time is long overdue. Now I have no particular beef about having to learn to say Mass again each new place I stop, just as long as it is the Mass and not somebody's imaginary play-period idea of what it should be. Ordinarily the Mass somehow manages to retain, even externally, enough of the same lovely ritual it always had, despite the sort of efforts to "make it more meaningful" which tend to conceal its meaning in arbitrary externals.

When would-be liturgists (and that epithet doesn't automatically exclude all of those who are considered experts even by someone other than themselves) go off in the wrong direction, you can be sure they're making one of two mistakes: they're trying to turn the Mass into either a *meal* or a *drama*, seemingly unable to understand that both words, when used about the Mass, are not used to denote its essence, but its accidentals. And so, they come up with either a big show, usually a poor man's musicale, or with a five-course meal—both of which shatter the whole spirit of the Mass, and neither of which would get a fairly competent critic's acclaim as good drama, music, or good food anyhow.

In the Mass the perpetuation of Christ's sacrifice on Calvary for men *is* the reality, and the "meal" and the "drama" are only there to assist in bringing out that reality, and not the other way round. If I want to show my solidarity with my fellowmen by having a meal with them, then by all means if we're all hungry let's have a meal—whether it's hamburgers and cokes or steaks and martinis—but let's not confuse it with

Some of the production numbers tend to push the liturgy into the background.

the Mass. And if I want to show the drama that is the Mass, then let's have a musicale, but let's have it on a stage before or after Mass. At Mass let's use both the meal and the drama bits as helps to bringing out the reality here—Christ perpetuating His sacrifice among us—so that *we*, two thousand years after the historical event, can participate in it with Him. It would have been a little silly to serve steaks or hamburgers at Calvary, even had that age been lucky enough to have a Beatles' accompaniment. I find, in fact, that the picture of the Mass being celebrated under fire on a hill in Iwo Jima looks much more like the Mass than that of many of the guitarists and bongo drummers who agonize it out musically on *their* front.

Most priests I've known have had such a vital appreciation of the Mass that if necessary they'd crawl to the altar daily to be able to celebrate the Sacrifice. And I feel the same way, resenting the sometimes heard expression, "I have to say Mass," as much as I resent the lay Catholic's sometimes remark, "I have to go to Mass on Sundays." Both of these are about like saying, "I *have* to be present at Calvary where Christ is dying for us."

I would imagine that most priests, while they love each Mass they've been privileged to celebrate, will remember a few occasions when the Mass stood out as more meaningful and memorable than others. Apart from my first Mass when the sense of unworthiness became well-nigh overwhelming, there are two Masses which stand out in my mind more than any others. There was the time in a little out-of-the-way place in Kansas, which boasted some one hundred young Catholic couples, at least that many young children, and no church. So we celebrated Mass in an old theater, and since it was too young a town to have any baby sitters, parents and children alike were jammed in there. Every now and then one of the kids would wonder aloud when the cartoons were coming on, and there was a constant hum of little noises—a hum, I felt, much like that which accompanies any good gathering of friends who are together for some common purpose. Since there was no altar rail and since we were crowded, the people knelt or stood or sat around the altar.

But I was *with* these people and not a mile away in some lofty sanctuary; and so we were together at this sacrifice and we all felt it. Actually since they were all around the altar anyhow, turning around to read the epistle and gospel was only a formality —and this long before someone officially discovered that an altar had two sides to it. I got through the epistle all right, despite some minor distractions from a lady directly in front of me who kept gently shushing the baby in her arms and the little guy reaching up to grasp her hand. During the gospel, however, one or the other of the children pushed her a bit too far, and she didn't just shush gently, but came out (during one of my pauses for breath, of course) with a nice loud "Shut up," which was startlingly clear to everyone —although it wasn't too clear that it had been aimed at her children and not kindly old Father. I started laughing and lost the place in the gospel—in the book, in fact—and then when I started reading again (you're not going to believe this, but it's true), the first words were, "Woe to those who are with child in those days." This broke us all up, so I closed the book and went on. But it did more than break us up—it united us further in that sacrifice as perhaps nothing else could have.

The other Mass I remember more than others took place in a gym out somewhere in Nebraska. It was the closing of a youth convention at which I had spoken, and it was my added privilege also to celebrate the Mass with the kids. Some five hundred of them were gathered around the slightly elevated platform and the altar, and they played their guitars and sang beautifully—not, this time, just for practice or to give a concert with the Mass as its setting, but as a genuine background for what was going on. You could see it, hear it, feel it; these kids and I were together in an earth-shaking experience, and the musical part of it wasn't itself that experience—the Mass was. The music, which fit so beautifully and wasn't just a bunch of songs "kids like to sing," brought out the sacrifice and enhanced its impression on us all. I'll never forget that Mass, nor how close those kids and I felt to each other in this sacrifice.

I guess the point I'm trying to make is that as far as I'm concerned, the one big thing I want to see accomplished in any liturgical changes is this sense of oneness at Mass, oneness with each other and with this ineffable Sacrifice. And it seems to me that closeness to the altar is of the essence here, and that not even having the priest face the other people there is going to do any good if they still can't see and be close enough to be part of the Sacrifice.

For the most part I've found the liturgical attempts of our day sincere and often even meaningful, with most people trying not just to preserve but to emphasize the essential element of sacrifice. If some of these sincere efforts were misguided, I'm sure the Lord understood—probably, in fact, a lot better than I did that bright day when I found a nun, not just *close* to the altar, but standing at the altar with me as I said Mass facing a group of retreatants. My surprise was probably not unlike that of Zachary when he suddenly discovered an archangel standing—or at least in place—next to him at the altar, the difference between Zachary and myself at this sudden burst of divine intervention being that it made *him* speechless.

As far as the musical background of the Mass is concerned, I really could not care less what instrument or instruments are made use of. If some feel that an organ helps, then let them go right ahead and *pulsare* their *organum* until the thing is all pulsed out. If guitar music helps to remind them more of Calvary than an organ does, that's fine too. And if they can achieve this effect better with bongo drums or a mouth organ or a tuba or a trombone or a pocket comb, then let them go to it. Similarly, if reciting prayers together or singing together or only keeping quiet and meditating together

An archangel appeared to Zachary at the altar, but not to me.

gets this result, I'm all for that too. And it seems to me from this distance that all these things could help on occasion, and none on other occasions. So the stumper for uninterrupted communal prayer at Mass might just be wrong, and the advocate of *only* what he calls guitar Masses could also be wrong, and the old frustrated operatic soprano or tenor who figures they're darned well going to sing the whole time might also be wrong. And yet all of them are sometimes right too—once they realize that we're trying to accomplish two things here: Having people realize that they *are* together, and at Calvary.

There *are* a few *ifs* here, obviously, the larger ones being: *If* the music *is* background and not just someone's showing off his talent or lack of same, or his love for singing, with the Mass itself pushed into the remote background since it only provides the occasion for the debut of this would-be musician; and *if* the music and the accompanying words actually do help to bring out the element of Christ's sacrifice and are not completely unconnected with it. I'd be less than honest if I didn't note here that I have run into occasions where all the would-be liturgist seemed to be trying to do was show off either a newly found singing voice or the latest plateau of his guitar-strumming—both of which could have remained hidden awhile longer without serious loss to either the liturgy or the world of music. I don't, in fact, quite understand why it is that almost anything is considered profound today if it's sung or yelled or whined over guitar accompaniment. And Christ seems to have done more with a hammer than with a guitar.

When I was teaching in high school, we used to work and exhort in season and out, trying to get our teen-agers to sing in church. And it never seemed to take. Now sometimes I'm beginning to see why they were so reluctant, and—again, *sometimes*—I wish they were reluctant again. They can not of course, be any worse than the French nuns who chanted the divine office so badly that St. Francis de Sales wrote to the then Holy Father asking to have them excused from the singing obligation. "If you think they're praising God," he wrote in essence, "you ought to hear them."

I'm not at all sure either that everyone in a given church or chapel is of the same mind and taste as the official or self-constituted "liturgy director." The cliche, in fact, that all young people must always have "guitar Masses" is simply, and as politely as I can put it, so much hooey. All too often the guitar is, in fact, the choice of a few, and those few usually haven't bothered to ask those many who are not present at their guitar Mass about the matter. And just as the ill-mannered protestors who desecrate the Mass are saying in effect, "Now that we have this crowd here, forget this sacrifice of Calvary and listen to something more important—me," so the potential musicians are often of the same attitude, as they do their thing in Calvary Hall.

The other day I got a letter from a Minnesota senior citizen attempting his second childhood. He seemed to think I had been mummified for years in Santa Barbara, as he told me with great glee and undoubtedly great zeal about all the advances in liturgy in the outside world—like Minnesota for instance. We have, he said, a guitar Mass every week and it really swings. It really grabs the audience. You really wouldn't believe it!

Now the fact is that I had said Mass in the midst of people, facing them if you will, and I had taken part in Masses accompanied by guitars while this guy still didn't know the difference between a guitar and a canoe paddle. But I don't resent his failure to know this so much as I'm alternately amused and revolted by his disproportionate glee at what he called a guitar Mass that "really swings." The very term "guitar Mass" is somewhat obnoxious, because it seems to put both guitar and Mass on the same level, and his "it really swings" somehow doesn't grab me when I realize, although he apparently doesn't, that he's talking about Calvary.

As I say, however, I'm all for whatever changes are going to make our liturgy more meaningful as well as for those which can make Christ's church more vital and effective while still remaining His Church. There are, I'm sure, some things I've enjoyed which must go also, such as some of the delightful bits of fancy one is exposed to in the Divine Office. I always got a kick out of reading, for example, that it was obvious even from his infancy that one Nicholas (December 6) was clearly going to turn into St. Nicholas, since *infans, cum reliquos dies lac nutricis frequens sugeret, quarta et sexta feria semel dumtaxat, idque vesperi sugebat: quam jejunii consuetudinem in reliqua vita semper tenuit.* This, rather literally translated, comes out: "As an infant, although he frequently imbibed his nurse's milk on other days, on Wednesdays and Fridays he did so only once, and that in the evening—a fasting habit he stuck with for the rest of his life."

And I also enjoyed the way St. Cecilia (November 22) told Valerian, to whom she had just been married off against her will, that she had vowed to remain celibate and she was darn well going to keep that vow. "Valerian," she is reported to have said on their wedding night, "I have a little secret to let you in on. I have a big tough guardian angel with me all the time and his only assignment is to guard my body."

Maybe, in our very good and undoubtedly very necessary reforms, we can get a bit too grim and humorless about things.

But if there is any one great ecclesiastical hangup today— especially, but not exclusively among the young—it's the confusion caused by would-be teachers, especially teachers of religion. I've already had something to say here about teaching in general, so I'll add only a few remarks about teaching religion. To be quite blunt about the matter: If there is a greater crisis of faith in the young today than ever before, *it is largely because of their teachers,* those teachers of religion, that is, who are passing little on to their students but their own hangups. And so that I won't antagonize these "teachers" any more than anyone else, let me add that I see a parallel here: For many years now, parents, with their permissiveness in the dating habits of the young, have allowed (sometimes even pushed) their children into situations which not even a mature adult could handle with complete equanimity. And here, in this all-important realm of faith, instead of teaching positively, all too many teachers of religion are only exposing their own doubts, frustrations, and—in many cases—lack of knowledge to people far more sensitive, in fact, than themselves.

I hasten to add that there are many, many fine teachers of religion—usually as unpublicized as they are proficient. At the same time, I keep running into young people who have never met such teachers and who, as a result, know absolutely nothing about their faith except how to question it. And while a complete adult can question things and still understand that questioning and denying are not the same things, the young person tends to make synonyms of *question* and *deny*. When he calls a thing into question, probing its reasons as he should, he tends to consider it denied until some miracle startles him into reconsidering. Unfortunately, the ordinary mortal doesn't make his way to heaven with the direct help of miracles. The permissiveness, the addiction to cliches, and all the other hangups are frightening when found in *any* teacher. But when you find them in the religion teacher, they're utterly terrifying.

Since one of my most recent major writing chores was a four-year high-school religion course, and since I've been doing a good bit of talking with both students and teachers on the matter ever since, I feel that I know something of the subject at first hand—at least as much, say, as the new teacher who's ready to hang up the whole course the first month. In fact, I undertook the arduous job of doing this course in the first place because of what I considered (and still consider despite the appearance of several more courses in the meantime) the inadequacy of existing series. This isn't to suggest that I feel my own work the final answer either, but I'd have been an utter fool to undertake such a job if I didn't think, from what I saw and tried to teach, that a course such as I ambitioned doing was terribly needed. I still run into kids who have just about finished high school and who have never had anything taught them in four years of exposure to religion classes. They've been the disciples of some of those great pedagogues whose only activity was to sit like some inscrutable Buddha, while the kids *discussed*—with never a word or answer or correction from the rapt teacher, absorbed undoubtedly in the contemplation of his own navel. Unfortunately, this is no exaggeration, incredible as it may sound to a genuine teacher, although I may, of course have exaggerated the extent of his study habits.

I've run into kids who didn't even suspect the real beauty and truth of their faith because they'd been exposed only to a few vapid clichés about the perfectibility of man, supplemented by a few out-of-context phrases from Teilhard de Chardin. Or sometimes they'd learned some very pretty truths of Christianity, but their teachers hadn't run the risk of dirtying up these nice, comfortable truths with any other truths—like the crucifixion and our share in it for instance, or the trial nature of our life here on earth as opposed to some unrealistic, sentimental dream of a heaven on earth.

And it was this sort of anemic masquerade for religion and its teaching which caused me to give six years of my life to studying and working out the religion course *Through Him, With Him and In Him*. . . . So far the response has made the effort worthwhile.

There are lots of things I'd like to say about these texts here but, unfortunately, they all sound like self-advertising, so I'll skip them. Let me only say that the books are based, generally, on *The Spiritual Exercises* of a friend of mine named St. Ignatius and they're called, respectively, *Living in God, Christ Lives on, The Life of Man in Christ,* and *Living in the Kingdom,* titles which might give some hint to the very perceptive that an attempt is made here to encourage people to *live* their faith rather than just trying to stave off death.

I've run into some interesting comments indeed (especially if you're a psychologist), directly or indirectly concerning this religion course—interesting and often pathetic. There were the two priests, in charge of selecting a high-school religion course for their whole diocese, who didn't take the time to read any of the available courses but picked one out solely and exclusively "because it was the shortest."

There was the nun who said that her girls wouldn't like my course (even though neither she nor they had read a word of it) "because of the color of the cover." When I mentioned that this was a new one on me and that lots of other girls apparently hadn't been bugged by this detail, she brought our meaningful dialog to its crashing conclusion by saying, "But those weren't California girls." First time I'd known the rest of the country was color-blind.

Nowhere is the teacher's responsibility greater than in the religion course. Nowhere else is it so vitally important to steer

the immature mind away from dilettantism. This will mean a
constant alertness to negative thinking, or what might well be
called destructive criticism, as opposed to a constructive attitude.
Political campaigns are all characterized by a good bit of this
sort of thinking, where the other party has done everything all
wrong, but the challenger has nothing better to offer either.
And the campus disorders are in much the same rut—they
consider a lot of things wrong, but have no idea what's right.

The young have a natural tendency, when they do become
dilettantes, to be negative in their thinking, constantly criticizing, never offering good substitutes, arbitrary (with their
personal opinions held up as the sole source of truth), and
finally cynical and pessimistic in their iconoclasm. Going with
this is the natural concomitant of immaturity which comes
quite naturally from a lack of experience—the inability to see
the whole picture, mostly since they simply haven't existed
long enough or ranged far enough away from the TV set or record
player to have seen it yet. Real maturity in the young always
contains the element of knowing and acknowledging that they *are*
young and that others may have seen more of the fullness of the
picture than they. Failure to acknowledge this indicates an immaturity even below their chronological age. Certainly it must
be clear that the teacher with this same attitude isn't a teacher
at all.

A by-product of this immature attitude is in the moral sphere,
where "opinion," or sometimes what-everyone-else-is-doing-anyhow,
is equated with "morality." This is, in fact, something of a characteristic of our age—as witnessed, for example, by the bishop who
felt that Friday abstinence could be retained in his diocese "because
most Catholics followed the law on it." Now I couldn't care less
whether there's a law of Friday abstinence or not. But to keep
the law *because* everyone seems to observe it, or to drop it *in case*
not everyone observes it, seems to me a frightening sort of reasoning.

Somehow the teacher has to put across to the young that
the term "moral" supposes eternal, objective values and truths, and
a basis, not in private opinion alone, but in human nature created
by God. It's our task, while still avoiding the very real danger of
exaggerated authoritarianism, to show the working of that true
authority through which God communicates His will to men rather
than His tapping each individual man on the shoulder and issuing
His orders to each of us personally and miraculously.

It is indeed wonderful that modern man seems to be learning
at last that he's not just an individual, but a member of society, of
the family of mankind, and of the Mystical Body of Christ. But

266

we can't forget either that man *is* still an individual with individual responsibilities, the most important of these—to which all others have to lead—being the individual responsibility of uniting himself with God, now and ultimately. Others can't do this for him, although they can help; and he in turn can do it for no one else, although *he* can help.

There is, in fact, the very real danger in our day that a person will turn to the social nature of man, knowingly or not, as only or partially an escape from himself. Sometimes it is, admittedly, unpleasant to contemplate oneself with all one's weakness and tininess; and it can be, for some at least, much less unpleasant to contemplate the ills of the world around him and the needs of his fellow man. And the real teacher will have to help his students avoid both extreme introversion and extroversion, and so to understand himself and his responsibilities and his nature both as an individual and as a social being.

Now allegedly for years the religion course has been at the bottom of the heap in the school, and teachers are said to have filtered down to it as it became apparent they couldn't teach anything else. Sometimes too it was allegedly presumed that anyone who was a priest or religious or a nice enough lay person was qualified to teach religion, even when he or she couldn't teach much of anything else.

You'll have to pardon the obvious irony of the "allegedly" above, but it's by no means certain that such was actually the case, at least not to the alleged extent. To some degree in fact, it might well have been the other way round—that some teachers, assigned to teach religion, saw in it only a second-rate course, "the same old stuff," uninteresting and therefore not deserving of their greatest efforts and dedication. Such a teacher may well have felt that the religion course was the drag course in the school.

It's certainly not at all surprising to find such an attitude on the part of administrators and teachers carrying over to the students. Nor is it surprising that many of the students came to consider religion the same old stuff—except for those fortunate enough to encounter some dedicated teacher who realized that one is supposed to give his greatest efforts to teaching *anything* assigned, whether it's the doctrine of the Trinity or more practical methods of janitorial service.

There were other reasons why students looked on religion as a ho-hum course—and why, incidently, as religion rises in its ratings today, it sometimes creates a new breed of teen-aged debaters and cynics. Some students are able to add, and so they could see that while other courses got time and credit in the school, religion didn't. They could also notice that whenever a class was dropped for a guest speaker or some other such act of God for the unprepared teacher, it was invariably the religion class which was scratched. Tragically, also, the students couldn't help but be affected by Father's dropping over from the rectory to "teach religion," especially since Father only showed up at all when he found the leisure, perhaps once or twice a week, and even then only cracked a few jokes which passed for the teaching of religion.

Young people aren't dented by anything short of a good-sized challenge, and it's not surprising that this sort of mediocrity and worse left them cold and worse. In other courses they often encountered interesting teachers, challenging subjects, and a lot of interest—at least sometimes. In religion they sometimes found only what they themselves best describe as "blah."

We *are* emerging. Sometimes we're only crawling out of this hole to fall flat on our faces a few times in the process, but we're coming. And while the spirit of negativism (discontent with the old, no matter how true) and of cynicism (the high-school debater's pose, that of the dilettante or instant theologian) can and, unfortunately, often do accompany our efforts today; still these are only by-products to guard against and not essential results of our resurrected enthusiasm. If we teachers have been partially responsible for the students' former apathy and even disgust with the religion course, it's our very grave responsibility now to see that our students don't emerge as carping critics and cynical decriers of anything old, as though "the old" were invariably a synonym for "incorrect." We have to give them the absolute best of the old *and* the new, the best of everything concerning truth, no matter who its particular agent or dispenser. If Plato or Aristotle or St. Thomas Aquinas said something worthwhile, it would be an immature mind indeed which would condemn it as not worth looking at because said so long ago. The student's mind *is*, in this respect as well as in some others, still immature. And it may never be anything else if he always draws an immature teacher.

One reason, if not indeed the main reason, why young people have so often considered the religion course as the same old stuff, and so not worthy of their attention, is simply that they saw no challenge there when they *were* simply rehearsed in the same old stuff again and again. There was no excuse for this, on the part of administrators, teachers, parents, texts, or anything else. And yet sometimes, such was the situation. The fact is that we seem to be discovering today something which, with any minimal knowledge of youth, we should have known all the time—that they play dead when mediocrity is held out to them and that they come alive only in the face of some enormous (and yet attainable and interesting) challenge.

The religion course ought to be regarded (and every student has to be made aware of this attitude) as the focal point of the whole Catholic school; and this, not just by those who teach religion directly but by every administrator and every teacher in the school. To attempt this with some pietistic course, or a skimpy or dilettante or esoteric one, would be a farce and would distort the whole school and its purpose. To do this with a vital course, a challenging yet achievable one which takes in every facet of the human personality and seeks to coordinate it, a course which pounds in the idea of living one's every action for God instead of just devoting a bit of time on Sunday to Him—this can be an eminently successful venture. It is, in fact, the only venture which makes Catholic education worthwhile: the education of a human being in every possible way and in line with the purpose for which he's been created. To educate as a sort of human lab experiment, or so as to induce skill in answering quiz-show questions, or to produce a well-trained intellect apart from God and man's destiny is sheer nonsense and a waste of time. It's also a waste of man and woman power, when that power has been trained for the part of a lesser mediator in imitation of *the* Mediator, Christ, bringing God to men and men to God.

With such an understanding on the part of administrators and all teachers, and with its enthusiastic proof in the actual, direct teaching of religion, the students will soon share the same attitude. Otherwise they may well continue to dedicate their lives to trifles (even such a seemingly huge trifle as the good life) and to be suckers for intellectual pride, cynicism, and materialism.

It may, in fact, be a modern heresy to say this, but where varsity sports now serve as the focal point for everything around the school, it is high time the religion course began to at least share some of that enthusiasm. When there is as much interest in religion, direct and indirect, as in some of the sports trophies in the case, then we'll be fulfilling ourselves to the utmost, getting involved in the right way, really loving as we should. In other words, when we make facts out of clichés, we'll have it made.

CHAPTER
TWELVE

*"Go sell
what you have"
—but don't stop there*

If your only source of information is that part of the press
I've thrown a few bouquets at earlier in this book,
◈◈ you're probably aware of the collapse of the religious
life along with the collapse of the Church. You'll sense, too, the
spirit of rejoicing in the earth-shaking, front-page news that Father
Nihil in Nowhere, Siberia, has married Sister Nadamás, his former
sacristan—not because of anything as common as that motivater
of lesser mortals, a sex urge, but because they couldn't identify
with the Siberians unless they married.

Then there was this diocesan priest in Minnesota (I'm not
sure what state he's in presently) who used to discourse learnedly
about many things—about anything you brought up, in fact—among
them his theory that religious orders were all through and good
riddance. Since it was my hunch that he was just another guy who
hadn't cut it in some religious order, I didn't pay much attention
to him at the time, except to deplore the example he was giving to
the young people he claimed to be helping.

Unfortunately though, this apostle of the superficial seems
to have many a loud ally today, not just technically outside of the
religious life, but nominally within it. It's no longer a question of
someone's only demanding from a distance, "Let's get rid of the
thing," much as did Voltaire in the case of the Church. But now
some of those who once voluntarily became part of one or another
religious order seem to think that, far from adapting themselves to
it and the conditions they once freely accepted, the whole order
(and the whole religious life, for that matter) ought to adjust itself to their ideas. And in some cases, their ideas come down to a
destruction of the very essence of the religious life, filtering it down
very often to some sort of ethical group of do-gooders who can
love everyone, at least in theory, with the possible exception of
each other.

I haven't the slightest doubt that the religious life is going
to continue to exist. But I also feel that it's in for some hard days,
especially numerically (just as it has been previously, in fact) and
that as a consequence its work is going to suffer proportionately for
awhile. Such a prospect is saddening of course, and yet there's a
certain amount of purification involved, once the disease runs its
course. I haven't the slightest doubt, either, that on some unpredictable future day some religious genius is going to come up with
a brand new idea: "Why," he'll ask, "don't we start a real, vital,
spiritually tough-minded religious order, dedicated more to the

glory of God than to the glory of men?" And somewhere a Benedict and Ignatius and Francis and Clare are going to die laughing at his originality.

When I was a kid, I remember a day when my mother threatened to have her lovely black hair cut just a bit shorter than that of many boys today. The thought was staggering, and we were all in revolt over it. And yet, since it did make for her greater comfort and efficiency, we saw eventually that it had to be done. The essential thing was that she remain our mother in every major sense, which she certainly did no matter what her hair might have looked like to us. And today one feels something of the same sort of emotion, as he envisions the new hairdo on his own religious order. As long as it's just a hairdo—or even a miniskirt for that matter—and she still remains essentially our mother, fine. But we don't want her bald or so mini-skirted she looks more like a stripper halfway through her act.

Like mother, the religious life can always use some renewing, or—to use a term which has become utterly stupid in its parroted repetition—updating. One always ran into smallness here and there in this life, a sort of pharisaical sticking with minor rules, for example, or even discourtesy under the aegis of religious practice. Once, for example, when I was moving from one house to another, I didn't receive any commendations, but I did get a touching note like so:

> ... you have permission to take with you, when you leave, the following items:
>
> (1) clothing and customary toilet articles,
>
> (2) your writings and notes,
>
> (3) crucifix, rosary,
>
> (4) a watch,
>
> (5) a Bible, book of rules, etc.

That "etc." by the way is mine, and not a slip on the part of the author of this memo. That little expression would have covered far too much—like a picture of one's mother, for instance, or maybe even his glasses.

But I mention this little bit of spiritual chintziness, not really as any gripe and certainly not as any indication that the religious life ought to be destroyed, but because I agree that smallness like this had and has no place in the religious life. This is only some of the bath water which ought to go down the drain, but I'm still against throwing the baby out with it.

274

I'm sure that *I'll Die Laughing!* could have been an even better seller than it was, had it all been done negatively and critically of my own order, of the religious life in general, of superiors and the whole bundle. I might well have just missed being proclaimed a sort of neo-John the Baptist with reverse English, a precursor of the cursers doing their thing today. I'm just as happy, however, that I didn't lose my head at the time.

Had I done that particular book in that particular way, it would have pleased a far different audience than it did—one, quite frankly, I couldn't care less about pleasing—the disgruntled and the superficial and the failures who rub their hands in glee when they see disloyalty coming from an organization they either hate or envy or both. Today you'd have to add a third term to hate or envy, and that would be something describing those who try to destroy because they either can't or won't live up to something they once voluntarily agreed to.

In all honesty of course, I could have concentrated on the overly tough superior, on the dull classes we sometimes encountered, on the poor rather than the excellent teachers we sometimes had, on what seemed to *me* the waste of a lot of time in our then "juniorate," and the fiasco of my own mini-tertianship. And yet those observations would have been far too subjective and so unfair. Why should I condemn the whole juniorate (which consisted of basic Bachelor Degree work) as an institution simply because I myself hated to study in what seemed to me a vacuum? Why should I criticize the tough superior when he might have been the source of great help in a more positive way to countless others and in some unrecognized ways to me? How could I criticize tertianship as an institution when I was unable to fill out the year myself?
To me, to condemn the religious life and my own order for subjective hangups like these would have been as irrational as the monk in West Germany who, a few years ago, tried to electrocute his superior who had appointed another monk to succeed him as the monastery's "chicken master." Not only that, but despite these and other minor personal annoyances, the course of study and training in the Society of Jesus at the time I went through it seemed to me psychologically well-nigh perfect. Even the things which were tough (maybe *especially* those, in fact) were of great, great value— unless one whiled away his whole time griping about them.

Among the trophy winners for causing the most confusion among Catholics today are those who gripe about their priestly and religious life, but who haven't the consistency to hang it up. And I find myself angry these days not so much at those who leave—them I mostly pity—but at those who stick around. They try to force changes which are so nearly essential that some excellent religious (who have given their lives to a religious order and its work) now begin to wonder if this isn't turning into something they never promised. There is, in fact, a coldness here, and no little cruelty. One religious of my acquaintance (a Ph.D. in his field) returned recently from the foreign missions and was "rejected" by one of our great universities, and told by his superiors that he "could look for work" on any campus he wished. Now that might be an academic spirit (and it's not even a very practical academic spirit when you cut it up and look inside), but it could never successfully masquerade as any sort of religious spirit. And this man has more *right* to a place in his order, which he's served for a number of years, than have any of those who rejected him on academic grounds. No wonder the young guy with a real vocation wants no part of what is presented to him as "the religious life," when it becomes only this sort of caricature of the life.

What right would *I* have had on entering the Society of Jesus to begin immediately to transform it into something essentially different, changing the things I myself didn't like? Of course I *did* like it. But I entered too, not just because of those things I thought I was going to like, but because of those that looked tough and challenging also. As time went on, when change seemed called for, all the radical changes seemed most necessary in myself and not in the Society of Jesus.

This is not to say that no change is good or necessary. The Church—as the perpetuation of Christ's life among men—has to be as modern as modern man. The religious life, so important to the life of that Church, has to be modern enough to help communicate that life—not to medieval man, but to modern man. But to change and modernize and update is not, or should not be, to destroy. Nor is change only for its own sake a rational thing.

There seems to be a ruthlessness and even a cruel thoughtlessness in those who stay within the superficial trappings of the religious life and try to change it essentially to suit themselves. Certainly the apostles of change for its own sake are destroying some religious groups, and this means that those who faithfully lived their lives in these groups are, to put it bluntly, out of a job and a home. Some of those who have brought on such change, on the other hand, have only been away from their original house a year or two, so there's no great thing involved in going back to what they've left. Just why they left it at all, or if in fact they really did, is the mystery. And then, of course, there's the longer term religious critic who tears the whole idea of the religious life to shreds, but who has, nevertheless, achieved a prominent position through that very life.

While some of the critics are doing their thing destroying

the religious life, they're also doing a yeoman job of wiping out some valuable apostolates. The inner city, if I understand the term rightly, *is* an important place to work. But so are the outer city and the country and the foreign missions and, sooner or later, outer space. "They are," as some obscure dramatist once wrote, "as sick that surfeit with too much as they that starve with nothing." Drop the work in schools entirely, even for something as important as inner-city-work, and we'll soon have no city at all to work in because education has to be the very first requisite to solving our problems. It is, in fact, my uncharitable conviction that the rush to the inner city is sometimes more a flight from a classroom or a typewriter or a library, or from whatever discipline is needed for working out long-range intelligent solutions.

But the sometime cliché "inner city" is usually joined to another cliché, "involvement," with both expressions thrown about by the initiate as though they had just discovered them. I'm afraid with all the uproar in the press and all the press the self-

Many a pastor is just too busy to get "involved."

styled gallant rebel gets, one is likely to forget the great number of priests and religious who *are* genuinely involved including a great number in the inner city and a great number elsewhere too. They're doing a thorough, unheralded job, these people, and they're the hope of the priestly and religious life and of the Church, despite their chosen obscurity. But they're the vast majority too, and I meet them at every Catholic Youth Organization convention I go to; in every group, in fact, I address. You can be sure, for example, that when you have a good retreat group or a good CYO convention, there's a great nucleus of priests and religious somewhere in the background working their heads off—and I've seen them all over the country, thank God. I only wish they were in the papers as much as the vocalists who know nothing about spirituality or the religious life and yet who profess to know everything about it. Those, in fact, who have the time to shout the loudest about involvement today are ordinarily those who often wouldn't recognize it if they saw it in the practical order.

There was poor, faithful old Brother Joe Jankowski who, when he died in Honduras, had a funeral to end all funerals, with the British Government ordering the flags to be flown that day at half-mast. And yet I never heard him so much as mention "involvement," and God knows where a computer would have stationed him. All Joe knew was how to serve God, day after day, plugging away at what really *was* his thing, without talking about it or writing letters to the paper about it or griping about his religious superiors and their lack of involvement. There was more apostolic zeal in Joe's slapping some market woman on the back and shouting "Hello, lady" than in 90 percent of those who constantly yell about the "non-involvement" of today's religious and who write letters to some editor similarly occupied.

I have in my possession a charming manuscript, unpublished naturally since it's not the stuff much of today's press cares about. It's written by a nun, old in years only, and among other truths she expresses beautifully and gently and humorously, she has this to say—with infinite tolerance and understanding:

> The new nun swings a guitar where we swung a rifle, brush ax or what-have-you, but she walks "in a great tradition" and I wonder if she will know more adventure or fun than her older sisters have known. The renewal can take my garb, but if it ever threatens my solitude and prayer, I may need my gun again.

The point that the new nun sometimes seems to miss is that the

Without the nun with a gun, Sister might not be playing her guitar today.

old nun was involved, so thoroughly and completely that she didn't have time to talk about it, much less write letters to the editor berating some imagined non-involvement of her predecessors. On the other hand, the old nun sometimes seems today to miss seeing or to misunderstand the involvement of the new nun too. Both have to reach a little.

Beyond a doubt, there are many dropouts from the religious—and priestly—life today. The truth is, though, that there always have been, the difference today being that some papers and magazines write up each one with such undisguised glee that one can get the impression that the whole crew—along with other creatures—is deserting a sinking ship. The fact is, though, that there are a lot of us "other creatures" who haven't scurried off and aren't going to. The difference is that unlike those who leave, we haven't called a press conference to explain to a zealous press and a panting public why we're staying.

There are always lots of reasons, most of them very personal, behind dropouts. But I believe the more valid those reasons, the

279

Today's most popular clerical press conference might well be subtitled, "Why I am copping out."

less a person would seek to publicize them, to rationalize his way publicly through the press or, if he only has an M.A. instead of a Ph.D., through some lesser means more in keeping with his degree of intelligence. I am, quite incorrigibly and rightly, proud of the order to which I belong. I'd be a pretty lousy Jesuit if I weren't. And so I feel a great sadness at those who, I feel, betray the spirit of that order. Nor can I remain completely unaffected by the obvious gloating of some publications, when no just other religious, but Jesuits are written up when they desert the promises they made. As one news magazine headlined it smugly, "And Now The Jesuits." In this particular article there is, I think, a most significant item. It seems that one Father Marius Schoenenberger, S.J., or formerly S.J., resigned as one of the regional assistants and as a member of the order. And as the article puts it, "Father Schoenenberger made his exit in a grand and confident manner. He called a press conference in the Sala Rosa of Rome's Cavalieri Hilton, ordered drinks set up for newsmen and explained why he was going. . . ." It is, in fact, very revealing that so many of those who depart the religious life—no doubt in the true spirit of the Christ they once promised to follow in this order—do so in a similarly "grand and confident manner." It's also interesting to notice how well the press welcomes this same grand and confident manner by giving them some fine publicity in return. Maybe those of us who stick around because we consider our promises sacred ought to throw a bash for the press now and then. Of course, it would be pretty dull stuff, but maybe if we "ordered drinks set up for newsmen and explained. . . ."

Many of those I've seen departing from my own order have not really surprised me, since I feel that the immature would have been such in any state of life. Or rather, I wouldn't have been surprised had most of them hung it up years ago. The one thing I hope every religious order and the priesthood avoids is any extreme attempt to keep such people from leaving it, at the expense of some essential elements of the religious life. And I only become angry at the whole situation when I encounter some excellent religious, in the face of just such a compromise, wondering if the religious order he or she joined really exists, essentially the same, anymore.

There are certainly some younger religious who are quitting the life also. Some of them are doing so for the same general reason as always—it's just not for them. I feel, however, that the reason some young religious are quitting the life is the same reason some with genuine religious vocations never enter it. And we'll come to that.

In those early years when St. Ignatius was just getting his Society of Jesus under way, he was often asked—sometimes, in fact, even pressured a bit—to form a co-ed branch of the Jesuits as well. Manfully, he resisted, and I'm with *him*. Even though this may be a cowardly attitude, however, I do have some excellent company, such as George Santayana who noted that "when men and women agree, it is only in their conclusions; their reasons are always different."

Or as a man who should have known better, Sigmund Freud, was to write rather pathetically near the end of his life, "The great question, which I have not been able to answer despite my thirty years of research into the feminine soul, is 'What does a woman want?' " And *that* is both discouraging and encouraging to us male types. I do not, of course, buy that anonymous male's flippant remark that he is all in favor of women taking up quilting or knitting, since it gives them something to think about while talking.

I have found, though, that one can criticize his fellowmen, if they're male types, and they either agree with you or they don't, either take it well or resent it. But in the latter case, they usually don't universalize too much or bear a grudge, preferring simply to slug you in the mouth for disagreeing with them and forget it. When you venture to criticize female types, however, the immediate reaction isn't always so much agreement or disagreement as the accusation, sometimes tearfully expressed, of your being a "woman hater." Nevertheless, especially since there's not one woman in my life I feel bound to please, I have to say with Professor Henry Higgins that it seems to me that when the ladies get hold of a thing, they sometimes tend to run it into the ground, where a man will more often be a bit more tempered in his approach. Just why this is, I shouldn't dare to suggest, so I'll try anyhow.

Some years back, Pius XII was so naive as to suggest that women religious ought to update their style of dress, because the yards and yards of material in their habits didn't seem, he said, appropriate today, nor conducive to attracting young girls to the life. A *New Yorker* article about the matter at the time concluded with the justifiably cynical remark that while Pius was undoubtedly the Pope, when it came to his telling women how to dress, the girls were going to regard him as just another man and hence completely ignorant in this sacred department. And so, for the most part, they did absolutely nothing about it.

Later on, however, once the ladies got the idea that a change in dress style was pretty much their own idea, they really got into the spirit of things, with some of them, as was only to be expected, going far beyond that *spirit of things.*

I've always felt that nuns, like priests, should be able to go incognito now and then—to dinner, to a show, or some such. I've always felt too that they should be able to relax in privacy or relative privacy among their fellow nuns or friends, dressed as they darn well wished. But I've felt too, and still do, that when they aim at complete anonymity even when doing their thing as nuns or generally when they appear in public, they've lost an element which—while not essential to their religious life—*is*, I believe, either essential, or darned near that, to their effectiveness. The same thing holds for men religious and priests, although the tendency for priests always to be unidentifiable as such doesn't seem as widespread, or at least as vehemently stumped for, as presently among some of the ladies.

In the latter category, one of my most ironical recollections is of a priest, hardly a Rocky Marciano type, ranting a bit against the cassock because "it makes me look feminine." Nobody told him, but he couldn't really blame that on any cassock—something or other had beaten the cassock to it by a lot of lengths. He would, in fact, have looked sort of cute even in a Green Bay Packers' uniform. On the other hand, one of the toughest characters

"I'm afraid the cassock might make me look feminine."

I ever met used to wear a kilt, and I never heard anyone suggest that it made him look feminine.

The fact is that while some priests and nuns apparently feel that they must dress to be unrecognizable as such, those they're supposed to be helping usually feel far otherwise. After a period of experimentation with lay dress for priests and religious at one of our large Catholic universities, it was discovered that while a slight majority of the young priests preferred lay garb, the vast majority of the lay people in the area preferred them to dress as priests. So it all seems to come down, ultimately, to whom one is trying to please. I've often admired the pride and obvious morale of a nurse in uniform. It's too bad if religious can't see the parallel. That doesn't mean one has to dress in medieval style either. But it does mean that one should be identifiable, and proudly so, as what he or she is. I doubt if many bishops give a hoot how the sisters dress, just so it borders on the neat and appropriate and gives some small hint (like an escutcheon of sorts, for instance, rather than a luck charm) that they're religious. What bishops do care very much about, as they must, is the whole concept, or "theology," of the religious life. If some religious are, in effect, destroying the religious life—even though masquerading that destruction under the word "renewal"—then no sincere bishop in the world could keep silent, even though he'll probably be accused of trying to tell women how to dress.

Somewhere else in this book I've mentioned that I am so fond of women that I get angry when I see one destroying her womanhood. And I can add here that I'm so fond of nuns that I can get very angry at those who would destroy their whole way of life and the very source of their spiritual effectiveness. I probably, in part, get equally annoyed at those who equate progress with destruction and those who oppose all genuine progress only because it wasn't the way they did it. And thus endeth this footnote.

CHAPTER
THIRTEEN

"To love pure and chaste from afar..."

Apparently, the most newsworthy character in the world today is the priest or nun who decides to ◇ ◇ ◇ marry and therefore becomes convinced that the practice of celibacy should be done away with entirely—for everyone. One can't help sensing an especially bitter tinge to the attack on celibacy by the ex-religious, ex-seminarian, and ex-, or soon to be ex-priest—but that I suppose we'll have to call beside the point, even if it isn't. And again, the news media lap it all up, with headlines like "Priest Resigns Duties To Wed Former Nun," plus a front page portrait of the happy couple. Had they not been ex-s , the notice of their wedding wouldn't have gotten beyond the "Vital Statistics" column near the want ads.

It's impossible to keep up with all the minutes of the meetings of the experts today, but some of their considered findings are more memorable and more often repeated than others. Not a few eminent religious meeting in solemn conclave have told us, for example, that close friendships between men and women can be psychologically profitable even to a religious. I can't say this pronouncement came as any great surprise to me, but it has always seemed to me that the human being, religious or lay, ought to take his friendships as they come. If he has to make a psychological thing of it to form and keep them—whether their object is a man or woman—he's already in big trouble, as he would be in any state of life. A person's friendships ought to be natural and relaxed and unstudied. If his friendships are mostly with men, fine. If he has a number of friends who are women, that's fine too. But he shouldn't have to go out deliberately to cultivate either type for psychological purposes.

I've had the good fortune to have some wonderful, understanding friendships with women as well as men, and I hope to continue to have. In fact, I get something of a wry charge out of the priest's lay pitier as he shakes his head in sympathy and says in effect, "All his friendships with women have to be platonic." And all the while the priest, especially if he's dealt much with the married, is probably shaking his head in sympathy and saying, "Poor guy, his friendships with all women but one have to be platonic." And the truth is that that last trick might be harder to pull off consistently than the first.

But you can't talk about a priest's friendships with female types without also talking about celibacy. There *is* a connection, apparently not always obvious to those who speculate about such matters. With all the publicity that a priest can get today by giving up on celibacy, as opposed to the lack of any press given the thousands of priests who persist in its practice, it would seem permissible that a guy who opted for celibacy a long time ago and thought enough of that promise to stick with it should say something on the subject.

Even a kindly, understanding priest like myself gets pretty well fed up with all this jazz about marriage being the only fulfillment, about a priest's not being mature enough at ordination time (why, he's hardly up to the use of reason yet, sometimes as youthful as twenty-six) to know what a promise of celibacy means, and about how impossible it's going to be for an unmarried priest to relate to the married. There seems a presumption on the part of these priests and their local fan clubs, that no other priest ever went through the temptation and concrete opportunity to give up on celibacy.

But the truth is that probably most priests have been faced, maybe not once but several times, with the sacrifice and sometime suffering involved in keeping their promise. I can't speak for every priest, of course, but I can speak for many—and most certainly for myself. Thank God, my own "agony of conscience" came, not from going against that conscience, but because of the decision to stick with it, despite the attractiveness of the "arguments" against it.

There's a sameness to all the critics of celibacy. They all seem to think that the priest faithful to his promise of celibacy is something of a zombie—unhampered or unbothered by the ordinary tendencies of a man—and that only a few more human and more humane priests are blessed with this human sensitivity (which seems sometimes to appear suddenly even up in the forties or fifties so that one wonders where it might have hidden out since adolescence). The spiritual ancestors of these experts in human relations were undoubtedly those who know for a fact that it was a cinch for St. Joseph to spend a celibate life in close proximity with a lovely woman.

There's no use arguing with people like these, because they're judging the hidden areas of interior feelings and motives; and the man who preserves an outer serenity along with at least occasional inner turmoil is a complete mystery to them. They understand far better the impulsive unrestrained acter on inner feelings than one who, for one reason or another (maybe sometimes even for the lowly motive of being part
288

of civilization), turns those feelings—like the legitimate desire to slug some fink—to some other purpose.

There have always been priests who have given up on
celibacy for one reason or another. But the main difference
between these precursors and those whose paths they are making straight is that the modern priest who reneges on his promise of celibacy often claims to be performing some heroic deed
rather than only going back on a promise freely given. He gets
written up as a man of great courage with individuality enough
to leave the 55,000 American clerical sheep munching the
ordinary, less tasty grass in their pasture. You can read the
newspapers forever and never come across much about the
priest who goes his priestly way, doing his job and living his
dedicated celibate life to the full. But let Father Elmer Sexaur
from Nowhere, Kansas, decide to marry and he'll rate headlines,
and often kudos, throughout much of the press.

The "fulfillment" bit is not the only flimsy myth dreamed
up in an attempt to turn broken promises into heroics. A few
old straw men are pulled into place to be blown over, too. We
used to fear sex, it's said, or treat it as something not very nice.
There were, in fact, religious superiors who thought this way,
and so they were over-protective of their subjects in this area.
Now however, the reasoning goes on, we know better, and so
the argument concludes in a great logical leap, *priests should
marry*.

Now admittedly there might have been, or there might even
still be, some priests who ranted and raved against extra-marital
sex to the point where they seemed to confuse it with marital sex.
I've never run into any priest like that myself, but he must have
existed because so many people claim to have heard him, or more
often, heard *of* him. It's perhaps true also that some religious
superiors (and that far more numerous selfless band of those
who felt it their duty to assist superiors in the care of their subjects) may have taken the duty of vigilance far too seriously.

When I was officially listed as studying philosophy at St.
Louis University, a superior told me that one of my fellow
Jesuits had informed him that I had been seen talking and—something clearly far more risky and perhaps risqué as well—even
laughing with one of the college girls. I practiced rather good restraint on this occasion, I think, since I could truthfully have told
him that I might have been spotted talking and even laughing with
more than one co-ed in those days and that, in fact, I found them
delightful to talk and laugh with and that, as a further fact, I
fully intended so to continue. But the idea of cutting down on
their laughter by marrying one or the other of them never got to

In my Jesuit youth I was once reported to superiors for holding meaningful dialog with co-eds.

the drawing board, or at least beyond it. As one of my Jesuit friends once told me in a kindly but truthful way, "There are a few lucky girls in this world—the ones who didn't marry you."

A balanced attitude here, even when a superior's point of view might have occasionally come from a bit right of center, always seemed to me both permissible and salutary. A pretty good (and she was both) friend of mine was coming through town once and invited me to have lunch with her, since she wanted to talk about something quite important —like the guy she was thinking about getting engaged to. I wasn't too sure about the local superior, since he was supposed to be a bit on the classically strict side. So I thought I'd best be honest and simply approached him with the question, "May I have permission to have lunch with a gorgeous blonde?"

He laughed like crazy, and in the midst of his laughter said, "Sure," with all the confidence of a man who recognizes a joke when he hears one. It worked fine, and only later did I think of what might have happened had one of the vigilantes seen me at lunch with said blonde and reported same, in his zeal for my soul, to that superior. There probably would have been an immediate reaction of "You don't say," closely followed by the sudden realization that he had, indeed, given me permission for exactly that.

Similarly, I always thought it a ridiculous regulation of some dioceses that a priest was not to ride a car, *solus cum sola,* as they used to say or literally, "male alone with a female alone." But if the rule seemed a bit silly it was still odder to see those who kept the letter of this law riding in the back seat of a car while their lady chauffeur drove—a far more suspicious arrangement, I would say, than the normal one. That was one rule I never took seriously except in its spirit.

Another of the clichés of the priest-protestor against celibacy is in the heartrending plea that he's lonely—an emotion he became conscious of rather abruptly, after many years of such "loneliness." There's really no answering this, since he probably was lonely at that. But there are at least a couple of things to add to the fact of his sad solitude. First of all, anyone is lonely on occasion, and I've met married people who were pretty darn lonely too. And secondly, I suspect these lonely characters would still be such, even in a well-stocked and well-stacked harem.

The "priest who wants to marry" hardly ever speaks only for himself, preferring to speak, far more generously, of the necessity for a "non-celibate priesthood." He seems in fact, to feel sure that others are even as he, and that although they now lack his courage, they once shared his immaturity. "I was," he'll tell you, "just too young when I was ordained to make that sort of decision." And of course, if *he* was too young, who else could possibly have been old or mature enough?

Now most of these self-confessed adolescents were at least twenty-six at ordination, or in many cases with Jesuits at least thirty at that time and usually even older. It's awfully hard to agree with a man who says he didn't know what he was doing at the age of twenty-six, whether he's telling you that he didn't realize what the promise of his priesthood and celibacy meant or that he didn't realize what his marriage vows meant. And this is especially hard to take at face value when the same person has already held himself up as an authority (often long before he's twenty-six) on many another item—such as the things he likes to disagree with in the Church. If he was too immature at twenty-six to know what celibacy meant, chances are he doesn't know now; a few years later, what marriage means either.

For myself, I didn't feel in any way precocious at twenty-one, but I did feel that I knew what I was doing when I took perpetual vows of poverty, chastity, and obedience at that age. I felt, still more, that I knew what I was doing when at the age of thirty-two I was ordained a priest. In other words, unlike some of today's twenty-six-year olds, I thought I had the use of reason by then. I also knew at that tender age that a promise or vow of celibacy wasn't any guarantee that I wouldn't want to hang it all up sometime in the future, but I still didn't intend my promise to read: "I'll be celibate unless and until I meet someone I love enough to change my mind . . ." or "until I get lonely . . ." or some such. We have to make some decisions in our lives which don't read: "only until further notice." And it isn't, in fact, just the priesthood that has an uncertain future, but many a choice—the state of matrimony, for example.

But the reneger on promises seldom if ever calls a spade a spade anyhow, and so the priest backing into the sea of matrimony often prefers to call it fulfillment, and involvement, and a new maturity rather than anything as common as a broken promise or a sex urge.

No sooner, in fact, is the priest going up the aisle (or through that sacred candlelit hallway to the J.P.) than he is immediately an authority on all that's wrong with the Church, beginning of course with her sticky ideas on celibacy. He likes to point to the fact that the Church has changed that old law about the faithful having to abstain from meat on Friday or telling women to wear what they call hats in church, and so quite obviously, she'll change the old law about celibacy some day too. (Incidentally, I wonder why none of those women stumping for ecclesiastical bareheadedness along with other dogmatic essentials has yet pointed out that the man who ruled that they should wear hats in church in the first place, Pope St. Linus, came to a rather significant end—he was beheaded.)

Now it really shouldn't take anyone of genius calibre to see that there's a medium large difference between giving up meat on Friday and giving up marriage all week. Christ, moreover, entrusted the exterior care of His Church to Peter and His successors and not to the whim of mankind; and so if the Church decides in the name of Christ, that her people are to stay away from meat on Friday for a few years, she makes that decision validly and legitimately.

But this subject is, of course, nothing as trivial as what one eats.

No one wants to beat a dead mockingbird, but at the same time, when sympathy for a man's plight—chosen contrary to what he once promised—goes to the extent of making him a hero and suggesting that all who do not follow his example are cowards, the time has come to point out a few things which may sound pretty unkind. Readers may remember a young priest who, a few years ago, got a tremendous press for publicly ranting and raving about his bishop. This young guy was, in fact, pretty well worshipped as a hero in the press, while his bishop was pilloried for every fault in the book and out of it. You don't see nearly so much publicity on this man in recent days, since he married in a hippie-type ceremony a lady with five children and since he now, I am told, lectures as an atheist. It just could be that a few of these little oddities had roots at that time, which the press in its eagerness to back the poor persecuted critic and tear down the authority, simply overlooked.

I know of one Jesuit who took off for the *loneliness* reason, saying that he hadn't a single friend in the community where he had lived. Of course, you had to move pretty fast to become his friend, since he always beat the whole crowd to the TV controls where he presided until it was time to go to his office or, later on, to commune with a new and finally found friend.

As I say, one prefers to be kind, but how can one be kind and untruthful? How can I, regarding those I've known who have gone this route, avoid calling self-pity by its own name —because here it is, to a degree that would make the self-pity of the adolescent (to whom it is fairly natural and so excusable up to a point) seem like raw courage! These are supposed to be *men*. And I pray for them, with sympathy. But they're not going to tell me that I'm wrong in sticking with a promise while they, in their emotional upheaval of self-pity, are the real men of courage.

There is responsibility and sacrifice to *any* life, and I doubt if the ordinary priest has much or perhaps any more of this to offer up (even when he discovers loneliness) than those in other vocations. Loneliness can show up anywhere, in the middle of a crowd or in a group of only two.

I'm similarly fed up with the billing these people get in the press with their "crisis of conscience," "distress and agony of decision" and all this. There is such melodrama over the distress and frustration of these poor men that we forget that they are men and not children, men who one day made an adult promise and are not now agonizing because that promise is hard to keep (although plenty of others *have* kept it), but rather because they have decided not to keep it any longer at all. And what a vast difference *that* makes in the whole picture. Christ "agonized" precisely because He was sticking with the will of the Father and not because He was about to rationalize His way out of it.

You don't have to counsel adolescents long, no matter what their age, before you discover that one of their big hangups is in looking in all the wrong directions to solve problems, and so becoming *escapists*. That's one reason a good psychologist can spot the alcoholic before he ever takes a drink, because he starts his practice of escapism so early.

Often enough the marrying priest thinks consciously or subconsciously that he's somehow going to solve all his problems, whatever they may be, through marriage. Had he himself been any sort of counselor, he could have recognized the utter inanity of this theory and could have known too that marriage by itself doesn't solve *any* problems, but can, in fact, create new ones. Many a girl has made the mistake of thinking that marriage would solve the booze problem of her fiancé, only to find that it made his condition worse.

I'm afraid the lonely priest is going to discover that marriage too—with its success and happiness—is built on a certain amount of self-denial and, yes, sadly but truly, solitude.

I'm afraid too—at least from those I've known—that the man who flunks out on his promise of celibacy may well flunk out on his marriage promise also. He may well be defeat prone, and then too if he felt one promise could be broken, why not another?

I've also noticed, in the ex-s I've known at first and second hand, a singular lack of a very fundamental element of true love and fulfillment and commitment and involvement and all the rest—they tend to have little or no sense of humor. To them —at least if one is to believe their words—love between man and woman is a dead serious thing with no room whatsoever for laughing at any of the ridiculous things lovers invariably encounter if they are really lovers. They're so grimly determined to be happy and fulfilled and non-frustrated that they seem unable to laugh off the frustrations which must inevitably occur when two people love one another.

Personal references are as distasteful to an author as they are to his readers, and I have already apologized for the numerous personal references here. But while I don't intend to run amok on such references now, I still wouldn't like it to be thought that McGloin is a guy who has lived his whole life in an ivory tower, insulated from mankind and above all from womankind. Let me add that had it not been for a sense of humor, I probably wouldn't be writing this particular book now. There were moments when the laughter came with difficulty, but with God's good grace, come it did—at least eventually. I must add too, simply and frankly, that I've often thanked God for letting me know someone who made others—attractive and loveable as they might have been—seem, on calm analysis at least, only a shadow of her, and only attractive to me because of some remote reminder they gave me of her.

If one is to be celibate, he must realize that celibacy is not in fact a denial of love at all. It's a positive life of love, in that one loves God and is able in that love to offer Him the sacrifice of the external elements of a human love to show his utter sincerity and willingness to prove that love in practice. And being a path of love, the life of celibacy is a happy life. If it isn't in fact happy, this so-called celibate isn't a real celibate at all but only some disgruntled griper who hasn't married—at least not yet.

While it's probably true that some religious superiors did, on occasion, become a bit overactive in safeguarding their subjects and their vow or promise of celibacy, there was also probably some reason for it. There aren't, after all, many plants in the hothouse which won't lean out in the direction of a little sunshine. It's well and good to say that one should be friendly with both men and women, but the fact remains that nature has so fashioned most of us that a man's friendship with a woman *can* (as it has) lead to a love that's personal and tending to be monopolistic and sexual.

It *is* quite true that a man can have a deep love for a woman and still preserve his life and vow of celibacy. It's also true that this sort of relationship can have many advantages, emotionally and psychologically. Unfortunately (or, if you look at it from another side, fortunately), one can't always predict when such a relationship is going to become so all-consuming that he'll consider his life of what he now begins to call lonely celibacy impossible. At that moment, not just ordinary virtue but heroism, and not just ordinary but exceptional grace of God is required. And one never can be sure that he's going to have a big enough supply of either one.

It's only good sense for a person to realize this fact, and still, not all those who theorize on the subject seem able to do this, as every now and then one of them blows the whole nice package of speculation in the practical order. There's no disgrace in a priest's being a bit restrained in his dealings with women—no more than for a married man, in fact, with all those attractive women he didn't marry. That's only good sense.

Here, as everywhere, balance and frankness and honesty are of the essence. For a man to act as if women didn't exist or were, when they did, never attractive is as dangerous as it is ridiculous. In fact, not a few of those I've known who were most reticent about even discussing the subject, who seemed to consider it a betrayal even to speak with a girl—except, of course, the unattractive ones and even then keeping a stern countenance—were just those who later became "too lonely" to hang on. A little easy friendship and talk and laughter might have helped them to unwind a bit before the whole spring snapped.

Perhaps one of the best implicit summaries of what I'm trying to say, and one which reflects the balance of the man who expressed it, came to me in a letter not too long ago. This young Jesuit is studying at a secular college and is something of a den mother and counselor to about six hundred co-eds. In writing to me about this, he said he "felt like a diabetic in a candy factory." Those I've known who have left the Society to marry in their declining years would never have been honest enough to come up with something that frankly and honestly put. Had they been, they might be more honest at present as well.

I suppose what I most resent today are those billed as comedians who, when they run short of material, openly sneer at the priest who leaves his calling to marry. It's as though they'd been waiting in the wings a long time and now they can finally point to some priests (although they never *say* "some priests," but only "priests") who are breaking promises like those they once chided others for breaking. Undoubtedly too, these hilarious comics get a certain satisfaction in seeing these poor ex-priests marrying and buying up all the old Nehru shirts.

But the truth is that celibacy is a positive thing, not negative. It's a release for greater love rather than a frustration from any. And while celibacy could, depending on circumstances, be a virtue for many people, still it's particularly fitting for the priest and his life. There is, in fact, no questio about its Scriptural basis, and the fact that most of the apostles seem to have been married has no more to do with opting for a married clergy than the fact that they were Jewish would have to do with opting for an all-Jewish clergy.

Ultimately and essentially, the life of a priest is one of *total* dedication to God and to the people of God, and it seems generally impossible (and so admits of the rare exception) to be completely dedicated to God and to all men while restricting one's personal love to one woman and one's own family. The fact is that there might also be a dedicated doctor or other professional who would do better not to marry either as far as his professional freedom of practice is concerned. The main difference is that the purpose of these latter professions isn't so universal and universally important as the purpose of a priest's profession—to lead all men to God.

It has to be admitted that celibacy is *not* essential to the priesthood. But it's darn close to essential to the practical excercise of that priesthood, and it would take an exceptional man to do both the work of the priest (and do it well of course) and the work of a married man (and do *that* well). Celibacy is, quite simply, a sacrifice made for some greater good. With no "greater good" involved it would, in fact, be pretty stupid—as would any sacrifice. And so even though celibacy is not intrinsically essential to the priesthood, I, for one, can't buy the idea of a generally married clergy. Far too many hangups are potential to the situation, even apart from the twenty-four-hour a day absorption which should be part of the priesthood. I've known the wives of a number of ministers and they've sometimes told me they're on a pretty conspicuous and uncomfortable spot. They have to be nice to everyone at all times, for one thing, no matter what the aggravation, and they don't dare wear better clothes or jewelry than anyone else. If the minister gets a wife a nice car or a watch, you can be sure the parishioners and the trustees are going to notice where their money seems to be going. Most parishioners will probably know for certain that their minister is giving more of his time to his family than he is to the sum total of parishioners—even if he's not. And the latter alternative can be a hangup too, since a family has some pretty demanding rights from its head.

There's a delightful book *How to Become a Bishop Without Being Religious*, by Charles Merrill Smith (Doubleday, 1965), with a most fitting dedication, "This is for Betty whom I married for irrelevant reasons," and an hilarious chapter on "Selecting the Clerical Wife." The author handles the subject lightly, satirically, and well; but it's still a potentially tragic and actually tough situation.

I feel that celibacy is the greatest bet there is on the afterlife and whatever God has reserved for us there. It's a living testimony to the world that the use of this lovely creature of sex is still a human choice and not something that man, like an animal, is driven to—or even unlike an animal, driven to indiscriminately and constantly instead of only periodically.

It's a wager, this celibacy, that there *is* a heaven, and that this world isn't it, try as man might to find or make his heaven on earth. Were the obligation of priestly celibacy to be legally lifted tomorrow, that legal release would still not do away with the advantages and love and purpose of celibacy, nor would it open the gates of paradise here and now.

Quite obviously then, celibacy can't be lived without faith. And I'm convinced that the marrying priest isn't marrying, despite his sometime protestations to the contrary, because of some sudden increase of faith so much as because of a debilitation of faith, as he finds himself aging and apparently missing out on something. I'm afraid too that the marrying priest, who once practiced, or should have, a very great detachment, is going to find that the more attached he now becomes, the more he fears losing the object of his attachment—through age or death or tiring or even wandering emotions. He's probably also going to find that if his priesthood required the sacrifice which is celibacy, marriage may release him from that sacrifice (at least sometimes) only to present him with a hundred others he hadn't even imagined.

Celibacy, in short, may be very un-modern. But Christianity is fairly un-modern too. And any variety of "Christianity" which can't reject a lot of the assumptions of this world isn't really Christianity at all. It can't for one thing, follow a crucified leader but must, like some of those awaiting the Messias of old, form a glorious Messias to its own liking rather than the One God had in mind.

For myself, because of this continuing sacrifice which is celibacy, I feel that I can face somewhat better the person who *is* suffering with Christ on the Cross; who has, for example, some incurable disease; or who has been deserted, say, by a loved one. Were I to go back on my promise, I don't think I could ever face anyone again and remind him of the sacrifice of the Cross—at least I couldn't without feeling like a hypocrite.

298

The "marrying priest" may have a few realistic surprises in store for him.

CHAPTER
FOURTEEN

I'll die laughing—still

Having been mildly critical of some of the critics of the religious life, I hasten to admit that not all *is* perfect with the ◈◈◈ religious life today, nor was it ever perfect for that matter. I also feel, however, that much that is allegedly wrong in that life has only lately appeared and was not noticeably present when I enjoyed the things I wrote of in *I'll Die Laughing!* I feel equally certain that many of the changes for renewal in the religious life are excellent; but where these changes become the forerunner of destruction, one can hardly be expected to welcome them with loud, sincere acclaim.

Some religious groups today have, for example, apparently been infected with some of the more serious diseases of the college campus, beginning with the blooper that the university is "for living rather than for learning." As a result of this presumption, *training* has become something of a dirty word in some novitiates and institutes. So novices and very near novices are teaching (even though they haven't really learned enough to teach yet in some cases) and discoursing learnedly on the religious life and its theology, having not yet studied it, been taught much about it, *or* lived it.

With my own limited charisms, I don't see how I could possibly have learned much without listening sometimes to men who had spent their lives studying in the fields I was supposed to be learning. Nor do I see how I could have picked up much about my faith or theology by only an occasional lecture, often from someone who dissented with Catholic theology, without at least previously having dug into the subject they were dissenting with. I think that those of us who entered the Society of Jesus back in those dark ages expected to learn something about it and then to become part of what we had learned. I doubt if more than a very select few of us dreamed we already knew much about it. There were those few, of course, who seemed to think they knew much more, intuitively no doubt, at each stage than their teachers and directors, but they stood out rather prominently in our midst and we didn't take them too seriously. How can you look on a guy as for real when he reads *Time* or even *America* during a theology class and then gripes that the class was no good? Seems to me all he had the right to criticize after such a class was *Time* or *America* and maybe not even them.

I don't mean to say that I've seen any particular know-it-all-ism in young religious today. What I *am* saying is that some of their guides—formal or informal—seem soon to convince many of them that there isn't much more to learn or at least that very few people are qualified to be of any help in the process.

There seems such an hysterical urgency today to plant even novices in the midst of some sort of apostolate that the whole thing would be incredible if it weren't happening. "Desert the desert" is the cry, as though being in temporary seclusion for learning and prayer were a terrible mistake. I can't help imagining the gung-ho, full-time activist offering Christ a copy of *Time* or a color TV set in *His* desert.

It is, in fact, my hunch that many technically termed leaders are piping young religious over a cliff. I've heard, for example, this sort of leadership philosophy: "Well, they're not going to have to go through the hard times *I* went through in the novitiate. . . ." And for "novitiate" you can read "juniorate" or "tertianship" or just about anything you wish, although you hardly ever hear: "They're not going to have to go through the hell *I* endured on first-class feast days."

It isn't hard to figure what the unadulterated activist would have been doing in the desert.

This might be called the self-made-man philosophy, the thinking of the man who doesn't want his children to have to put up with the hardships he endured. So what does he do? He deprives his kids of the very things which *made* him, thinking he's doing them a favor.

The fact that *I* might have run into some difficulty as a novice or a junior shouldn't be enough motivation for eliminating those difficulties for the present-day novice or junior. Cutting them out might well only be an insult to him—and leaving his need for a challenge unfulfilled and setting him up for headlong flights from the difficulties he'll have to face later on. An over-sterile, over-protective atmosphere can make one a sucker for a later disease, since he's never had any chance of building up any immunities.

Unfortunately, not even all official religious leaders are above an over-catering to the young on occasion. There are those, in fact, who seem to want to be recognized (much as the aging politician, I feel, who is beating the drum for an eighteen-year-old voting minimum) as the great befrienders and sometime defenders of youth. "Youth must be served," they say, in a burst of originality, "since they are the hope of the future."

Now I'm all for serving youth—in fact, I tried to serve youth darn near exclusively for a long stretch of my life and I still do a little serving on occasion. But you don't serve youth at all by lying to them, and lie to them you do when you tell them they're the only people of importance in the world or in a given religious community. A few of those old has-beens over thirty in a community are, in fact, sometimes doing quite a job at their own thing, and the young can learn a lot from them unless they only sit back to be served. It's also to be hoped—and the young know this perfectly well until someone in his second (or perhaps retarded first) childhood tells them differently—that youth, as well as *being* served, must also sometimes serve a bit.

I remember being referred to as the hope of the future myself as we went through the Jesuit course, and once the training period was finished, figured the future was here at last and the hope had arrived. But then I never seemed to catch anything about the present, hearing instead about some new hopes of the future even then coming up. And the remark I had heard after a young Jesuit priest had pronounced his final vows, "There's a young man with a fine future behind him," began to make some sense. I'd like to see a little attention to the present of the religious life as well as its future.

We're a bunch of lovers today—at least no one can doubt it if they're listening to us. There is a constant discussion of *love*.

and allied *desiderabilia* (that's Latin, man!) even on the part of those whose nearly full-time vocation is that of agonizing reappraisal. There is, in fact, so much such talk that there isn't a lot of time left for loving; and instead, there seems to be a growing impersonality in at least some religious communities and a loss of any semblance of solidarity and warmth. The newcomer to the religious life sees his elders running off to so many meetings, conducting so many surveys, that they don't really have time for much personal contact with him. They'll survey him and put an IBM card in the machine which will, when you push a button, come up with the dope on what he is or should be doing; but they won't have much time to talk with him, much less listen to him.

We are, I fear, becoming as impersonal in some respects as computers and credit cards and all the rest. Sometimes in fact, one's dealings with a superior can have all the warmth and recognition of a conversation I once had with a certain credit card company. I had applied for their credit card, and the phone conversation went about like this:

> I:
> Jesuit Residence.
>
> LADY'S VOICE:
> Good morning. We're checking on the credit reliability of a Father Joseph T. McGloin. I wonder if you might vouch for him?
>
> I:
> Of course. No problem there at all. He's perfectly reliable.
>
> L.V.:
> Fine. Thank you. (Sounds like typing.) Now I wonder if I might ask you for a character reference for Father McGloin?
>
> I:
> Father McGloin is one of the finest persons I've ever known. Certainly I can give him a character reference. He's reliable, balanced, wonderful.
>
> L.V.:
> Well that's fine. Thank you so much.

(More sounds of typing.) Might I ask
to whom I am speaking?

I:

Father McGloin.

L.V.:

Father McGloin. I see. Would you
mind spelling that and giving me the
initial?

I obliged, to the accompaniment of more typing, and then a final crisp
"Thank you." And so help me, that was the end of the conversation, and I got the credit card!

I may be all wrong, but it seems to me that there's getting to
be less and less room today for the Jesuit slob, that poor benighted
guy who plugs away and works his head off and prays a bit, and
never gets chosen for any of the committees. All he's capable of is
doing all he can for the poorest of the poor on the missions, or
bringing a little light of learning into the unsuspected darkness of
the freshman mind of a Monday, and he's getting turned into, not
so much Henry Glutz, S.J., as Henry Glutz, IBM.

On this present plateau of my approaching old age, I signed
up for a course at one of our Jesuit colleges, and when it came
time to fill out the part about tuition, I was told quite seriously,
"We'll hold off on filling that in. I'm not sure whether or not
Jesuits get the religious discount." And hey, you know what?
They didn't and I didn't. Big deal.

But my few gripes re what seems to me an over-servicing of
youth and a sometimes growing impersonality in the religious life
are superficial and minor when compared with my next suggestion
to the Holy Spirit. At the heart of our greater casualties in the
religious life today, and also I am convinced the central reason for
fewer vocations, is one great phenomenon: the draining of the
genuine challenge from religious training and the religious life. If
there's one thing a young guy doesn't want today—nor did the really
young ever want it—it's a breeze. And sometimes, in some places,
that's exactly what directors of the religious life seem to be doing
—offering him or her an unchallenging life, a great big fat career
of blah.

Some years ago one of our Jesuit priests did a little informal
survey about vocations at one of our relatively large universities.
There were quite a few young guys who, on entering college, had
been all gung-ho about becoming Jesuits. Come graduation, none

"A Jesuit is only another business man—in a cassock."

of them wanted any part of it. In checking with them about what had caused this change of mind, they came up with some pretty embarrassing answers: "A Jesuit is only a business man in a cassock," they said. "If I want 'an academic career,' I can have one just as easily outside of the Jesuit order." And finally and most enlightening and embarrassing, "There's no challenge in the Jesuit life."

Now *there's* a tragedy—that these young guys knew nothing (or still worse had unlearned everything) about the inner spiritual life that's supposed to motivate a religious in even his most ordinary actions. They apparently knew nothing about the more than six-thousand Jesuits on the missions, although they probably knew something about the Peace Corps. It just may be that with the academic preoccupation of some religious orders these days, there's a diminishing appeal to the American boy or girl who still considers the studies a means to a greater end. Sometimes, in fact, even while bemoaning the casualties and making the early stages of the religious life ridiculously easy, religious superiors and their advisors make entrance into the religious orders so strict that they may well eliminate many of the daring and the believers in great challenges. It's almost as though, sometimes at least, the attitude towards accepting candidates into the religious life is similar to that of the southern governor when he was made aware of the troubles caused by the prisoners in his state pen. "We're just," he said with complete seriousness, "going to have to get a better brand of criminal." And it's my own two-bit contention that by looking for perfection, especially academic perfection, in the applicant to the religious life, we may well be turning aside some of the finest potential religious there are—some who might rise to the challenge, when given, even better than some of the initially more perfect. Nor can I buy the philosophy of one provincial I met, who will accept only college men and no more high-school graduates. God's grace doesn't necessarily wait for college, and many of our greatest Jesuits have begun as only high-school graduates.

This kindly old author is, in fact, fed up to here with the gripes about "no vocations" when the possible vocation candidate is offered a life with no challenge. What young guy or gal who wants to set the world on its ear is going to be attracted by a life he feels he can have any number of other places? How can any girl, wanting to devote herself to a genuine religious life, possibly see any resemblance to that life in three women sharing an apartment; with maybe one of them supporting the others, with no real prayer life, no community life, no dedication except to a vague preoccupation with "their own thing"—which only means doing what they feel might be in at the moment—no solidarity so that they can produce results as a unit, and hence no mutual help, companionship, or love at home? They are driven (if that's the word) by only some vague sentiment they call love which loves either those one chooses or those it's popular to "love" at the time.

There was an enormous joy in our lives when we went through the Jesuit course in that old stone age I was part of. And nobody ever had to *tell* us we were supposed to be *joyous*—we just were. I said Mass a couple of years ago for a group of nuns, and apparently, someone had recently told them they were supposed to radiate happiness, because at Communion time every face looking up at me had the most forced smile I have ever seen. Now I'm all for smiling, and there's no happier time than when receiving Holy Communion, but there's something ghastly about an on-cue smile —sort of like the spontaneous audience applause at a TV show.

I miss, somehow, the spontaneous joy in the religious life— lost maybe in countless agonizing reappraisals. I miss the unrestrained laughter I heard once in an elevator when several priests and nuns were going up to their respective respectable floors in a Marquette University dorm. As we ascended, one of the nuns who had just gotten on looked at me and asked, "Did you push the sisters' button?"

One theologian of my acquaintance—who took off, incredible as it seemed to all of us, to marry another super-adult—used to come up with such sparkling little gems of original wisdom as "A scholar knows no holiday," and "If a teacher has the truth, he can't possibly be dull."

Then there was the young Jesuit who registered a formal protest on the bulletin board about the community blast being thrown for one of the Jesuits on his golden jubilee. "We have no right," the protest went, "to spend money this way." Seems to me Christ had something to say to one of His followers when he too griped that "this could have been sold for much and the money given to the poor." Anyhow this young guy was far too holy and, I hope still, too solemn for us. He left shortly thereafter, no doubt to sell all he had, if anything, and give it to the poor rather than wasting any time in tributes to people who had given fifty years of service to those poor and lots of others as well.

I miss, I'm afraid, the spontaneous laughter of those who neither weep nor laugh on cue, but who tend to laugh even when they weep because they know why they're doing both. Where some neo-religious seem ready to overthrow the whole system because they're subjected to what they consider some pretty poor instructions and classes from time to time, we could look at a great Jesuit brother, Willy Teson, and only say, "This lucky guy has slept through more than fifty years of exhortations."

An occasional new nun may sometimes seem ready to desert her vows at the first drop of the word fulfillment, but she's still dead sober when holding dialogue on the whole subject. She'd undoubtedly have been shocked at a short telephone conversation I once was a small passive part of, and which struck me and the Sister I refer to, as hilarious.

I:

Is Sister X available?

THICK FEMALE GERMAN ACCENT:

One moment. I will see.
(Fairly long, silent wait, about the length of a decade of the Rosary)

GERMAN ACCENT:

Ach, Sister cannot come to the phone.
She is having an affair in the yard.

But enough of my gripes and my lauding of *temporis acti.* The fact is that the religious life *is* still a valid, positive life, and while its renewal is ever desirable, its destruction is not. And I especially resent those who leave this life telling the world *it* can't survive—the psychological implication seeming to be because they couldn't survive it.

Not only is the whole genuine religious life vital and valid, but that bugaboo of the ultra-activist, the contemplative life, is similarly so—yes, Virginia, even, maybe especially, in our day. If one has any faith at all, he must know that the best thing one can do for another, when all is said and done, *is* pray for him. The contemplative doesn't go somewhere to *escape* from the world (if he does he's a phony) so much as to help it in the way God seems to be pointing out as the best *for him.* And as such, it's no one's prerogative to criticize him for it, just because it doesn't happen to be the critic's thing. Of course, the latter may well admire far-eastern contemplation—which can so easily be introversion—but then that's getting to be *in*, and it *is* so restful, especially in a Nehru jacket. The true contemplative lives out a song without words, but this critic—the activist—often enough only lives out a lot of joyless words without a song.

I can never forget that my own choice of the religious life came, finally, from the conviction that there had to be more to life than the other possibilities seemed to hold out—to me, at least. It wasn't any "escape," since I didn't want to leave the things I was leaving at all, much less "escape from" them. But I wanted this *more*, because it seemed the way to fulfill *my* life.

I have a friend who graduated from Biz Ad School, saw all the little commuters with their briefcases, and said too, "There must be more to life than this." Today he's a fine free-lance photographer and artist.

At the time *I'll Die Laughing!* came out, I had only recently finished the then Jesuit course of studies and training in the religious life. The introduction to this book ends up like so: "With all the work and sweat that have been part of the past twenty years or so, there has been so much enjoyment that I could not call the account of those years anything other than what I did." And it still holds. The religious life, so far (I still feel, stubbornly, like I might be some small temporary part of "the hope of the future"), has brought me an enjoyment I had never dreamed possible. And I hope that fact has come through in this sort of *Quintodecimo Anno* of that earlier work. I suspect that if time permits, I'll be stubbornly laughing, even at whatever sufferings may be involved, if I ever get the chance to do a *Quadragesimo Anno* of the whole bit. But I won't, of course, so you'll just have to realize that somewhere or other, I'll be laughing.

In that earlier day there was, too, a certain religious spirit in the Society of Jesus which I tried to outline briefly in that book. I still believe what I said then, that:

> The Society of Jesus is an army of men whose purpose is outlined in their rules, "the salvation and perfection of their own soul and the salvation and perfection of their neighbor with the divine grace." There is, too, a single purpose, common to all members of the Society and that purpose is stated in the Latin motto, *ad majorem Dei gloriam* (usually abbreviated A.M.D.G.), which simply means "for the greater glory of God."
>
> As an army, the Society has a spirit far different from that of the military with secular purposes. We Jesuits operate under a King who loves each one of us, Christ, and this King of ours has commanded us to love one another. Our general, St. Ignatius, passed that order down when he wrote in the very first rule of the Society that "The interior law of charity and love is to help thereunto (that is, to the attaining of our purpose) rather than any exterior constitutions."
>
> In our army, there is an attitude not found in any other army. Ours is a life of *joyful* service, a life of love with the co-operation of those around us and above us. You find among Jesuits a certain joy in a common worthwhile purpose and a comradeship in sharing that purpose.
>
> Like any soldier, the Jesuit has to take orders, and he goes wherever, and whenever, he is sent. This means that he must not become too attached to any particular place, persons, or type of work. Although a Ph.D. in Greek, he could be told to teach mathematics (though of course that would rarely happen). A great preacher might be given a writing job. Such orders are given with a view to serving the greater glory of God *as a unified body*.

312

For attaining his purpose—the salvation of his own soul and that of his neighbor—the Jesuit has a variety of means at his disposal. Among those means are a number of daily spiritual push-ups, including an hour of prayerful meditations each morning. Through prayer he strives for union with God, and the closest possible union with the suffering Christ is sought through dedication, sacrifice, and penance. The Jesuit seeks to be so completely divorced from material things that he will be "as one who being dead to the world and to self-love lives only to Christ our Lord."

A Jesuit learns to imitate, not the world he has left, but Christ whom he has come to serve. The rule tells him to "abhor wholly and not in part what the world loves and embraces and to accept and desire with his whole strength whatsoever Christ our Lord loved and embraced. For as worldly men, who follow the things of the world, love and with great diligence seek honors, reputation, and the credit of a great name upon earth as the world teaches them, so those who follow Christ must seek slanders and injuries and wish to be held and accounted as fools without at the same time giving any occasion for it, in imitation of Christ." Thus to the Jesuit it is not always the better thing to defend oneself, even if accused falsely, though there are occasions when the truth should or must appear. But in the imitation of Christ, it is sometimes more perfect to endure even false accusations in silence.

Too, the Jesuit should seek always his own "greater abnegation and continual mortification." Nor should he stop with only resisting a temptation to a given sin, but rather should try to cultivate the opposite virtue. That means that if a man tends to be proud, not only must he vanquish pride but conversely he must embrace humility.

A Jesuit endeavors to possess values so perfect that first things are always put first; and he esteems spiritual gifts and virtues "of greater moment than either learning or other natural or human gifts."

The imitation of Christ causes the Jesuit to be poor as He was poor, and his "diet, apparel and lodging will be such as become poor men," choosing for his own use "the meanest things of the house." It also causes him to be especially obedient, to such an extent that orders received from his superior are to be obeyed as though from God himself. The humility which distinguishes his personal life must inform his feelings toward the Society of Jesus as well. While the Society is the only vocation for him, nonetheless he will conceive of it, with respect to other orders, as the least of all.

The following paragraph which is known as the *Sum and Scope of the Constitutions* describes what Jesuits should and can be:

Men crucified to the world, and to whom the world itself is crucified, such would the rule of our life have us to be; new men, I say, who have put off their affections to put on Christ; dead to themselves, to live to justice; who, with St. Paul, in labors, in watchings, in fastings, in chastity, in knowledge, in long-suffering, in sweetness, in the Holy Ghost, in charity unfeigned, in the word of truth, show themselves ministers of God; and by the armor of justice on the right hand, and on the left, by honor and dishonor, by evil report and good report, by good success finally and ill success, press forward with great strides to their heavenly country, and by all means possible and with all zeal, urge on others also, ever looking to God's greater glory. This is the sum and aim of our Institute. This is what a Jesuit novice is told to aim at for the rest of his life.

Now, by present standards in an age of instant evolution, that was written a long time ago. But if you were to study current Jesuit documents you'd find that we still buy it, completely, for our own day and in our own day's way. We are, in a word, still in business, and probably more so than ever, with a bit more freedom to swing where freedom is required—and by "swing" I mean not just "swing" but "swing at."

No one reading even a major portion of this book can accuse me of glossing over the things which seem to me drawbacks in the religious life today nor, in fact, some of those of past days. But one thing ought to stand out, and if it doesn't I've goofed it up somewhere—and that is that I love this Society of Jesus and have the greatest hopes that it will continue to be the Society I entered, unquestioningly dedicated to Christ and the champion of His Vicar on earth. Quite naturally, with that sort of stubborn attitude, kindly and gentle as I am by nature, I can become quite angry when I see or hear a Jesuit acting like something else, betraying the Society he once voluntarily entered and in which he once made a promise which he knew was perpetually binding—to live a life of poverty, chastity, and obedience, and with a unique sort of dedication to Christ's Vicar on earth, the Holy Father.

But the fact that there are a few such misguided people in this Society shouldn't surprise anyone, much as it shames those of us who love her. To seek to condemn the whole Society for a few, however publicized, oddballs is as completely unjust as drumming out the whole apostolic college along with Judas. Earlier in this book I mentioned that my attitude towards both ultra-liberals and ultra-conservatives, religiously and politically and every other way I can imagine at the moment, is "a plague o' both your houses." And the same holds here. I have before me an article, which really could only have proceeded from someone inspired by a psycho-pathic hatred brought on by God knows what—envy perhaps—who writes little endearments like this: "Jesuit training alienates man from Christianity.... The Jesuit is taught that the bishops of the Church ... are fools.... Loyalty to the Society comes before loyalty to the Church.... The Jesuits regard *Time* as a quasi-Catholic magazine...."

I've used a technical term here, "psychopathic hatred." But if the writer of this sort of bilge really believes that bit about *Time*, he's not just the victim of a psychopathic hatred, but of illiteracy as well. At any rate, with our relatively few Jesuits (there are about 36,500 still to be heard from publicly) whose public utterances have not been in keeping with the spirit of the Society, sooner or later, some such idiot was bound to emerge and condemn the whole Society for the stupidity of a few and call, as he does, for the ex-tinction of the Society. Which gives you an idea of why I deplore the ultra on either side of center—they both want to throw out the baby with the bath, both for different reasons, but both equal-ly unjust to baby.

The religious life is still a life of love, but not love in some sentimental, vague sense so much as the love which is built on sacrifice and self-forgetfulness in seeking the will of God and the good of mankind before one's own. The religious life is still a life of the greatest, really genuine, freedom since the vows—freely pronounced—don't so much restrict as free one for a broader scope of love and service. Certainly I can serve God a lot better by being free of those things I have vowed to give up, even though all these things were pleasant in themselves and not easily given up.

Finally, this religious life is still a life of complete, not partial dedication to a cause—a foolish cause, no doubt, in the eyes of the material-minded, and yet the greatest cause in the mind of one who sees life whole and not just in its material aspects. The religious life is still, in a word, the quest of an impossible sort of dream.

EPILOGUE

Living
to
beat hell!

We seem to be living in a day when those who are supposed to be speaking or writing publicly about their beliefs spend ◈ ◈ most of their time on what they don't believe. In the meantime, the vast numbers of those who have positive beliefs are seldom heard from—not always through their own fault, but often because there isn't nearly as much market for belief as for unbelief. It's something of a parallel with the relative publicity given a man or a woman walking down the street fully clothed and one without any clothes. It seems fitting then that I bring this book to a close with a short thing on what I *do* believe. Although *all* my beliefs are shared by many and *some* of those beliefs by a lot of others, there are certainly other people who have an essentially different set of beliefs from mine. And I have in general the greatest respect, not always for the beliefs of others, but for those others themselves and their right to so believe. I can't always respect only the *sincere* beliefs of others, since sincerity—essential as it is to real belief—is not the only essential. A madman, after all, can be perfectly sincere—or an assassin. And so I respect the beliefs of others when those beliefs are well thought out and prayed out. And I expect in turn the same respect for my own beliefs.

I believe what I said in *I'll Die Laughing!,* and none of the shouting from those bogged down in the rut on the right nor the weird hysteria of those on the left have caused me to alter those beliefs. They have prodded me into restudying it all more intensely, a discipline that has only strengthened my faith—as the questioning and digging and probing led, not to denial, but to greater and still more confident affirmation.

I believe in God. That's where it all starts and ends. But I don't believe in any god created by man's imagination: some benevolent old guy with a beard, "the man upstairs" bit, or some ineffectual old would-be philanthropist, some absent-minded ethereal type who forgets about mankind now and then.

No, the God I believe in is a perfect Being—perfectly everything, in fact, including perfectly attractive and beautiful and knowledgeable and, above all, lovable. He is, in fact, worth working for and waiting for, infinitely beyond the sum total of all attractiveness and lovableness a guy can see here on earth, or even in space.

I believe that God created man, however He went about it, either by some built-in evolutionary process or also with some separate acts of creation along the line. I believe, moreover, that

319

this creative act of God is an act of complete unadulterated love, because God didn't stand to gain a thing from it, but mankind can. And this *is* Love—to love enough just to give, to share, and not to count either the cost or possible returns on the investment. As Father Walter Farrell, O.P. (I think) put it so accurately: "The effort of love is not to enjoy itself but to renounce itself, and it becomes itself only by leaving itself."

I believe that God created me for this purpose: to find my fulfillment, my love and happiness in Him and to use the partial fulfillments and loves and bits of happiness of here and now as means to Him. I believe, in fact, that God put me here in this life to last out a time of trial before reaching this complete fulfillment and unadulterated happiness in Him. And so I believe that as soon as a man forgets about or rejects the *trial* nature of this life, he can't solve a single human problem rationally; and as long as he keeps that fact in mind, he's got hold of the principle for solving any problem. And this isn't any evasion or postponement of the problem, but rather a facing of the problem in the light of reality.

I believe that God created a lot of things to help a man achieve this final goal of his, and so I believe too that all the things within my horizons are either to be used to get me to God, or to be adjusted until they do help, or else not used at all. This is, in fact, the big job of a man with a free will—to turn the things that might block his way to God into things that help.

I believe, moreover, that since we are destined for this perfect love and happiness and fulfillment in God and since this present period of trial is a means of getting us there, that the whole scene is a joyous one—not just the naturally enjoyable parts of it, but the tough parts as well. There is, in fact, no sadness even in suffering and tough intellectual decisions when their purpose is to bring us to Him. The only real sadness is wasting things, like using them the wrong way and imagining them ends in themselves instead of recognizing them for what they are—means.

The sick and handicapped, in fact, often have an insight into this earth-shaking fact which goes essentially deeper than that of the totally hale and hearty. There was my friend, Mary Ellen Kelly, who could move only her hands, a few inches at a time, and her eyes, but who managed to write a whole book of love to God, *With The Dawn Rejoicing*.

I believe that of all the things we can say of God, the most important thing is that He really *is* Love, that He creates love, that we're meant for love, and that we can find no fulfillment outside of it. And I believe that every iota of human love is great in itself, yes, but it's only a hint and a shadow of what the vast, infinite

320

love of God, which awaits us, is like. And so human love too is a means of getting us to God—and if it isn't, it's only a prostitution of love.

And so I believe too that we love God in loving His creation, maybe especially the creatures that make up mankind—and woman-kind too. I may have occasionally satirized the girls here at times in my great admiration for what a real woman *should* be, but I think in general that God found a pretty good use for that spare rib. I've sometimes felt, in fact, that He might have done just a bit too much of a good job in that department on occasion, but I'm sure that even this seeming overdoing of a good thing had some good reason in His Providence.

I believe that if a man uses his head and doesn't let his emotions dictate to it, he'll have to see that God must, indeed, be, and he can come to know quite a bit about Him too. But I believe too that God knows that this is a pretty tough job, and so He began at one point in history to tell us a little bit about Himself. He told us, in fact, more and more, until finally He *showed* us Himself as

"Well, now that you ask for suggestions about the extra rib, I do have this wild idea . . . "

well. And I believe that Jesus Christ actually is God, and that the true Christian is one who really follows this Christ, this crucified Savior, in fact.

And so I don't believe that a Christian can possibly be one who looks for his heaven here on earth, but he's one, rather, who uses earth to get at the real heaven.

I believe that Christ came, not for a small group of people in a small corner of the world for a brief period of history, but for all men of all time. And I believe that Christ perpetuates Himself, therefore, through His Church. And so I believe—as I always have from the day I first was able to believe anything, even down through the times of personal doubt and study—in what is sometimes referred to in print these days with a hidden sneer at its archaic ring as "the established Church." It is, moreover, my belief that this Church in which Christ perpetuates Himself today and as long as this world will last is essentially the Catholic Church. And since I do know that and believe it completely, *for me* there is no salvation or achieving of God, my purpose, anywhere else. Naturally, I can't speak for others.

I believe that Christ so constituted His Church that as God generally has, He operates through human agents, and so I believe that when the Holy Father speaks, in his department, of course —which is the area of the knowledge of God, of belief in Him, and of God's law—he expresses God's Will for us. I can't see any big deal of faith in the guy who'll believe when the Lord personally taps him on the shoulder and says "Believe it, bub,"—at least not so long as we're in a state of trial whose greatest test is faith and whose greatest aide is humility.

I believe that Christ, within His Church, perpetuates Himself through His sacraments so that we get some share in His life: a kinship with Him through baptism; we share His strength through confirmation; we experience His forgiveness and the help we need to avoid sin in the sacraments of penance and anointing; we acquire His vocational strength in the sacraments of orders and matrimony; and we gain a greater love for Him in the Sacrament which really *is* Himself perpetuated in a special way, the Holy Eucharist.

I believe that Christ perpetuates Himself in a special way in the sacrifice of the Mass, giving us today the chance to be really present at the sacrifice which saves us; and I believe that He stays among us in the sacrament of the Eucharist in some sacramental way that no philosopher can explain. Certainly I believe that if Christ could change water into wine and could heal the sick and could, in fact, have become man in the first place, that He has no trouble remaining among us in this Sacrifice of the Mass and in

322

His continued Presence in the Eucharist on the altar. I believe Him when he says, "This is My Body. This is My Blood. Do this in memory of Me."

I believe that for this time of trial, God gives man certain tests to pass, certain laws to keep, and that today the interpreter of those laws is His Church under His Vicar, the Holy Father. Since we *are* on trial, however, I don't believe it possible that we can always see all the reasons for God's law, as voiced for us through His Church. I believe, moreover, that historically from time to time God tries mankind, almost as a unit, in some special way. I believe too that if we could see all the reasons for God's every law, we wouldn't have to exercise any faith—and that would destroy the whole idea of our being on trial, by faith, and on our way to heaven.

So I believe that God has given us a moral law which sometimes calls for some sacrifice, bordering in fact, on occasion, on heroism. But I also believe that we follow a leader who was crucified, and *that* was, you might say, at least mildly heroic.

I believe that when a Catholic objects to this moral law of God as expressed and interpreted by His Church that he's acting, psychologically, as did Adam and Eve, whose essential sin was setting themselves up in place of God as the judges of good and evil, despite what God had told them to the contrary. And I can't buy the guy who will, indeed, nod piously and accept God's law in categories in which he's not particularly tempted anyhow, but who raises a great hue and cry about God's representatives not really being such when something in the law they express goes against his wishes. I'm just a bit suspicious of the objective judgment of the divorcée who declares, "I believe that the Church is right in keeping celibacy for the clergy, but I don't believe what she says about divorce and remarriage."

And I have a similar tendency to doubt the complete good will of the "marrying priest" who would say "I buy the Church's stand on divorce but not on celibacy."

I believe that both puritanism and license are wrong, and so you can't really say that one is worse than the other; but if I had to give a trophy for last place in my own estimation, it would have to go to puritanism. True, the person who lives by license offends God by violating His Law, but puritanism insults His intelligence and doesn't even acknowledge any joy in His gifts. Life is to be enjoyed—its pleasures when they're the ones He approves and its sufferings, somehow or other, when they're such that they're clearly His will also.

I believe besides that a man can go beyond what's demanded of him by narrow duty or rule, to show, even now, the love of God for which he is made and so to lead others to profit from the trust

323

he shows in his own faith. I believe that married people can do this in many ways, but I believe that there are some men and women God wants to give witness to this faith in a special way, by sacrificing marriage and by living "the life of the counsels" in the religious life. I don't care to argue with anyone about the relative *heights* of the married or religious states, but I do feel, at the same time, that of itself the religious life is a more daring bet on the afterlife than is marriage.

Within the religious life I believe in my own order, in the Society of Jesus, an order, *I* feel, dedicated in a special way to the Church and loyalty to Christ's Vicar. Quite naturally, since I owe so much to this Society and to the spirit St. Ignatius built into her, I love her. I get a lump in my throat when I hear "The Star-Spangled Banner" sung with spirit, and I get a similar feeling when I hear the *Suscipe* or "Take, Lord, and receive," a song expressing a Jesuit's vowed dedication to Christ under the standard of Ignatius. I think this is a thing called morale, and if it's corny to have it, I am hopelessly corny.

I believe in America—not an America ashamed to speak of God, not a materialistic America, but an America true to her spiritual beginnings and ideals; an America ready to use her tremendous material and technological advantages the way men are supposed to use all creatures, as the means to a higher goal.

I believe in youth, yes, and I believe in infancy and middle and old age as well, because I believe in and love men as creatures of God and as my brothers. And I believe in you who have had the patience to read this book and maybe even the foolhardiness to buy it. Forgive me for its shortcomings and believe, with me, that it was done because I firmly believe with a huge, brilliant child, Mr. Gilbert Chesterton, that anything that is worth doing is worth doing badly.

I can sum up all my beliefs, I think, at least in substance, in a simple, timeless paragraph of one Iñigo de Loyola, soldier:

> Man was created to praise, reverence and serve God our Lord, and by this means to save his soul; and the other things on the face of the earth were created for man's sake, and in order to help him in the pursuit of this end for which he was created. And so it follows that man must make use of these created things in so far as they help him to achieve his purpose, and in the same way, he ought to leave them alone in so far as they get in the way of its achievement. And so it is necessary that we make ourselves indifferent to all created things, in so far as it is left to the liberty of

our free will to do so and is not forbidden, in such a way that we do not, as far as we are concerned, wish for health rather than sickness, for wealth rather than poverty, for honor rather than dishonor, for a long life rather than a short one—and so, in all other things, desiring and choosing only those which most lead us to the end for which we were created.

Amen to that, man—that *is* living.   In fact, to live like that is happiness enough to make a man eventually die laughing.